teach® yourself

understanding tax
for small businesses

D0241032

teach®
yourself

**understanding tax
for small businesses**
sarah deeks

J. S. Andrades
21.3.2007

For over 60 years, more than
50 million people have learnt over
750 subjects the **teach yourself**
way, with impressive results.

be where you want to be
with **teach yourself**

For UK order enquiries: please contact Bookpoint Ltd, 130 Milton Park, Abingdon, Oxon, OX14 4SB. Telephone: +44 (0) 1235 827720. Fax: +44 (0) 1235 400454. Lines are open 09.00–17.00, Monday to Saturday, with a 24-hour message answering service. Details about our titles and how to order are available at www.teachyourself.co.uk

For USA order enquiries: please contact McGraw-Hill Customer Services, PO Box 545, Blacklick, OH 43004-0545, USA. Telephone: 1-800-722-4726. Fax: 1-614-755-5645.

For Canada order enquiries: please contact McGraw-Hill Ryerson Ltd, 300 Water St, Whitby, Ontario, L1N 9B6, Canada. Telephone: 905 430 5000. Fax: 905 430 5020.

Long renowned as the authoritative source for self-guided learning – with more than 50 million copies sold worldwide – the **teach yourself** series includes over 500 titles in the fields of languages, crafts, hobbies, business, computing and education.

British Library Cataloguing in Publication Data: a catalogue record for this title is available from the British Library.

ISBN-10: 0 340 92741 0
ISBN-13: 978 0340 927410

First published in UK 2006 by Hodder Education, 338 Euston Road, London, NW1 3BH.

This edition published 2006.

The **teach yourself** name is a registered trade mark of Hodder Headline.

Typeset by Transet Limited, Coventry, England.
Printed in Great Britain for Hodder Education, a division of Hodder Headline, 338 Euston Road, London, NW1 3BH, by Cox & Wyman Ltd, Reading, Berkshire.

The publisher has used its best endeavours to ensure that the URLs for external websites referred to in this book are correct and active at the time of going to press. However, the publisher and the author have no responsibility for the websites and can make no guarantee that a site will remain live or that the content will remain relevant, decent or appropriate.

Hodder Headline's policy is to use papers that are natural, renewable and recyclable products and made from wood grown in sustainable forests. The logging and manufacturing processes are expected to conform to the environmental regulations of the country of origin.

Impression number   10 9 8 7 6 5 4 3 2
Year   2010 2009 2008 2007

contents

about the author		x
01	**introduction**	**1**
	what is this book about?	2
	using this book	3
	who is this book aimed at?	3
	be commercial about tax	4
	keeping it legal	5
	advisers	6
02	**which taxes do businesses pay?**	**8**
	taxes and duties checklist	9
	income tax	10
	corporation tax	13
	capital gains tax	15
	inheritance tax	18
	National Insurance	22
03	**how the tax system works**	**26**
	raising taxes	27
	the Budget	27
	HM Revenue and Customs	28
	self-assessment	28
	tax returns	28
	tax year	30
	records	30
	completing your tax return	32
	late returns	33
	paying your tax	35

	correcting errors	38
	enquiries	38
	discovery assessments	41
	can I appeal?	41
04	**starting a business**	**42**
	working on your own	43
	sole trader	43
	limited company	44
	comparison of trading through a limited company rather than as a sole trader	46
	company or sole trader?	47
	working with others	48
	partnership	48
	limited liability partnership (LLP)	48
	notifying HM Revenue and Customs	49
	starting to trade	49
	personal services	50
	casual income	51
	notification process	52
	what does being registered with HM Revenue and Customs mean?	53
	other notifications	53
	expenditure incurred before the business starts	54
	financing the business	54
	anticipating tax payments	55
05	**profits**	**58**
	choice of year end	59
	accounts	64
	tax return	65
	income	65
	expenses	67
	problem areas	72
	profits	77
	how much tax do I owe on my profits?	80
	recap case study	82

06	**losses**	**87**
	claiming income tax losses	88
	company losses	96
	capital losses	97
	loss claims for business Investments that go wrong	101
07	**equipment**	**102**
	on which items can you claim capital allowances?	103
	types of capital allowance	105
	calculating capital allowances	107
	cars	115
	capital allowance claims	110
	increasing your claim	119
	leasing businesses	121
08	**employees**	**123**
	who is an employee?	125
	paying employees	128
	taxing employees	129
	taking on a member of staff	131
	deductions	133
	statutory pay	137
	employer's National Insurance	140
	taxing perks	141
	tax-efficient perks	146
	construction industry	148
09	**premises**	**151**
	working from home	152
	renting premises	155
	buying business property	155
	selling business property	160
10	**VAT**	**163**
	what is VAT?	164
	when do I need to register for VAT?	166
	what is the rate of VAT?	170

	records and VAT returns	173
	complications	177
	special schemes	180
	cancelling your VAT registration	183
11	**pensions and insurance**	**185**
	paying into your own pension	186
	employers and pensions	193
	state pension	194
	insurances	195
12	**incorporating a business**	**198**
	when is the best time to incorporate?	199
	closing down your self-employment	200
	starting a limited company	203
	minimizing capital gains tax	203
	the advantage of running a business with share capital	210
13	**closing a business**	**213**
	closing down an unincorporated business	214
	closing down a limited company	219
	VAT de-registration	220
	closing down your PAYE scheme	220
14	**selling a business**	**223**
	what are you selling?	224
	case study – shares or assets?	228
	will you receive cash or shares?	230
	reducing capital gains tax	231
	an alternative course of action	234
15	**passing on a business**	**236**
	giving away your business	237
	what happens to my business when I die?	239
	making a will	242
16	**putting it all together**	**243**
	Nina's Kitchen	244
	starting to trade	244
	getting organized	245

buying new equipment   245
tax return time   246
moving on   252
taking on staff   252
VAT registration   253
completing the second tax return   253
completing the first VAT return   254
rewarding staff   254
completing employer end of year returns   255
PAYE inspection   255
completing the third tax return   255
paying a pension   256
paying a sick employee   256
loss   256
completing the fourth tax return   257
where next?   258

appendices

01 rates and allowances   259
02 key dates   285
03 glossary   290
04 further information   299

index   **302**

about the author

Sarah Deeks has a degree in law and practised as a Chartered Accountant for 16 years working as a sole trader, a partner and a director of a small limited company. During this time she helped her many clients with their day-to-day tax problems. Sarah has been writing about tax since 1988. Her practical knowledge of the tax world, unique approach and incisive style enable her to communicate this most difficult of subjects to the lay reader. She has written and contributed to a number of tax books and journals for LexisNexis Butterworths and Tottel Publishing.

Acknowledgements

With thanks to my husband Martin for ensuring that the book answers his questions.

01

introduction

In this chapter:
- about this book – how it works; who it is for
- being commercial about tax
- myths, avoidance and evasion
- choosing an adviser

What is this book about?

Teach Yourself Understanding Tax for Small Businesses teaches you how tax affects a small business from its conception to its demise. It is based around the real-life decisions that business people have to make every day. So if you are wondering about the tax implications of operating as a sole trader or a limited company turn to Chapter 4. Thinking of employing someone for the first time? – Chapter 8 covers the tax consequences. Is VAT registration on your mind? – check out Chapter 10.

You probably have a reason for buying this book. Are you about to start a new business or expand an existing enterprise? Perhaps you want to feel more confident when dealing with your advisers or the tax authorities? Does tax bamboozle you? If so read on. I cannot promise a ripping yarn or a laugh a minute but you will learn to avoid some of the pitfalls that so often plague new ventures and understand the tax consequences of the various decisions you will make as a business person. You will also find that your increased knowledge takes the terror out of dealing with your tax affairs enabling you to have more meaningful and equal consultations with your bankers, accountants and other financial advisers.

Tax is a vast and complex subject but the content of this book is specifically targeted at small businesses so you do not have to wade through irrelevant details to find the answer to your question. In spite of its size the book offers a wealth of information about the tax consequences of all those expensive decisions from buying property to incorporation, and it contains a detailed glossary for those hard-to-understand terms as well as a calendar of important dates. I have taken liberties with some of the jargon to make it more understandable for the tax novice and whilst reading the book will not turn you into an expert overnight it will make you aware of where tax impacts on your business preventing potentially expensive mistakes.

Teach Yourself Understanding Tax for Small Businesses is not about how to fill in forms because HM Revenue and Customs produce comprehensive guidance to help you complete your returns but it tells you where to get the forms and the assistance you need via numerous Internet links.

This book may be suitable background reading for new students of tax, law, accountancy, business and finance but as it does not include any legislative references it cannot substitute for your student texts.

Using this book

This book is up to date at 31 July 2006 but tax is a constantly changing subject. In addition to changes which are announced in the annual Budget (see Chapter 3), court cases, statements by the tax authorities and new legislation need to be taken into account on an ongoing basis. You will need to keep your knowledge current by regularly checking HM Revenue and Customs' website.

The book has been designed so that it is easy for you to keep it up to date. All the important numbers such as tax rates and allowances are largely confined to tables in Appendix 1. These include space for you to update them each year until 2010 with Internet links telling you where to obtain the most recent figures.

The book has been written so that you do not have to read it all but can refer simply to the chapter that interests you. You will find it useful to have some background knowledge, so the first three chapters are recommended reading for everyone. These give you an introduction to income tax, corporation tax, capital gains tax, inheritance tax and National Insurance. You will also learn how the tax system works, when forms have to be completed and what happens if you fail to comply. Having mastered the basics you can then turn to the chapter relevant to the decision you are making.

This book is no substitute for advice from an experienced practitioner who can take all the facts and circumstances of your business into account. If you are considering an expensive purchase or making a complex decision, you should always seek professional help (see Advisers).

The law in Scotland and Northern Ireland differs from that in England and Wales. So if you are buying or selling property, or undertaking a legal transaction such as writing a will or securing a debt, you may find that some of the terminology differs.

Who is this book aimed at?

This book is aimed at the smallest businesses. You are most likely to be a sole trader but you could be a partner or trade as a limited company. Often your business will just be you but you may have some help from your spouse, partner or another member of your family. As time goes by you may take on a few employees.

It is a book about the average man or woman in the street who just happens to be running a business rather than working in a job. You will not necessarily be a particularly high earner but simply trying to make enough profit to pay the bills and provide you and your family with a decent standard of living.

You may be unsure about using this book because you think that you have no head for figures. If so be reassured that you can use it irrespective of whether you failed or succeeded at school maths. Everyone learns in a different way, so the book includes different styles of learning. Every point is described using as little jargon as possible and the words are reinforced by practical examples and case studies. There are checklists and tables for quick reference and regular recaps to reinforce your knowledge. As you will see in the next section, mastering business tax is as much about your attitude to it as being able to perform complex calculations.

Be commercial about tax

Being in business is about making money. Paying tax on those profits and transactions is part of business life. If you focus too much energy on saving tax at all costs, you will take your eye off the ball and may miss a valuable commercial opportunity.

Tax is just a percentage

Would you like to pay £1 million in tax? I would! It would mean that I was making a profit of £2.5 million. This is a simple concept but one often over-looked. If you concentrate your efforts on making more money by getting that extra sale or increasing your fees, even after paying tax you will be richer. In the million pound scenario – you earn £2.5 million, the tax authorities take 40% of it (£1 million) and you get to keep 60% of your profits (£1.5 million). For every extra £100 you earn, your income rises by at least £60. This is how your wealth increases not by you spending time trying to reduce your tax bill.

Spending to save tax

Beware of complicated tax-saving schemes and the temptation to make unnecessary purchases just to save tax. Paying into a pension might be a good idea but you should be aware that to reduce or eliminate your tax liability will cost you more than the original tax bill and may strap your business for cash. Buying new equipment might be acceptable if you need it now and had planned to buy it, but many people make inappropriate purchasing decisions just to avoid paying tax to the government. In other words do not let the tax tail wag the commercial dog.

Failing to budget for tax

Failing to budget for tax is one of the principal reasons why businesses fail. No one likes paying tax, least of all once or twice a year in a large lump sum depending on whether you trade as a company or sole trader. If you forget to do anything about it, or like an ostrich put your head in the sand and hope it will all turn out for the best, your finances may get rocky. If however you start your business on the right footing, adopt good business practices and allocate funds to pay your tax regularly throughout the year, you should always be able to meet your tax liabilities when they are due even if it is irksome to part with the money.

Risk

If you were going to invest in a new business, you would probably want to know how risky the new venture would be. We all have different attitudes to how much risk we like in our lives and so it is with your tax affairs. Playing risk games with your tax will ultimately take up more time and effort than keeping your affairs low-key and up to date. If it gives you a buzz trying to find ways to reduce or avoid paying tax, good luck to you. You may have saved tax but you will probably have increased the risk that HM Revenue and Customs (HMRC) will enquire into your affairs and this in turn will have a significant cost in money and time. At the other extreme you may be someone who does not sleep unless they know that their affairs are in perfect order. If so reduce your worry and find a good accountant (see Advisers).

Keeping it legal

Having read this far into the book, you may be wondering why you need to bother with tax at all. Surely there must be a way round dealing with the tax authorities? Myths abound about how a friend of a friend has never been sent a tax return in spite of being self-employed for ten years. The simple answer to this scenario is that failing to deal with your tax affairs is illegal. It is not up to the tax authorities to send you a tax return. It is your responsibility to make sure that they know you exist so that they can send you a form to complete. Failing to pay your tax in this way is called tax evasion and you could face criminal prosecution when the tax authorities discover what you have done. I say 'when' not 'if' because with increased cross-checking between different government departments, concerted 'spill-the beans' campaigns and international co-operation, it is very hard to evade tax for your whole life.

Tax evasion is a wide-ranging concept and includes under-stating your income or claiming a tax deduction for expenses which are not permitted. Once again tall tales circulate about which expenses you can off-set for tax. If you are in doubt refer to this book, HMRC's guidance or seek professional advice otherwise you could find yourself with significant fines or a criminal record.

Whilst evading tax is illegal, avoiding paying more tax than you need to is legitimate. You are at liberty, within the constraints of the tax system, to organize your affairs however you wish. So if you want to pay pension contributions to reduce your tax, or claim loss relief in a certain way because it is more effective, the tax authorities do not mind. The tax legislation is however littered with provisions known as anti-avoidance measures which restrict your actions. So you cannot for example avoid tax by paying funds into an offshore bank account or undertaking a series of artificial transactions.

Advisers

After you have read this book you may decide that doing your own taxes is not for you. It all depends on whether you are someone who believes that using specialists will save you money in the long run, or whether you want to save their costs by dealing with the tax authorities yourself at the risk that you make a few mistakes along the way.

Few businesses even small ones manage without professional advisers and most consider their costs to be a necessary expense of being in business and budget for them accordingly. Reading this book should help you to get the best out of your adviser and feel more comfortable using them in a number of respects. Firstly you will know when to ask for help, secondly you will understand more of their advice and thirdly you will feel more in control of the relationship because you can ask for specific help rather than paying them to provide you with the background information that a book like this contains.

So how do you go about finding an accountant to help you with your business taxes? Personal recommendation is obviously best so ask around. Failing that, contact one of the professional bodies which regulates accountants. These are listed in Appendix 4. Anyone can call themselves an accountant but unless they are professionally qualified there is little recourse should things go wrong. Do not be afraid to interview several advisers when making your decision – most offer an initial free consultation so that they can assess your needs and you can find out what they can do for you. Reading this book will help you to ask them the right questions. Overall trust your instincts. You are hoping that this will be the start of a long and fruitful relationship, so personality and approachability are just as important as technical expertise.

Recap

- Reasons to read this book include: you are thinking about becoming self-employed, you have to make a key business decision, you are having problems with HM Revenue and Customs, you want to have more meaningful discussions with your accountant or you want to save money (tax, penalties or both).

- This book is most suitable for you if you are a sole trader, a director/shareholder of your own limited company, or you run a business with your spouse, partner or another relative.

- Everyone should read the first three chapters of the book and then refer to the other chapters as necessary. There are numerous cross-references to highlight other sections of the book that might interest you.

- Tax is just one aspect of your business' financial affairs. Try to take a commercial and pragmatic view about it, invest in a good adviser and it will take up minimal time and effort.

- There is no magic to saving tax but it will usually cost you more than the tax you save.

- Remember – arranging your tax affairs to minimize your tax bill is legal. Evading tax is illegal.

02 which taxes do businesses pay?

In this chapter:
- checklist summarizing which taxes businesses have to pay
- essential questions answered: Who has to pay income tax, corporation tax, capital gains tax, inheritance tax and National Insurance? What is each tax charged on and at what rate? Are there any exemptions or pitfalls? How is the tax paid?
- simple calculations

At this early stage it is helpful to develop an understanding of the full range of taxes that businesses have to pay. This will help you to get to grips with your tax obligations and to have more informed discussions with accountants and other professionals about your business set-up.

Taxes and duties checklist

The following checklist summarizes all the main UK taxes and indicates whether they apply to sole traders, partners or companies. There are four direct taxes (so called because they tax income, profits and gains): income tax and inheritance tax paid by individuals, corporation tax paid by companies, and capital gains tax paid by both individuals and companies. There are also four types of National Insurance. All employers irrespective of whether they are sole traders, partners or companies will pay Class 1 employer's contributions on their directors' and employees' wages. Indirect taxes such as VAT are charged on expenditure.

Direct and indirect taxes and National Insurance are administered by HM Revenue and Customs (see Chapter 3). Rates and council tax are administered by your local authority.

Tax	Sole traders	Partners	Companies
Direct taxes			
Income tax	Yes	Yes	No
Corporation tax	No	No	Yes
Capital gains tax	Yes	Yes	Yes
Inheritance tax	Yes	Yes	No
National Insurance			
Class 1 employee's contributions	No	No	No
Class 1 employer's contributions	Yes	Yes	Yes
Class 2	Yes	Yes	No
Class 3	Yes	Yes	No
Class 4	Yes	Yes	No
Indirect taxes			
VAT	Yes	Yes	Yes
Excise duties	Yes	Yes	Yes
Stamp duties	Yes	Yes	Yes
Local government			
Rates	Yes	Yes	Yes
Council tax	Yes	Yes	No

In addition to the taxes listed above there are a number of taxes, levies and duties that apply to specific industries such as aggregate extraction, waste management, power generation, oil, shipping, air transport, haulage and insurance.

This chapter examines all the direct taxes and National Insurance. VAT is dealt with in Chapter 10. Rates and council tax are covered in Chapter 9.

Income tax

Who pays it and what is it charged on?

Income tax is principally paid by individuals. It is charged on the:

- Trading profits of sole traders and partners (see Chapter 5);
- Employment earnings including salaries, wages, perks, tips, commission, holiday pay, sick pay and maternity, paternity and adoption pay (see Chapter 8);
- Pensions including the state pension;
- Some state benefits such as jobseeker's allowance and income support;
- Income from property (rental income, ground rents, insurances and lease premiums);
- Income from savings and investments (bank and building society interest and share dividends);
- Miscellaneous income from settlements, estates, trusts and casual and one-off receipts.

Although most sources of income are taxed some are exempt from income tax including:

- Statutory redundancy and some payments for loss of your job (see Chapter 13);
- Pension lump sums on retirement (see Chapter 11);
- Some state benefits and sickness policies;
- Individual savings accounts (ISAs) and Child Trust Funds;
- National Savings certificates and premium bonds;
- Tax credits.

Most people living in the UK are liable to pay tax on their income (including their business profits) regardless of whether the money is earned here or overseas. If you live abroad (are non-resident) you still have to pay UK tax on your UK income. If you have been living overseas for some years (are not ordinarily resident in the UK), or come from overseas (are non-domiciled) different rules may apply and you will need to seek professional advice about this aspect of your affairs to ensure that you complete your tax return correctly.

Collection

Income tax is collected as follows:

- Under self-assessment for sole traders, partners, those with property income or more complicated affairs (see Chapter 3);
- Through the PAYE system for employees, directors, pensioners and the recipients of some state benefits (see Chapter 8);
- By deduction at source from bank and building society interest.

Calculation

Calculating income tax can be complicated depending on the number of different sources of income that you have. Persevering with the numbers is however worthwhile because it may help you to manage your income tax liabilities better (see Chapters 4 and 5).

Before you start your calculation you need to add together all your sources of income to arrive at your total income for the tax year and refer to Appendix 1 for the tax rates and allowances for the appropriate tax year. You should then work through the following steps to calculate the tax on your business profits:

1 Everyone is entitled to earn or receive a certain amount of money before they owe any tax. This is called your personal allowance. It increases slightly each tax year and is £5,035 in 2006/07. Some older people receive a higher allowance. The personal allowance is deducted from your income before you pay tax.

2 After you have deducted the personal allowance from your income, the first part of your income is taxed at 10%. This is known as the starting rate of tax. The amount of your income that is taxed at 10% increases slightly each year and is £2,150 in 2006/07.

3 The next part of your income is taxed at 22%. This is called the basic rate of income tax. The amount of income charged to basic rate tax changes slightly each year and is £31,150 in 2006/07.

4 Any further income you receive is taxed at 40% – the higher rate.

Example

Ben is a self-employed electrician. His annual profits are £40,000. He calculates his income tax liability as follows:

Tax year 2006/07	Step	£
Profits		40,000
Personal allowance	1	−5,035
Income subject to income tax		**34,965**
Tax due		
£2,150 at the 10% starting rate	2	215.00
£31,150 at the 22% basic rate	3	6,853.00
£1,665 at the 40% higher rate	4	666.00
Total income tax owing		**7,734.00**

Ben will also owe Class 4 National Insurance (see National Insurance).

Savings and investment income

Dividends and interest are taxed differently from trading profits, salaries and other sources of income.

- UK dividends are paid with a 10% tax credit. If your total income is taxed at either the starting rate or the basic rate you owe no further income tax on your dividends even though the dividend tax credit is less than the basic rate of income tax. If your total income including dividends means that you have to pay higher rate tax, instead of paying 40% tax on the dividend you pay tax equivalent to 25% of the dividend you receive. For example, a £100 dividend will add £25 to your tax bill if you are a higher rate taxpayer.
- Interest is usually paid with 20% income tax deducted at source. If you pay tax at the starting rate you will be owed a tax refund. If you pay tax at the basic rate you owe no further tax on your interest even though tax is deducted from your interest at a lower rate than basic rate income tax. If your total income including the interest results in you having to pay higher rate tax, you can deduct the 20% tax that you have already paid on your interest from the higher rate tax you owe.

Corporation tax

Who pays it and what is it charged on?

Corporation tax is paid by companies on their profits and gains for an accounting period. Profits include all of a company's sources of income including investment and property income. Company profits are calculated in broadly the same way as those for sole traders and partners (see Chapter 5) but with some important differences in the way that financial transactions (interest paid and received and profits and losses on loans) are treated. Companies, but not sole traders or partners, can claim a tax deduction for expenditure on goodwill and intangible assets, and depending on their trade may be entitled to tax credits for research and development and to clean up contaminated land.

Corporation tax is charged on the profits of all UK resident companies and non-resident companies who trade in the UK through a branch or agency.

If your company is a member of a group of companies it is still taxed on its own profits but groups are treated differently from companies in some respects including the treatment of their losses. If you have a group of companies you will require an accountant.

Dividends

If your company pays a dividend there is no tax to pay on it but the dividend is not a tax-deductible expense when calculating your corporation tax bill. Dividends are paid with a 10% tax credit and as you learned in the section on income tax, unless the recipient is a higher rate taxpayer there is no further income tax to pay on the dividend. Dividends which the company receives are not liable to corporation tax but they are taken into account when claiming small companies' marginal relief (see Calculation).

Collection

Corporation tax is collected under self-assessment (see Chapter 3).

Calculation

Calculating your corporation tax liability is straightforward once you have worked out your taxable profits because there are only two tax rates; one for small companies and one for all others (see Appendix 1). The only complication occurs if the company's profits exceed the small company threshold (£300,000) but are less than the upper limit of the marginal relief band (£1.5 million). In this situation the profits are taxed at the full corporation tax rate but reduced by marginal relief. This is calculated according to a set formula which is:

1 The marginal relief fraction (see Appendix 1) multiplied by:
2 the upper limit of the marginal relief band (see Appendix 1) less profits (which at this stage must include dividends received by the company plus their tax credits) multiplied by:
3 the company's profits charged to corporation tax divided by the profits as calculated in stage 2. If the company has not received any dividends you can ignore this stage.

You must remember to claim marginal relief in the company's tax return.

Example

Ali Enterprises Ltd made a corporation tax profit in the 2006 financial year of £390,000 and it received no dividends. The company's corporation tax liability is:

- £390,000 × 30% = £117,000. This is reduced by marginal relief.

Marginal relief is calculated as follows:

- 11/400 × (£1,500,000 – £390,000) = £30,525.

The company therefore owes corporation tax of:

- £86,475 (£117,000 – £30,525) – a corporation tax rate of 22.17%.

Small companies' marginal relief is reduced if the company's accounting period is less than twelve months or if it has any associated companies. Marginal relief cannot be claimed by close investment-holding companies. You will probably need an accountant to help you work out whether you have any associated companies.

Capital gains tax

Who pays it and what is it charged on?

Capital gains tax is paid by individuals (sole traders and partners) and by companies who pay it as part of their corporation tax bill. Essentially it is charged on the profit you make from selling a capital asset; the profit or gain being the difference between the price you acquired the asset for and the price you sold it for. Assets owned before March 1982 are subject to special rules.

Capital gains tax is charged on a wide variety of assets such as:

• Property used in your business including your home if you use part of it exclusively for work (see Chapter 9) and property rented to tenants;
• Shares in private companies and traded on the stock market;
• Some compensation for the loss of assets; and
• Goodwill and intellectual property.

Not all assets are liable to capital gains tax. Those which are exempt include:

• Your home but not any part used exclusively for work;
• Transactions between spouses and civil partners;
• Cars and other machinery and assets with a useful life of less than 50 years (but not where capital allowances have been claimed (see Chapter 7);
• A disposal by one trading company of a substantial shareholding (10% plus) in another;
• Personal items (chattels) sold for less than £6,000;
• Gambling winnings and prizes;
• Most life insurance proceeds;
• Assets passing on death (see Inheritance tax).

Most people are liable for capital gains tax on all their assets regardless of whether they are situated in the UK or overseas. If you live abroad for five or more whole tax years most disposals of assets while you are overseas are not liable to capital gains tax but you have to pay capital gains tax on assets used in a UK business. If you come from abroad (are non-domiciled) you are only liable for capital gains tax on your overseas assets in some circumstances.

Collection

For individuals, capital gains tax is collected through the self-assessment system and paid on 31 January (see Chapter 3).

Calculation

Calculating your capital gains tax can be complicated because there are a number of deductions or reliefs that you may be able to claim to reduce your liability. Your entitlement to these reliefs depends on whether you trade as sole trader or partner, or as a limited company.

Indexation allowance can be claimed by companies. It can also be claimed by sole traders and partners on assets acquired between March 1982 and 5 April 1998. It is calculated by applying the increase in the retail prices index for the period you owned the asset to the cost of acquiring it. If you are a sole trader or partner, indexation allowance is given for the period of ownership to 5 April 1998. From that date you may be entitled to taper relief.

Rollover relief can be claimed by any business which replaces certain business assets one year before they are sold and up to three years afterwards. Rollover relief can be claimed on a number of assets including land, buildings and goodwill (see Chapter 9). The new asset does not need to be the same type as the asset being disposed of. Claiming rollover relief may waste your entitlement to taper relief. If you are considering investing in a replacement asset, professional help is advisable.

Taper relief can be claimed by sole traders and partners. It reduces your gain by a set percentage depending on whether the gain arises because you have disposed of a business asset (which is tapered at a higher rate) or a non-business asset (which is tapered at a lower rate) (see Appendix 1). There are many detailed conditions which must be met and deciding whether an asset qualifies for the higher rate of relief is not as simple as it may sound. Advice will be necessary to maximize your claim to this relief.

Annual exemption: individuals (sole traders and partners) but not companies are entitled to an annual exemption. It serves a similar function to the personal allowance in income tax. If your gains are less than the annual exemption you do not have to pay capital gains tax (see Appendix 1).

The basic capital gains tax calculation is outlined below. You will need to prepare a calculation for each capital asset you sell or dispose of in the tax year. If you make a loss on an asset you can deduct it from your gains. The steps in a capital gains tax calculation are as follows:

1 Work out your sales price deducting any selling costs such as agents' fees.
2 Calculate the cost of buying and improving the asset. Add on any purchase costs to this number such as stamp duties, legal costs and agents' charges.
3 Deduct the purchase costs from the disposal proceeds. If you have made a loss there are no further reliefs to claim. Refer to Chapter 6 to make sure you use your losses effectively.
4 If you have made a gain claim indexation allowance if appropriate and then rollover relief if you are replacing the asset.
5 Taper any remaining gain (see Appendix 1).
6 If you are a sole trader or partner claim the annual exemption (see Appendix 1).
7 Any remaining gain is taxed according to the highest tax rate that you pay on your income. This means that the gain could be taxed at 10%, 20% (not 22%) or 40% (see Appendix 1).

Example

In June 2006 Simon sells a freehold shop which he bought in May 2000. He has always used the shop in his business. Simon cannot claim indexation allowance because he bought the property after 1998. He is not replacing the shop with another business asset so rollover relief does not apply. Simon is a basic rate taxpayer even after including the gain on the shop and he calculates his capital gains tax liability as follows:

Tax Year 2006/07	Step	£
Freehold shop sold June 2006 (after deducting selling costs)	1	150,000
Freehold shop purchased May 2000 (including acquisition costs)	2	–100,000
Gain before taper relief	3	50,000
Taper relief – 75% as the shop is a business asset owned for more than two years	5	–37,500
Gain after taper relief		**12,500**
Annual exemption	6	–8,800
Taxable gain		3,700
Capital gains tax at 20%	7	**740.00**

Inheritance tax

Who pays it and what is it charged on?

Inheritance tax is charged on the value of your capital assets when you die and paid by the executors of the estate. It is also charged on some transactions occurring during your life, for example gifts made within seven years of your death and transfers of assets into a trust. Inheritance tax is not paid by companies.

Inheritance tax is charged on all your assets apart from those listed below. There is no exemption for your home as there is with capital gains tax. Indeed, the value of the family home is often the reason why people have to pay inheritance tax. Exempt assets include:

- Amounts left to a spouse or civil partner unless they come from abroad (are domiciled overseas) when a limit of £55,000 applies;
- Certain business and agricultural assets (see Chapter 15);
- Amounts bequeathed to charities, heritage bodies and political parties.
- Decorations for valour and compensation paid to Second World War victims.

No inheritance tax is due on the first part of your estate assets. This is known as the 'nil rate band' (see Appendix 1). If the total value of your assets when you die (your estate) is less than this amount you do not have to pay inheritance tax.

Most people are liable to inheritance tax on all their assets irrespective of whether they are located in the UK or overseas. If you come from overseas (are non-domiciled), you are liable for inheritance tax on your UK assets. Deciding your domicile for inheritance tax is complicated and you will require professional advice.

Calculation

It can be useful to understand the basic inheritance calculation so that you can regularly appraise whether you have an inheritance tax liability. If you have a business you will need to make arrangements about what happens to it when you die and you may want to plan your affairs to minimize your inheritance tax liability (see Chapter 15).

The following steps demonstrate how to perform a basic inheritance tax calculation:

1 Work out the value of the estate assets. Detailed valuations are often required, for example of real estate, shares, businesses and personal items. Liabilities such as loans can be deducted.
2 Deduct the funeral costs;
3 Deduct the value of any bequests to spouses and civil partners, business and agricultural property qualifying for relief (see Chapter 15) and exempt gifts such as legacies to charities;
4 If the value of the estate is below the relevant threshold (see Appendix 1) there is no inheritance tax to pay.
5 If the value of the estate is more than the relevant threshold, inheritance tax is calculated at 40% on the excess over that threshold.

Example

Paul, a wholesaler of cleaning products dies unexpectedly in January 2007. His business is valued at £200,000 and qualifies for business property relief. He leaves the business to his brother. He owns the family home jointly with his wife. The house and his personal effects are worth £400,000 and he has shares and investments worth £30,000. In his will he leaves the house, personal items and investments to his wife. Paul also owns a flat in Ibiza valued at £100,000 which he leaves to his daughter.

There is no inheritance tax liability. The business assets qualify for business property relief and the bequests to his wife are covered by the spouse exemption. This leaves the flat in Ibiza valued at £100,000. As this is below the nil rate threshold (see Appendix 1), no inheritance tax liability arises.

If Paul had been a single man with no wife, who had left his entire estate jointly to his daughter and brother, the inheritance tax calculation would be as follows assuming his funeral costs were £5,000:

	Step	£
House		400,000
Investments		30,000
Flat in Ibiza (Note 1)		100,000
Business		200,000
Total value of estate	1	**730,000**
Funeral	2	–5,000
Business property relief (Note 2)	3	–200,000
Estate after business property relief		525,000
Exempt threshold	4	–285,000
Taxable estate		240,000
Inheritance tax at 40%	5	**96,000**

Note 1: The flat in Ibiza is subject to inheritance tax even though it is located abroad because Paul is domiciled in the UK. There may also be taxes to pay in Spain. If so some of these may be deducted from Paul's UK inheritance tax liability but his executors will require professional advice.

Note 2: Business property relief and agricultural property relief are considered in more detail in Chapter 15. Deciding whether assets are business assets or agricultural assets is not always clear-cut and you will need professional advice.

Gifts

One way to reduce your inheritance tax bill is to give away your money while you are alive. The following gifts are exempt from inheritance tax:

- £3,000 per tax year to any person or combination of people, plus a further £3,000 in the first year that you make a gift;
- Up to £250 per tax year to any number of people;
- Regular gifts out of income (not capital), for example £50 per month to your daughter;
- Amounts paid to support your family, for example maintenance settlements if you are divorced or separated;
- Gifts made upon the marriage or civil partnership of any person up to the following amounts: £5,000 from a parent, £2,500 from a grandparent or other relative and either party of the marriage or civil partnership to the other, and £1,000 from anyone else.

You can also give away larger sums of money and provided that you survive for more than seven years after making the gift no inheritance tax is due. If you die within the seven-year period the gift may become liable to inheritance tax. These gifts are known as 'potentially exempt transfers' because they may be exempt or they may not – it all depends on when you die, the nil rate band at that time and the amount of any other potentially exempt transfers you have made in the previous seven years. If you die between three and seven years after making the gift any inheritance tax due on the gift is reduced.

Pitfalls

You may now be thinking that it would be a good idea to give away your assets over and above the nil rate band to your children (or other relatives) whilst you are alive and provided that you live for seven years all your inheritance tax problems will be solved. You may also be thinking that if you need the money back again or you need to use the assets you have given away at sometime in the future that this would be no problem because 'it is all within the family'. HM Revenue and Customs have thought of these possibilities. In most situations conditional gifts (known as 'gifts with reservation of benefit') are liable to inheritance tax. In some cases they are liable to income tax under rules known as 'the pre-owned assets legislation'.

National Insurance

Who pays it?

National Insurance is paid by people who are self-employed and partners, employees, employers and those who are none of these but who wish to voluntarily protect their entitlement to the state retirement pension. Young people aged under 16 do not have to pay contributions even if they work and those in full-time education between the ages of 16 and 18 are credited with contributions for that period. If you are over state retirement age, no contributions are required and if you do not work because you are looking after children you can claim home responsibilities protection which reduces the number of years you require to qualify for a full state pension. Special rules may apply if you come to the UK to work or you go abroad.

National Insurance is divided into four classes. For the rates at which contributions are due, see Appendix 1.

- *Class 1* National Insurance is paid by employees (including directors) and employers. It is based on a percentage of the employee's salary, bonuses and some perks but it is not charged on dividends. Contributions entitle you to claim jobseeker's allowance, incapacity benefit, state pension and state second pension (see Chapter 11). Class 1A National Insurance is paid by employers on staff perks such as company cars whilst Class 1B contributions, also paid by employers, is charged on amounts paid under a PAYE settlement agreement (see Chapter 8).
- *Class 2* contributions are paid at a flat weekly rate by those who are self-employed and in a partnership. This includes spouses and civil partners who are also business partners. The payments protect entitlement to the state pension, incapacity benefit and maternity allowance. For details about registering to pay Class 2 contributions see Chapter 4.
- *Class 3* National Insurance is a voluntary weekly sum paid by those who have not earned sufficient income to make the year qualify for National Insurance purposes. Paying Class 3 contributions protects your entitlement to the state pension and other benefits in some circumstances. If you are considering paying voluntary contributions you should take advice as in some cases the payments may not increase your pension or benefit entitlement.

- *Class 4* contributions are paid by self-employed people and partners based on a percentage of their profits. They give no entitlement to benefits or pensions.

Collection
- *Class 1* National Insurance is collected through the PAYE system (see Chapter 8).
- *Class 2 and 3* contributions are paid by monthly direct debit or quarterly payment to the National Insurance Contributions Office (NICO), part of HM Revenue and Customs.
- *Class 4* National Insurance is collected through the self-assessment tax return as part of a sole trader or partner's tax bill (see Chapter 3).

Exemptions
If you are self-employed or a partner you can claim 'small earnings exception' which exempts you from paying Class 2 contributions if you expect your trading profits to fall below a certain threshold (see Appendix 1). To apply for exception you should complete form CF10, see **www.hmrc.gov.uk/selfemployed/fagcf10.shtml**.

If you pay Class 2 contributions when you could have been exempt you can claim a refund. Given that Class 2 contributions are only a small weekly sum most people pay them irrespective of their earnings to protect their state pension and benefit entitlement.

Multiple jobs or self-employments
If you are both employed and self-employed in the same tax year, you may pay Class 1 contributions on your employed income and Class 2 and Class 4 contributions on your self-employed earnings. Depending on how much you earn it may not be necessary for you to pay all this National Insurance as there is an annual maximum limit on the total contributions that you need to make. To prevent you overpaying you can apply for some of the contributions to be 'deferred' by completing form CA 72 A or CA 72 B, see **www.hmrc.gov.uk/leaflets/nic.htm**. If you have two employments or directorships you may also need to notify NICO so that you do not overpay National Insurance contributions. If you have not applied for a deferment you may be able to claim a refund if you overpay contributions.

Irrespective of the number of self-employments you have you only need to pay Class 2 contributions once. Different rules apply to Class 4 National Insurance. Here the profits from all your self-employed businesses must be added together to calculate your liability.

Calculation

Each type of National Insurance is calculated differently:

- Class 2 and 3 contributions are calculated as weekly sums at a fixed rate for the tax year.
- Class 1 National Insurance is based on the employee's or director's earnings above the 'lower earnings limit' multiplied by the appropriate percentage. Once earnings reach the 'upper earnings limit' a reduced rate applies.
- Class 4 contributions are calculated at a given rate on the sole trader's or partner's profits falling between the lower and upper limits. Where profits exceed this limit, contributions are charged at a reduced rate.

The following example illustrates how Class 1, 2 and 4 contributions are calculated.

Example

Jane is a self-employed physiotherapist who makes a profit in 2006/07 of £35,000. She pays Class 2 National Insurance of £2.10 per week (£109.20 a year) by monthly direct debit to NICO.

Jane also pays Class 4 contributions through her self-assessment return as follows:

- 8% of profits between £5,035 and £33,540 a year = £28,505 × 8% = £2,280.40.
- 1% of profits above £33,540 a year (£35,000 – £33,540 = £1,460 × 1%) = £14.60.

Her total Class 4 contributions are £2,295.00 (£2,280.40 + £14.60).

If Jane employs Harriet as a part-time receptionist paying her £150 a week, Harriet will pay Class 1 employee's National Insurance contributions on the part of her salary above the weekly threshold of £97 per week. This comes to £5.83 per week (£150 – £97 × 11%). Jane deducts this sum from Harriet's wages.

Jane will also pay Class 1 employer's contributions of £6.78 per week £150 – £97 × 12.8%) on Harriet's salary. Jane pays both parts over to HM Revenue and Customs (see Chapter 8).

Recap

- If you run a small business in the UK as a sole trader or partner you will be liable to pay income tax on your business profits plus Class 2 and Class 4 National Insurance.
- If you run a family company you should consider the National Insurance savings of paying a dividend rather than a salary – but watch out for the many pitfalls (see Chapters 4 and 11).
- If you trade as an unincorporated business consider the National Insurance consequences of a spouse or civil partner working in the business being alternatively your employee or your business partner (see Chapter 4).
- Remember that tax rates, allowances and thresholds change each year so you will need to update the figures in this chapter in April each year (see Appendix 1 for details of how to do this).

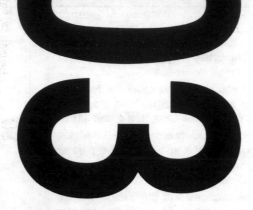

03

how the tax system works

In this chapter:
- tax returns
- paying tax
- record keeping
- important dates
- enquiries

In the last chapter we looked at which taxes businesses pay. This chapter considers the administration of the tax system – how taxes are introduced and changed, what you must do to comply with your income tax, capital gains tax and corporation tax obligations and what happens if you fail to do so. A number of important dates are outlined and a full diary of these is included in Appendix 2.

Raising taxes

Raising taxes is a fundamental part of Government economic policy and the extent to which tax affects small business changes according to the political agenda. For example, if the government wants to encourage new small businesses in order to create employment or generate economic growth, it will offer enterprise incentives such as reduced tax rates and increased allowances for investment in equipment.

Taxes can be levied by Parliament and local authorities. Each year the Chancellor of the Exchequer decides how much money to raise from taxing individuals and companies and how that money is to be spent. Rather like running a small business the Chancellor has to balance the books, so if less tax is collected, the amount that can be spent on health, education and welfare is accordingly reduced unless money is borrowed to cover the shortfall.

The Budget

The Chancellor sets out how much money will be raised from taxation and how it will be spent in an annual Budget. This is usually held in the spring but an interim report on the nation's finances is delivered each autumn (this is called the Pre-Budget statement).

The Budget coverage you see on the television usually focuses on the price of a pint of beer and the cost of your car tax but these aspects are only a small part of what the Budget is about. Major changes to all the taxes outlined in Chapter 2 take place following the Budget in an annual Finance Act. These changes, many of which have a significant impact on business, receive little or no publicity except amongst finance professionals.

HM Revenue and Customs

HM Revenue and Customs (HMRC for short) are responsible for all the taxes set out in Chapter 2 except rates and council tax. Inheritance tax is dealt with by Capital Taxes Office (see Chapter 15), National Insurance is administered through the National Insurance Contributions Office (NICO) and Stamp duties are dealt with by Stamp Taxes Division (see Chapter 9). HMRC also handle many employer-related functions including tax credits, the national minimum wage, statutory sick pay, maternity pay, paternity and adoption pay (see Chapter 8).

If you have reason to complain to HMRC you should refer to their Code of Practice (COP) 1 – 'Putting things right – how to complain' (see **www.hmrc.gov.uk/leaflets/cop1.htm**).

Self-assessment

Individuals are responsible for self-assessing their liability to income tax, Class 4 National Insurance, some student loan repayments and capital gains tax. Companies have to self-assess their corporation tax.

Self-assessment places the responsibility on you as an individual or company to correctly calculate how much tax you owe and report this to HM Revenue and Customs by completing an annual tax return. HMRC will neither agree nor disagree with your self-assessment unless they enquire into your return which they can do for a certain length of time after the form has been submitted (see Enquiries).

Self-assessment also requires you to pay your taxes on time. Although HMRC usually send you a reminder near the due date for payment, if they fail to do so it is still up to you to pay any tax owing at the right time otherwise you will be charged interest and may face a surcharge (see Paying your tax).

Tax returns

You self-assess your tax liabilities by completing an annual tax return.

Individuals

Individuals are sent a form around the end of the tax year (5 April). It must be completed with details of your income, gains and claims to allowances for the tax year just ended. It must be returned to HMRC by 30 September if you want them to calculate your tax, or if you are an employee or director to include underpaid tax of up to £2,000 in your tax code (see Chapter 8). This filing date is extended to 30 December if you submit your return over the Internet. The final date that you can file the return and avoid a penalty is the 31 January which follows the end of the tax year (see Late returns) although if you are not sent a tax return or a notice to complete one until after 31 October, the filing date is three months from the date that the form is issued. You can choose to file a paper return or you can file it electronically via HMRC's website by following the links from 'Do It Online'. From 2008 all paper returns must be filed by 31 October.

If you have not been sent a tax return and think that you need to complete one, you must tell HMRC by the 5 October following the end of the relevant tax year to avoid a penalty. If you are self-employed you should be sent a return or a notice to complete one unless you have forgotten to tell HMRC about your business or moved address and not informed them. Make sure that you notify the tax authorities within three months of starting your business otherwise you will be fined £100 (see Chapter 4).

Companies

If you trade as a limited company, the period covered by your tax return is not the tax year but your accounting period and this varies from company to company. The return must usually be filed within twelve months of the end of the company's accounting period. Different dates apply if the accounting period is longer than twelve months. If it is late the company will be charged a penalty. You cannot ask HMRC to calculate the company's corporation tax so you may need to seek help from an accountant to do this. HMRC have a strong preference for company returns to be filed electronically (follow the links from 'Do It Online').

Employers

If you have employees or trade as a limited company, you must complete and submit an employer's end of year return (forms P35 and P14) before 19 May (22 May if they are filed electronically). The submission date is 6 July for forms P11D and P9D. By 2009/10 all employers will have to file their end of year returns electronically (see Chapter 8).

Tax year

The tax year runs from 6 April in one year to 5 April in the next. The tax year 2006/07 means that it starts on 6 April 2006 and ends on 5 April 2007. These unusual dates are the result of an historical anachronism. Personal and employer tax returns are completed for a tax year and should include all the transactions falling between 6 April and 5 April. Company returns are completed for an accounting period not a tax year.

If you are self-employed your accounting year does not have to coincide with the tax year and you can select any date you like. Many people however choose to prepare their accounts to the end of the tax year because it is simpler. You can also prepare accounts to 31 March and this is treated in the same way as if you had prepared the figures to 5 April (see Chapter 5).

Records

When you run a small business you must keep accounting records detailing all your transactions. If you are unsure how to maintain suitable records, you could refer to *Teach Yourself Small Business Accounting*, seek advice from an accountant or attend a bookkeeping course run by your local Business Link, see **www.businesslink.gov.uk**.

There are no hard and fast rules about how you should keep your accounting records because every business is different. They can be hand written or computerized. You may use an accounting software package or you can record your transactions on a spreadsheet. Irrespective of which method you use you must make sure that you do not lose the records. If you keep them on a computer you should take regular printouts and back up the system. If you keep a manual book you should periodically photocopy the pages.

Your accounting records should as a minimum achieve the following:

- **Record your income.** This might include a list of daily totals from your till or a running total of invoices sent to customers. You must retain your till rolls, copies of your invoices, appointment books and work diaries.
- **Record sums paid into your business bank account.** You must identify the source of all sums banked into your business bank account. You should also keep records of amounts paid into any private bank account (for example share dividends, transfers from other accounts, personal drawings or gifts). You must retain your bank statements and supporting papers such as paying-in books.
- **Record all your business expenses and sums paid out of your business account.** You need to keep records of who you have paid for business purchases and services, when and how much you paid them and the means of payment (bank transfer, cheque, cash or credit card). You must keep receipts for all business expenses as well as cheque books and credit card statements. You will need to find a satisfactory way of filing your receipts particularly if you have large numbers of them so that they do not get mislaid.

In addition, to maintaining these records, at your accounting year end you will need to work out and keep records of:

- The people who owe you money (debtors);
- Those who your business owes money to (creditors);
- The value of your stock, any work in hand and uncompleted contracts;
- Cash on hand including your till float and any petty cash;
- The equipment and assets used in your business (see Chapter 7); and
- Private motoring adjustments (see Chapter 5) and sums included for your home costs if you work from home (see Chapter 9).

To complete your personal tax return, you will also need to keep records of your non-business financial transactions such as:

- Employments, pensions received and state benefits;
- Rental income;
- Income from savings and investments;
- Pensions contributions paid;
- Gift aid payments to charity;
- Capital gains, for example from the sale of shares.

How long do I need to keep my records for?

If you are self-employed you need to keep your accounting and tax records for five years ten months from the end of the tax year. This means that for the tax year which ended on 5 April 2006, you must keep the records until at least 31 January 2012 (longer if HMRC enquires into your return). If you are trading as a limited company you must maintain your accounting records for six years from the end of your accounting period (again, longer if HMRC enquires into your return). If you fail to keep records HMRC can fine you up to £3,000.

Although you need to keep records to support the entries in your tax return, you do not need to send them to HMRC when you submit your tax form. The only time they will want to see them is if they launch an enquiry (see Enquiries).

Completing your tax return

This book does not explain in detail how to complete your tax return as HMRC publishes comprehensive guidance and helpsheets for individuals which can be accessed on **www.hmrc.gov.uk/individuals/fgcat-individualtaxreturn.shtml**. For information about company returns refer to **www.hmrc. gov.uk/ctsa/index.htm**.

Individuals

There are two versions of the paper tax return, a short tax return (SA 200) and the full version (SA 100). If HMRC has sent you the short form you should check the guidance notes to ensure that you are eligible to complete it. You must complete the full return if you are:

- a company director;
- a partner;
- self-employed with sales of more than £15,000, multiple businesses, loss claims or if you want to change your accounting date.

Even if you are entitled to complete the short return, you may choose not to because it does not include a space to explain how you have prepared your accounts. For example, to provide details of the private use of your car, or use of home allowances. If HMRC need this information to appreciate that your self-assessment could be too low and you have not supplied it, they could raise a discovery assessment at a later date to collect extra tax (see Discovery assessments).

The full version of the return requires you to complete supplementary pages for each employment or directorship, self-employment and partnership. You do not usually need to submit accounts with the return but if your business is complex or the accounts show details not reflected on the return, you might want to send them to HMRC to ensure that you have made full disclosure. If you submit them you should highlight the reason why you are doing so. Alternatively you could use the additional information boxes on the return to provide any information which you think will help HMRC to understand your form better. Irrespective of whether you submit your accounts, you must make sure that the tax return form is fully and correctly completed.

Companies

Companies must complete a form CT 600 and file it together with accounts and computations. There is a short version of the form which can be completed by most small companies. The returns require the completion of a number of supplementary pages most of which do not affect small companies. Forms, supplementary pages and a completion guide can be accessed on **www.hmrc.gov.uk/ctsa/returns.htm.**

Late returns

Individuals

If you fail to send in your tax return by the final filing date HMRC can raise their own assessment of your tax and Class 4 National Insurance. This assessment will be cancelled once your own return is submitted. If your return is late you will usually be charged an automatic penalty of:

- £100 if the return is not filed by 1 February (you usually have one day's grace after the 31 January filing deadline) but if you owe tax of less than £100, the fine is limited to the tax you owe. If you are owed a refund, you cannot be fined.
- A further £100 if the return is not filed by 31 July (or six months from the filing date if later).
- If the return is still outstanding on the following 31 January, a fine equal to the tax due.

- HMRC can in some cases charge a penalty of £60 per day for persistent failure to file a return.

The only way that these penalties can be reduced is if you had a 'reasonable excuse' for not submitting the return on time. HMRC interprets this very narrowly and in most cases it would only work as a defence if you had been seriously ill from the date the return was issued. Normal domestic dramas and another person's ill-health are rarely sufficient for you to claim that you had a reasonable excuse for not completing your return on time.

Although the penalties for failure to submit a tax return on time may not seem particularly significant if the return is less than six months late, this is unlikely to be the end of the story. If you have not paid your tax because your form is outstanding you may also owe interest and surcharges (see Paying your tax late). Taking penalties, interest and surcharges together plus interest on outstanding penalties and surcharges, the costs may be much higher than you expect.

Companies

If you send in your tax return after the final filing date you will be charged an automatic penalty (which cannot be mitigated by claiming that there was a reasonable excuse) as follows:

- £100 if the return is up to three months late but £500 if it is the third successive return to be filed late.
- £200 if the return is more than three months late but £1,000 if it is the third successive late return.
- If a company fails to deliver a return and pay the corporation tax for more than 18 months, it will be fined 10% of the unpaid tax for a return submitted between 18 and 24 months after the filing date and 20% of the unpaid tax for returns filed more than 24 months late.

Employers

If a business fails to submit their employer end of year return on time, the following penalties are charged:

- For forms P35, P14 and P11D(b): £100 for every 50 employees for each month or part of a month for which the return remains outstanding. This means that an employer with three employees who files their employer return three months late faces a £300 penalty. The fine is limited to the total tax and National Insurance contributions deducted from your staff during the tax year.

- For forms P11D and P9D: £300 for each outstanding form plus up to £60 per day if the failure continues. An incorrectly completed form can attract a penalty of up to £3,000.

Paying your tax

Some people work out their own tax bill and know how much tax to pay but many people rely on HMRC to calculate their tax for them. HMRC's calculations are not always correct because errors can occur when the information is transferred from your tax return to their computer system (unless you file your tax return online). You should therefore check any tax calculation carefully to ensure that it includes all your sources of income. If you retain a copy of your tax return this should be fairly straightforward. If HMRC ask you to pay too little tax it is up to you to have the calculation corrected otherwise you could be liable to interest and surcharges if they discover the underpayment at a later date.

Details of how to pay your tax are given on HMRC's website, see **www.hmrc.gov.uk/howtopay/menu.htm**.

The dates on which you pay tax differ for individuals and companies.

Self-employed individuals and partners

Most self-employed people pay two equal tax payments on 31 January and 31 July. These payments are based on the amount of tax you paid in the previous tax year and are called 'payments on account'. They are deducted from your total tax liability for the year. If your tax liability is more than the payments you have made on account you must make a 'balancing payment' the following 31 January. If your payments on account exceed your tax liability the excess will be refunded to you or deducted from your next tax instalment.

Example

Magdalen's self-assessment for 2005/06 is £3,300. She has to make payments on account of her 2006/07 tax liabilities of £1,650 on 31 January 2007 and £1,650 on 31 July 2007. She works out her tax for 2006/07 when she completes her tax return in August 2007 and it totals £3,500. Magdalen has paid £3,300 as two payments on account of £1,650 but she still owes HMRC £200 which she pays on 31 January 2008.

On 31 January 2008 Magdalen owes her first payment on account for 2007/08. This is half of her total tax bill for 2006/07 so she pays £1,750 (£3,500 divided by 2) making her total tax payment on 31 January 2008 £1,950 (£1,750 + £200). On 31 July 2007 she pays a further £1,750 on account. She works out her 2007/08 tax when she completes her tax return in September 2008 and it comes to £3,000. As Magdalen has already paid two tax instalments of £1,750 i.e. a total of £3,500, she will receive a refund of the £500 she has overpaid. Her payments on account for 2008/09 will be £1,500 per instalment.

Recap

On 31 January you may have to pay two lots of tax – a balancing payment for the previous tax year and a payment on account for the current year.

No payments on account

If your income tax for the previous tax year totalled less than £500 you do not have to make any payments on account. Payments on account are not required if more than 80% of your tax bill is covered by tax already deducted under PAYE or from other sources (e.g. bank interest).

If you are just starting in business you will probably make no payments on account in the first year. This means that when you prepare your first tax return you will owe tax for the whole of your first year plus you may have to make a payment on account for the next tax year. If you have not planned for these tax liabilities you may find that your business gets into financial difficulties. Chapter 4 tells you how to keep track of your tax liabilities when you start up in business. Budgeting for your tax bills once you are an established business is considered in Chapter 5.

Reducing your payments on account

If you expect your profits in the current year to be lower than those for the previous tax year so that your payments on account will exceed the tax you owe, it is possible to reduce them by completing form SA 303 (see **www.hmrc.gov.uk/selfemployed/faqsa303.shtml**). You need to be careful if you are considering this course of action because if you reduce the payments below the amount you owe you will be charged interest on the shortfall. You may also have to pay a penalty if HMRC considers that you have been negligent in your calculations.

Paying your tax late

It is tempting to think that tax comes at the bottom of your pile of bills but if you pay your tax after the due date you will be charged interest at a set rate which changes from time to time (see Appendix 1). You may also incur a 5% surcharge if you have not paid your tax by 28 February and a further 5% surcharge is levied on any tax still unpaid by 31 July. Interest is charged on any unpaid surcharges and penalties so if you are late with your tax payments, the costs can soon mount up. Taxpayers who pay their tax late probably also face an increased risk of an enquiry.

Companies

Most companies have to pay their corporation tax nine months and one day after the end of their accounting period. Companies with annual profits above £1,500,000 have to pay their tax quarterly. If a company pays its corporation tax after the due date it will be charged interest (see Appendix 1). This can be deducted from the business profits.

Employers

The dates by which you must pay over the PAYE and National Insurance deducted from your employees' wages to HMRC are set out in Appendix 2. Interest is charged on sums still outstanding on 19 April after the end of the tax year (22 April if you pay electronically).

Correcting errors

If you discover that an entry on your tax return is incorrect after you have submitted the form you have twelve months from the official filing date to amend it. If you have underpaid tax as a result you will have to pay interest and surcharges if appropriate (see Paying your tax late). In some cases HMRC can charge a penalty.

The tax authorities have nine months from the date you file your return to correct any obvious errors on the form. If they do this you should check why they want to make the alteration and if you are unsure about the changes they have made you should consider taking professional advice. You will need to do this quickly as you have to reject HMRC's amendment within 30 days.

Enquiries

HMRC will never tell you that they are satisfied with your tax return and because it is up to you to self-assess your tax they have a right to check the form in detail. This process is called an enquiry, investigation or audit. HMRC handles tax enquiries in accordance with a number of Codes of Practice, see **www.hmrc.gov.uk/leaflets/c11.htm**.

If HMRC starts an enquiry into your return, it does not necessarily mean that you have done anything wrong. Some enquiries are selected entirely randomly to give the tax authorities information about how accurately taxpayers are completing their forms. The majority of enquiries are however chosen because HMRC considers that the form may contain one or more errors and that you may have underpaid your tax as a result. Some enquiries are into just one aspect of the return; others will scrutinize all the entries on the form. HMRC use a variety of means to select returns for enquiry. The most common are:

- Information supplied by third parties or collected by HM Revenue and Customs;
- A suspicion that your profits, drawings or salary are not sufficient to support your lifestyle;
- Your return appears to be out of line with your previous years' forms or returns filed by other similar businesses in your area.

Notifying the start of an enquiry

A tax enquiry is a formal process and HMRC must tell you that an enquiry has started by issuing a written notice. The notice must be sent to you within a year of the official filing date for the return. If you are a sole trader this usually means that if your return has to be filed by 31 January 2007, HMRC have until 31 January 2008 to start an enquiry for that year. If you file the return after 31 January or amend it, the period in which HMRC can enquire into the form is extended. It is worth checking that HMRC has adhered correctly to these dates because notices are sometimes issued incorrectly.

The passing of the final date for opening an enquiry into a tax return unfortunately does not give you any certainty that HMRC are satisfied with it. They can 'discover' underpaid tax for up to five years ten months following the end of the tax year (for individuals) and six years (for companies) if they can prove that your tax return contained insufficient information to enable the tax authorities to fully understand the entries you have made on the form. This period is longer if you have been fraudulent (see Discovery assessments).

What do I do if my return is chosen for an enquiry?

If you receive a notice informing you that HMRC is enquiring into your tax return, you will almost certainly require help from an accountant who specializes in dealing with the tax authorities on these matters. A tax enquiry should be taken seriously as it is likely to have financial consequences for your business. If a tax underpayment is discovered due to under-declared income or over-claimed expenses or reliefs, not only will you have to pay the tax but interest and penalties on top. A shortfall in one year may also lead to HMRC reviewing the position for previous years, so depending on the amount of unpaid tax you could end up paying the tax authorities a significant additional sum. HMRC now deals with all taxes so an underpayment in one field may lead an enquiry in another, for example PAYE or VAT. You could also have to repay some of your tax credits.

What happens in an enquiry?

An enquiry will involve HMRC scrutinizing your accounting records. They may also ask to see private bank statements, contracts etc. You can refuse to let them see documents that you do not consider relevant to the enquiry but if you do not co-operate with HMRC any penalty they charge may be higher. Ultimately HMRC can issue a notice obliging you to hand over the documents they require. To challenge this notice you would have to appeal to the Commissioners (see Can I appeal?). HMRC also have powers to search premises and seize documents in more serious cases.

Once they have looked at your records, HMRC will request a meeting with you and your accountant if you have one. HMRC use these meetings to find out as much as possible about your business. They may ask to visit your business premises but you can refuse if it is inappropriate. Sometimes they will gather information about your business by pretending to be a customer or client. HMRC are experienced in interviewing taxpayers and you are likely to find meetings with them intimidating unless you take someone with you.

During the meeting the officer handling the enquiry will usually discuss any aspects of your return that they have problems with. Afterwards they may ask you to supply additional information, or you may wish to provide it to counter their allegations. To conclude the enquiry HMRC will either suggest you amend your self-assessment or they will amend it for you. If you disagree with HMRC's amendment you can appeal against it (see Can I appeal?). In some cases you may reach a negotiated agreement (called a settlement) with HMRC about the extent of any underpayment together with interest and penalties. When the enquiry is over HMRC should issue a closure notice informing you of the fact.

Fees and insurance

If you engage an accountant to help you with the enquiry you will not usually be able to deduct their costs as a business expense in your accounts if it turns out that you owe additional tax. It is possible to take out fee protection insurance to cover the costs of an experienced adviser to help you in the event that your tax return is chosen for an enquiry. In most circumstances these costs are also not tax-deductible. No insurance policy will cover the cost of any additional tax you owe as the result of an investigation into your affairs.

Discovery assessments

Once the final date for enquiring into your return has passed (see Notifying the start of an enquiry), HMRC can still raise a tax assessment if they 'discover' that you have underpaid tax because you provided too little detail on your return to make them aware that it included contentious or subjective entries. Most small business people should make written disclosure of their accounting policies, adjustments and valuations to avoid the possibility of a discovery assessment being raised. The full version of the tax return includes space for you to explain your transactions. Alternatively you can submit supplementary information with the form.

Can I appeal?

If you disagree with HM Revenue and Customs and cannot resolve the matter you can appeal to either the General Commissioners or the Special Commissioners. If you disagree with the Commissioners' decision on a point of law you can appeal to the High Court and ultimately to the House of Lords. The Commissioners' findings about the facts of the case cannot usually be appealed to a higher court. The costs of dealing with an appeal can be significant and you will need to obtain information about your chance of success before undertaking this course of action.

> ## Recap
>
> The tax system places the onus on you to:
>
> - inform HMRC that you need to complete a tax return;
> - keep records of your financial transactions;
> - fill in the form fully and accurately;
> - file it on time; and
> - pay any tax due.
>
> If you fail to do so you will face additional costs in the form of interest, penalties and surcharges. HMRC police the tax system by enquiring into certain taxpayers' affairs each year. Keeping on top of all these requirements can be burdensome for a small business and you may find it cost effective to use an accountant to help you to avoid the pitfalls.

04

starting a business

In this chapter:
- choice of business medium
- self-employment versus limited company – a checklist
- am I really self-employed?
- notifying HM Revenue and Customs
- pre-trading expenditure
- business finance
- anticipating tax payments
- recap case study

When you start a business, you have to decide whether to operate as a sole trader, partnership or limited company. There are many commercial and practical reasons for operating as one type of business rather than another and the choice of trading medium affects the amount and type of tax you pay.

Working on your own

If you decide to set up in business on your own you have to choose between trading as a limited company (being incorporated), or working as a sole trader (being self-employed). You may also want to review whether it is advantageous to form a limited company if you are already self-employed and your business is expanding (see Chapter 12).

Sole trader

Operating as a sole trader is the simplest trading method. No formalities are required apart from notifying HM Revenue and Customs. The disadvantage is that you are personally liable for all your business debts. This means that you could have to sell your house to pay your creditors if the business fails. There are ways to partly protect yourself such as owning your home in joint names but you should take legal advice.

Operating as a sole trader is most suitable for people who do not take many risks. They often work from home or a rented room and sell their own services rather than manufactured goods, for example therapists, consultants, artists and writers. Many trades people such as electricians and plumbers are also self-employed.

Sole traders are responsible for the following taxes:

- Class 2 National Insurance paid at a weekly flat rate by monthly direct debit or quarterly payment;
- income tax and Class 4 National Insurance paid on their trading profits;
- operating PAYE on their employees' pay; and
- registering for VAT if necessary.

Limited company

The biggest advantage of trading as a limited company is that you are not personally liable for any business debts. If your enterprise fails, whilst you may lose all the assets in the company and your shares will be worthless, your personal property is protected unless you have had to pledge the assets to the bank to secure a loan or overdraft, or you have been fraudulent.

Operating as a company is most suitable for riskier businesses which require greater capital investment (such as equipment or stock), or where a large bad debt, poor period of trading or claim could destroy the business. Trading as a company may be necessary if you want outside investors to put money into the venture.

If you are considering incorporating a company you should seek professional advice. It is easy to form a company but much more complicated to close it down (see Chapter 13). You may also be surprised to discover that you cannot take any money out of the company apart from your salary, a dividend or to reimburse expenses as the company's money is separate from your own. There is also far more paperwork and bureaucracy to contend with.

Limited companies are responsible for the following taxes:

- paying corporation tax on their profits;
- paying VAT if VAT registered;
- operating PAYE on employees' salaries.

Directors' salaries and perks

As a company director you are an employee of the company and have to pay income tax and employee's National Insurance on your salary under the PAYE system (see Chapter 8). The company has to pay employer's National Insurance on top of your salary. This can add considerably to the cost of trading through a company. You will also have to pay income tax on many of the perks that the company provides you with (for example a car or private medical insurance) and once again the company has to pay employer's National Insurance on these.

Dividends

As well as being a director you will probably also own shares in the company. If the company is profitable some of the profits can be paid to you as a dividend. Dividends can also be paid to other members of your family who are shareholders. The dividend is paid with a tax credit and provided that you do not pay tax at the higher rate you have no further tax to pay (see Chapter 2). Unlike a salary, no employee's or employer's National Insurance is paid on dividends. This favourable tax treatment has led to many small businesses paying their company directors small salaries and large dividends to save tax and National Insurance. HM Revenue and Customs does not like owner-managed companies saving tax in this way and they now prevent some dividend planning by tax rules known as 'IR35' and 'the settlements legislation'. IR35 stops you saving tax and National Insurance by using a company or partnership to provide personal services where you would otherwise be considered to be employed by your client (see Personal services). The tax authorities may use the settlements legislation to stop you saving tax by paying dividends to members of your family who earn less than you do and pay tax at a lower rate as a result.

If you decide to trade as a limited company and want to take significant dividends from the company you will require professional advice otherwise you risk completing your self-assessment return incorrectly and you could have to pay extra tax, penalties and interest if HM Revenue and Customs enquires into your return (see Chapter 3).

Comparison of trading through a limited company rather than as a sole trader

Limited company	Sole trader
Directors' salaries are paid under PAYE with income tax and National Insurance deducted when the salary is paid. Employee's Class 1 National Insurance is paid at a higher rate than self-employed contributions.	Sole trader's drawings are not taxed. ✓ Self-employed Class 2 National Insurance is paid at a flat weekly rate irrespective of the amount of your profits.
Employer's National Insurance is paid on directors' salaries by the company.	No employer's National Insurance is paid by a sole trader. ✓
Company profits (after deducting directors' salaries) are charged to corporation tax. This may be charged at a lower rate than income tax.	Profits are taxed at income tax rates. Class 4 National Insurance is also due.
Many company perks are liable to income tax and National Insurance.	Perks are treated as drawings and are not liable to tax and National Insurance.
Dividends can be paid. In some circumstances these may save tax and National Insurance but HM Revenue and Customs have ways of preventing certain types of dividend planning.	Dividends only apply to companies.
Company money is distinct and separate from your own. You can only take money from the company as a salary, dividend or to reimburse legitimate business expenses. If you take other money from the company it may be illegal and you will still be taxed on it.	There is no legal difference between the money belonging to the business and your own funds. You should however keep accounting records which accurately record all the business transactions.

Limited company	Sole-trader
Some tax reliefs for research and development, goodwill and intellectual property are only available to limited companies.	Sole traders and partners can not claim these tax reliefs.
As a director and employee you will be entitled to benefits not available to sole traders and partners such as statutory maternity pay, jobseeker's allowance and the state second pension.	Sole traders are not entitled to the same state and pension benefits as employees because they pay National Insurance at a lower rate.
Tax relief is available to some private investors under the enterprise investment scheme.	No enterprise investment scheme tax relief is possible.

Company or sole trader?

There is no easy way to tell whether you will be financially better off trading as a company rather than a sole trader as it depends on a number of factors including:

- How much profit the business makes;
- How much money you need for your personal use;
- The amount you need to leave invested in the businesses; and
- The scope to pay significant dividends.

An accountant will be able to undertake calculations to help you decide whether to form a limited company; however, they can only ever be a guide as to whether using a limited company is the best option. You should bear in mind three things:

1 Business profits, your investment requirements, tax rates and the law change continually.
2 Running a company is more complicated than being self-employed and your adviser may have a vested interest in recommending incorporation to increase his or her fees.
3 Forming a company is straightforward. Getting rid of one is not.

Working with others

If you decide to set up in business with other people you have the following trading options:

- A limited company (most co-operatives are also constituted as companies) (see page 44);
- A partnership; and
- A limited liability partnership;

Partnership

A partnership is similar to a sole trader but with several people jointly running the business. There is no limit on the number of partners you can have but where a large number of individuals are involved it may be simpler to form a limited company. A partnership differs from a limited company in that it is not a separate business entity except in Scotland. Each partner is bound by the actions of the other partners and your personal assets may be at risk if the business fails. A partnership agreement may be required but it is not compulsory. If you are planning to set up a partnership you will need professional advice.

Partnership profits are shared between the individual partners in the way that they have agreed amongst themselves. Each partner is taxed as if they were running their own self-employed business and pays Class 2 National Insurance, and income tax and Class 4 National Insurance on their share of the trading profits. A partnership is responsible for:

- operating PAYE on its employees' pay;
- VAT registration (if necessary).

Limited liability partnership (LLP)

LLPs have been available since 2001 and combine some features of a limited company and some of a partnership. Like a company, the members of an LLP are not personally liable for the business debts. Provided that they are not negligent, even if the LLP becomes insolvent, the individual members only risk their partnership investment not their homes and other assets.

The income tax treatment of most LLPs is like an ordinary partnership. The profits are shared between the members in the way set out in the members' agreement. Each partner is taxed as if they were running their own self-employed business paying Class 2 National Insurance, and income tax and Class 4 National Insurance on their share of the trading profits. The LLP is also responsible for:

- operating PAYE on its employees' pay; and
- VAT registration.

If you are planning to set up a limited liability partnership you will require professional advice as there are a number of formalities which must be complied with.

Notifying HM Revenue and Customs

Irrespective of whether you choose to operate as a sole trader, partnership, LLP or company, when you set up a business you have to notify HM Revenue and Customs about the following events:

- Starting to trade;
- Taking on employees (see Chapter 8);
- Needing to register for VAT (see Chapter 10).

Starting to trade

One of the first things to decide is the date that the business starts trading. If you fail to notify HM Revenue and Customs on time you may be penalized (see Notification process). With a limited company, LLP or partnership this is fairly straightforward. You will probably have purchased a company 'off-the-shelf', drawn up a partnership or members' agreement and opened a business bank account in readiness for your first trading transactions. With a self-employment, determining a start date may be more complicated particularly if you have previously undertaken similar work as a hobby. There are no hard and fast rules for deciding when a hobby turns into a business and it depends on the facts of each particular situation.

Case study

Basil works full-time for the local council and is a keen gardener. He often grows more plants than he can use himself so he sells the spare ones to his friends and neighbours. He estimates that he earns about £100 a year by doing this which he reinvests in seeds and compost.

Basil is probably not self-employed. He does not grow the plants to make a profit. The money he makes is not his main source of income and he only spends his leisure time working in the garden as he has a full-time job. The people who buy from Basil would probably not consider that he was running a nursery.

Basil's circumstances change. He is made redundant and as he is not working, grows more plants. He starts selling these from his front garden and once a week sells some of them at a car boot sale. He takes £1,000 in three months. Basil is almost certainly self-employed. He grows and sells plants to supplement his income and spends many hours a week doing so. He now takes risks and grows plants only for resale. His customers probably think that Basil is a commercial grower.

The main facts to consider when deciding when to register as self-employed are:

- Do you aim to make a profit?
- Is the income significant to you?
- Do you spend several hours a week on the business activities?
- Would an impartial member of the public think that you were in business?
- Do you risk losing money?

Personal services

If you provide personal services, for example you mainly sell your time and labour and not a product, HM Revenue and Customs may not always consider that you are self-employed. Instead you could be treated as an employee. There is no easy way to tell whether you are employed or self-employed for a particular contract and once again it depends on the facts. In tax language, the main distinction between employment and self-employment is as follows:

- are you providing a contract *of* service (in which case you are an employee); or
- fulfilling a contract *for* services (when you will be self-employed)?

The fact that you do not receive holiday, overtime or sick pay are not important and do not necessarily point to you being self-employed. The main factors that indicate a self-employment are:

- You decide how, when and where you work rather than someone telling you what to do and giving you orders.
- You could send a substitute to do the work, for example your own employee.
- You risk making a loss, for example if you make a mistake you have to correct it in your own time.
- You provide your own equipment and not just the small tools that an employee might provide.
- You work for several people or businesses at the same time and have several different clients on your books.

For further information see HM Revenue and Customs leaflet IR56 'Employed and Self-employed'.

If you try to circumvent these rules by providing personal services through a company or partnership, HM Revenue and Customs can use the IR35 rules (see Limited company) to prevent you saving tax and National Insurance. They do this by pretending that the intermediary company or partnership does not exist and tax you as if you were directly employed by your client.

Casual income

Sometimes a person will be neither self-employed nor employed but simply receiving a casual (often one-off) payment for work undertaken or services provided, for example selling a photograph to a magazine. In this case there is no need to follow the notification process below but the income will need to be declared to HM Revenue and Customs on a self-assessment return. If you do not usually receive a return you must tell the tax authorities that you need to complete one by 5 October following the end of the tax year in which the payment fell, otherwise you will be liable to a penalty. There is space on the tax form to enter casual income not declared elsewhere on the return. If you are unsure whether you should be registered as self-employed you may need to ask an accountant.

Notification process

HM Revenue and Customs must be notified within three months from the end of the month in which you begin to be self-employed that you are in business. If you fail to do so you will be fined £100.

When you set up in self-employment or join a partnership you must complete HM Revenue and Customs form CWF1 'Becoming self-employed and registering for National Insurance Contributions and/or tax'. The form can be downloaded from **www.hmrc.gov.uk/startingup/register.htm** or completed by calling the Self-Employed Registration Helpline on 08459 154515. The form requires the following information:

• Name and contact details;
• National Insurance number;
• Continuing employments (if any);
• Start date;
• Nature of the self-employed work;
• Trading name and contact details;
• Details of any business partners.

If you are over state retirement age you do not need to pay Class 2 National Insurance. If you already complete a self-assessment tax return there is no need to notify HM Revenue and Customs.

Building industry sub-contractors must separately register under the Construction Industry Scheme, **www.hmrc.gov.uk/selfemployed/iwtapply-for-a-cis-registration-card-or-tax-certif.shtml** (see Chapter 8).

If you have set up a limited company you must notify your local HM Revenue and Customs business support team, **www.hmrc.gov.uk/bst/work.htm**. You should also notify your tax office that you have become a company director so that they can send you the correct self-assessment tax return pages to complete in due course.

If you have appointed an accountant to help you, you will need to sign form 64–8 authorizing HM Revenue and Customs to deal with them on your behalf. This can be withdrawn by you at any time by informing the tax authorities.

What does being registered with HM Revenue and Customs mean?

Once you have informed HM Revenue and Customs about your business you will start paying Class 2 National Insurance unless you are exempt (see Chapter 2). At the end of the tax year (5 April) you will be sent a tax return which must be completed with details of your business income and expenses (see Chapters 3 and 5). The form must be returned no later than the following 31 January (30 September if you want HM Revenue and Customs to work out your tax bill) otherwise you will be penalized. If you have incorporated a company, the company also has to complete an annual self-assessment return.

Being registered with HM Revenue and Customs does not mean that you are automatically treated as self employed in all circumstances (see Personal services). It is up to the person or business with whom you contract to determine whether you are employed or self-employed for that particular piece of work. If you want to dispute your employment status you should take professional advice before you speak to HM Revenue and Customs.

Other notifications

When you start a business there are various other organizations that you should notify depending on your circumstances.

Tax credits

If you receive Child Tax Credit because you have children, or Working Tax Credit because you have a low income or disability, you may need to inform HM Revenue and Customs about your new business venture depending on whether you think your income for the current year will be more or less than it was previously. If you anticipate your income rising by more than £25,000 a year you should inform HMRC otherwise your tax credits will be overpaid. If you expect your income to fall, notifying your change in circumstance could increase your award straight away. For further information see **www.taxcredits.inlandrevenue.gov.uk/HomeNew.aspx**.

State benefits

If you are in receipt of state benefits, you are required to inform the Department for Work and Pensions about the new business as it is a change in your circumstances.

Business rates

If you are renting or purchasing business premises, or modifying your home to provide accommodation for your business you may be liable for business rates paid to the local council (see Chapter 9).

Expenditure incurred before the business starts

As we have seen in this chapter it is not always clear when a business actually starts trading. Often you will have incurred expenditure many months, or even years, before the business finally gets off the ground. Provided that you have kept a record of these pre-trading expenses, any money spent up to seven years before the business starts trading is a tax-deductible expense of the first accounting period.

Equipment (including cars) purchased before trading commences can be introduced into the business valued at the asset's current market value. The item then becomes eligible for a 25% capital allowance. This is deducted from your taxable profit and saves you tax (see Chapter 7).

Financing the business

Raising sufficient finance to start a new business is often difficult for budding entrepreneurs. The tax consequences and implications for your choice of trading medium are considered in the following paragraphs.

Bank loans and overdrafts

The interest on business loans and overdrafts is allowable as a business expense and reduces the taxable profits (see Chapter 5). The loan or overdraft repayments have to be met out of the profits generated by the business and they are not deducted from your taxable income.

Partnership loans

A partner can obtain tax relief on the interest on a loan taken out to invest in a partnership. No relief is available for investment in some types of LLP.

Loans to invest in a company or co-operative

Individuals (provided that the investor and company meet various conditions) can obtain tax relief on the interest on a loan taken out to invest in a small company or co-operative.

Private investors

You may find that friends, family and other private investors want to invest in your business. If so you will probably need to trade through a limited company. Where a company qualifies for the Enterprise Investment Scheme, an investor can obtain tax relief on their investment provided they hold onto the shares for a set period of time (see Appendix 1). When the shares are sold they are also exempt from capital gains tax provided that the investment and the company satisfy detailed rules. You will require professional advice if you want to raise funds for your business in this way.

Anticipating tax payments

For sole traders and partners there is often a significant time delay between earning profits and paying the tax on them particularly in the early days of a new business. If you forget this, you may have an unpleasant surprise when your first tax bill arrives. Sole traders and partners pay income tax and Class 4 National Insurance on 31 January and 31 July each year but not during the first year of a new business (see Chapter 3). This can cause financial difficulties if the liability is not anticipated well in advance.

Example

Adam starts a self-employed business on 1 July 2006. His profits for the nine months to 31 March 2007 are entered on his 2006/07 tax return. The return is submitted to HM Revenue and Customs in September 2007. Adam's tax bill for 2006/07 comes to £5,000 and is due for payment on 31 January 2008.

In addition on this date he has to pay £2,500 (half his liability for 2006/07) as a payment on account of his potential tax bill for 2007/08. This makes his total payment on 31 January 2008 £7,500.

Adam paid no tax during the first 19 months of his business because he was newly self-employed. He then has to pay a large amount all at once. If Adam has not planned in advance for this tax bill he could face financial problems especially as he has to pay a further £2,500 only six months later on 31 July 2008.

There are two ways to plan for potential tax bills. The first is to do nothing and if necessary to borrow the money when the liability falls due. Be aware that banks do not like lending money to pay tax bills and if you have to borrow funds to pay your tax, the interest is not tax-deductible as personal tax payments are private expenditure and part of your drawings (see Chapter 5). The second approach is to put money aside on a regular basis to meet the liability. It can be difficult to know how much to allocate for your tax bills particularly in the first year of trading, as you will probably not know how much your profits will amount to. As a very general rule, if your profits are between £15,000 and £30,000 and you provide services rather than manufacturing a product or running a shop, your tax bill will usually be 15–20% of your takings or sales. If you run a shop or manufacturing business the percentage will usually be lower than this. It may also be useful to know that if you make a profit equivalent to average earnings (about £22,000) your annual bill for income tax and Class 4 National Insurance will be approximately £5,000. Budgeting for your tax bills is considered further in Chapter 5, How much tax do I owe on my profits?

Recap case study

Jasmine leaves her job in a city hairdressing salon to set up in business as a mobile hairdresser. She reviews the advantages and disadvantages of trading as a sole trader or a company and decides that because the business is not particularly risky that she will operate as a sole trader under the name 'Jasmine Hair'. She takes out a business bank loan and acquires a small van along with the necessary scissors, appliances and products. Jasmine starts visiting customers on 1 May.

On 1 June Jasmine notifies HM Revenue and Customs that 'Jasmine Hair' started trading on 1 May. She completes form

CWF1 and starts paying Class 2 National Insurance contributions by monthly direct debit backdated to 1 May. She expects to take £1,500 a month from customers in her first year of trading and does not need to register for VAT. She decides not to do so voluntarily.

Jasmine starts to keep records of her business income and expenses following the system set out in *Teach Yourself – Small Business Accounting*. She is concerned about how much tax she will have to pay so she puts 15% of her takings away at the end of each month in a separate deposit account.

The following April Jasmine receives her self-assessment tax return. She remembers to claim tax relief on the business loan interest and some towels and gowns that she purchased before she started trading. She also makes a note to claim capital allowances on the van and hairdressing equipment she purchased.

When Jasmine comes to pay her income tax the following 31 January plus a payment of half as much tax again as a payment on account for the current year, she is pleased to find that she has more than enough put away in her tax account to meet the bill.

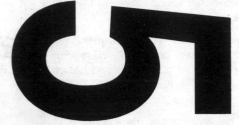

profits

In this chapter:
- choice of accounting year end
- calculating your business profits
- which expenses are tax-deductible?
- special situations
- how much tax do I owe on my profits?
- recap case study

By now you will probably have decided whether you are going to operate as a sole trader, partnership or limited company and you may have started trading. This chapter helps you with the next stage – choosing a suitable accounting year end, understanding how your taxable profits are calculated and learning which expenses are tax-deductible. This information will enable you to keep accurate accounting records from which you will prepare your tax return in due course.

Choice of year end

Within the first few months of starting your business you should choose a suitable accounting year end date to prepare your first accounts to. After it has passed, you will need to draw up accounts or make entries on your tax return to reflect all the trading transactions for your first accounting period. This period is unlikely to be for exactly twelve months and will probably be between six and eighteen months long. In subsequent years you will usually prepare a statement of your income and expenses on an annual basis unless you change your accounting date or cease trading.

Sole traders

If you are a sole trader or a partner, there are two basic choices:

- A year end which coincides with the end of the tax year (5 April or 31 March); or
- Another date (usually extended to the last day of the month for convenience). This date may be the anniversary of your starting the business or another convenient date, for example a date occurring during a quiet period if the business is seasonal or to coincide with one of your VAT returns if you are VAT registered.

Using an accounting date other than 5 April or 31 March will make your tax affairs more complicated particularly in the first two years. You may need to take advice so that you calculate your profits correctly.

You will not save tax by your choice of year end date because the income tax system is designed to tax all your profits over the lifetime of your business. There are however good reasons for selecting one year end over another:

- If your profits are on a rising trend you may defer a higher tax bill for a year by using a year end other than 5 April or 31 March (see the Example of Linda). The disadvantage is that you may owe more tax than you expect in a subsequent tax year or when you cease the business.
- You need to use a year end which gives you enough time to prepare your accounts so that you can submit your tax return on time.

Example

If you started trading early in the year, say on 1 February 2006, you may be tempted to use 31 January 2007 as your accounting year end. In the first tax year you will either have to submit your tax return with provisional entries or send in the form late – not an auspicious start to your self-employment. This is because your 2005/06 tax return which has to be submitted by 31 January 2007 requires you to include two months' worth of the profits from your accounts. As your year end is not until 31 January 2007 it is impossible to file an accurate return on the due date. If you submit your tax return with provisional entries you will pay tax based on estimated figures and if you pay too little tax as a result, you will be charged interest.

Using a year end of 5 April or 31 March

Many sole traders select 5 April as their accounting date. As it is the end of the tax year it makes completing the tax return as straightforward as possible. You can also use a date of 31 March and the tax authorities treat it as if it is 5 April. This means that:

- If you choose 31 March as your year end, your tax return for the year to 5 April 2007 will show your income and expenditure for the period 1 April 2006–31 March 2007.
- If you use a 5 April date, your return for the year to 5 April 2007 will include your accounting transactions for the period 6 April 2006–5 April 2007.

If you use either a 5 April or 31 March date, it is unlikely that you will have traded for a full year by the time you come to draw up your first set of accounts. In this case your return will show your profits or losses from the date you started to trade to either 5 April or 31 March even if this period is only a few months long.

Example

Anil starts his business on 1 November 2006. He wants to make completing his tax return as straightforward as possible and chooses an accounting date of 31 March. His tax return to 5 April 2007 shows his transactions from 1 November 2006 to 31 March 2007.

Preparing accounts to another date

If you decide to use an accounting date other than 5 April or 31 March it may be for commercial reasons to fit in with your trading cycle. For example, a nursery school might adopt 31 July to coincide with the end of the school year.

A date which is not either 5 April or 31 March will result in profits being taxed more than once in the early years. This is not necessarily as bad as it sounds, particularly if your profits are increasing. Tax relief is given for these 'overlap' profits when you cease trading, or in some cases if you change your accounting date. You will need to calculate your overlap profits and enter them on your tax form each year.

Example

Linda starts up a business as sole trader on 1 July 2006. She decides to prepare her first accounts for a year to 30 June 2007. She calculates her profit as £16,000.

- Her tax return to 5 April 2007 will tax profits of £12,000 covering the period from when she starts the business to the end of the tax year. This is the period 1 July 2006–5 April 2007. She calculates her profits by taking nine months out of the twelve-month accounting period. That is £16,000 × 9 months divided by 12 months = £12,000.
- Linda will also use the accounts for the year to 30 June 2007 to complete her tax return for the tax year to 5 April 2008 because this is a set of accounts which ends in the tax year covered by the return (6 April 2007–5 April 2008). Her taxable profits for 2007/08 are therefore £16,000.
- You may have noticed that Linda has already paid tax on nine months' worth of these profits (£12,000) in the previous tax year to 5 April 2007. These profits which are taxed twice become Linda's 'overlap' profits. Linda can claim relief for these if she ceases to be self-employed or she changes her accounting date to a date nearer to 31 March within the tax year (see Chapter 13).

- Linda's second set of accounts for the year to 30 June 2008 show a profit of £20,000. The profits will be taxed in the tax year to 5 April 2009.
- From then on Linda will always use the accounts to the accounting date falling in the tax year until she ceases her business. This is known as the current year basis of assessment.

You might find it easier to understand this in table form.

Tax year	Accounting period	Months taxed	Taxable profit	Overlap profits
2006/07	1 July 2006–30 June 2007 (12 months)	1 July 2006–5 April 2007 (9 months)	£16,000 × 9/12 = £12,000	
2007/08	1 July 2006–30 June 2007 (12 months)	1 July 2006–30 June 2007 (12 months)	£16,000	£12,000 (1 July 2006–5 April 2007)
2008/09	1 July 2007–30 June 2008 (12 months)	1 July 2007–30 June 2008 (12 months)	£20,000	

If Linda had used a year end of 31 March, making profits for the nine months 1 July 2006–31 March 2007 of £12,000; year to 31 March 2008 of £20,000 and year to 31 March 2009 of £22,000, her taxable profits would be as follows:

Tax year	Accounting period	Months taxed	Taxable profit	Overlap profits
2006/07	1 July 2006–31 March 2007 (9 months)	1 July 2006–31 March 2007 (9 months)	£12,000	
2007/08	1 April 2007–31 March 2008 (12 months)	1 April 2007–31 March 2008 (12 months)	£20,000	
2008/09	1 April 2008–31 March 2009 (12 months)	1 April 2008–30 March 2009 (12 months)	£22,000	

Using a 31 March year end increases Linda's profits in 2007/08 and 2008/09 because her profits are on a rising trend. She may therefore prefer to use 30 June as a year end because it gives her a cash-flow advantage by deferring some of the profits (and tax) to a later tax year. The disadvantage is that she is not up to date with her tax liabilities. If you use a year end other than 31 March or 5 April it is important to keep track of your tax liabilities on a regular basis; see 'How much tax do I owe on my profits?' later in this chapter.

Linda has apportioned her accounting profits by reference to whole months. It is also possible to divide them on a daily basis which will give a slightly different result. Whichever method you adopt, you should be consistent and use it in subsequent years.

Changing your year end

It sometimes turns out that the year end date you have chosen is inconvenient. You can change it in the second or third tax year without complication but after that you have to meet various conditions for the change to be effective. You are likely to need help from an accountant to help you make the calculations and comply with the requirements laid down by HM Revenue and Customs.

Partners

Partnerships are taxed in a similar way to sole traders and the choice of a partnership year end is governed by the same factors.

Each partner is taxed on his or her share of the partnership profits as if they were a sole trader carrying on an independent business. This means that if partners join or leave the partnership, the new or retiring partners will be taxed differently from the others. You may need professional help with these calculations.

Companies

If you trade as a limited company your choice of accounting period is not related to the tax year. Instead you should select any date (usually a month end) that suits the business' trading pattern. You can make up accounts for longer or shorter than twelve months but a longer period is split into two periods, one for twelve months and one for a shorter period. This will require the completion of two tax returns.

Example

Turtle Ltd starts operating on 1 October 2006 and prepares its accounts to 30 September 2007. Its corporation tax liability is based on the profits for the twelve-month period. There is no need to apportion the profits and there are no overlap profits.

If Turtle Ltd had decided to prepare its accounts to 31 January 2008, it would have two accounting periods:

- 1 October 2006–30 September 2007; and
- 1 October 2007–31 January 2008.

The next accounting period would be for the year to 31 January 2009.

Accounts

Having selected a suitable accounting year end date, we now look at how you prepare accounts from your books and records for tax purposes. In order to calculate your tax bill you need to draw up a trading and profit and loss account which summarizes your income and expenditure for the accounting period. Most businesses apart from those which are very small, also prepare a balance sheet setting out the business' assets, liabilities and capital at the selected accounting date. The accounts are then used to complete your tax return.

This chapter does not tell you how to maintain accounting records (see Chapter 3) or how to prepare 'double-entry' accounts from those records, instead it looks at how to present your accounting records for tax purposes and considers which expenses are tax-deductible. For information on bookkeeping and accounting you should refer to *Teach Yourself Small Business Accounting*.

Accounts are prepared according to specific rules known as generally accepted accounting principles (GAAP). This means that they have to include at the accounting year end:

- Outstanding debtors (people who owe you money) and creditors (people to whom you owe money). The only exception to this rule are barristers and advocates who can work out their profits for the first seven years based on the income they have received or the fees that they have delivered;

- Stocks of materials and goods, and work-in-progress valued according to set criteria (see Problem areas – Stock and work-in-progress);
- All your income, even on contracts which you have not completed at the year end; and
- Liabilities only when they become due.

An accountant can help you prepare accounts that comply with accounting principles. If your business has complex transactions or you are unfamiliar with bookkeeping and accounting, using a professional will minimize the risk that you will make mistakes in completing your tax return.

Tax return

If you run a small unincorporated business it is not necessary to prepare formal accounts for HM Revenue and Customs. Instead details of your income, expenditure and balance sheet (if you prepare one) can be entered directly onto your tax return. You may however need to give formal accounts to your bank manager, other financiers and mortgage lenders.

If you trade as a limited company you will require accounts for shareholders and Companies House as well as the tax authorities.

Income

The first stage to working out your accounting profit is to calculate your income. Income is also called turnover or sales revenue. It represents the money you have earned in your accounting period from selling goods or services. If you run a shop or other business where you do not make sales on credit, working out your income is relatively straightforward. If you sell goods, or supply services on credit (i.e. your customers do not pay you straight away), then you must adjust your sales receipts for opening and closing debtors (that is for the amount that customers owed you for goods or services supplied before your accounting date). You add your closing debtors to your sales figure and deduct your opening debtors from it. If you are paid in advance you will need to consider whether you should adjust your income figure for this receipt.

If you supply services over a period of time you must include a proportion of this income (including any profit that you will eventually make on the contract) even if you do not invoice your client for the work until after your accounting year end. This is a new rule and if you make an adjustment to a set of accounts ending on or after 22 June 2005 to take this extra income into account, you may be entitled to 'spread' the adjustment over the following three to six years depending on the size of the adjustment and the amount of your profits. You may need professional help to make this adjustment and claim the spreading relief.

Turnover includes not just sales of goods or services but commission received, tips and gratuities, payments in kind, recharged items and disbursements. It is usually expressed excluding (net of) VAT (see Problem areas – VAT). If you receive income from which tax has been deducted you should include the total payment before tax on your return and make a separate entry for the tax.

Turnover excludes interest received on a business bank account, rental income and profits from selling assets all of which must be shown separately on your tax return form.

The more adjustments you have to make to your sales income or turnover, the greater the chance that you could make a mistake in calculating the figure. You also need to be able to calculate turnover accurately in order to work out whether you need to VAT register. If you are approaching the VAT registration limit you should take extra care when calculating your sales to make sure that you register on time and avoid a penalty (see Chapter 10).

Examples

Maggie runs a newsagents. Her taxable sales turnover for the year to 31 March is calculated as follows:

- Total of her daily till takings book excluding VAT; *plus*
- Customers yet to pay their accounts for papers delivered before 31 March; *less*
- Amounts owed by customers calculated the previous 31 March.

Desmond is a self-employed plasterer. He sometimes works for private clients but he usually sub-contracts for a large building company who deduct tax from his payments. He charges his time by the half day and adds the cost of materials on top. His sales turnover for the year to 5 April is calculated as follows:

- Total value of invoices raised for the tax year, including recharged materials, tax and invoices which have not yet been paid; *plus*
- Any work undertaken up to 5 April but invoiced in the following year; *less*
- Sums owed by clients and work-in-hand calculated the previous 5 April.

Desmond will claim a deduction for the tax he has already paid and for the cost of his materials on his tax form.

Spencer is a freelance author. His only income in the tax year is an advance for a book he is writing. At 5 April he calculates that he completed 75% of the work on the title, with 25% left to complete in the next tax year. His sales turnover for the year is calculated as follows:

- Advance from publisher; *less*
- 25% carried forward to the next tax year to represent the uncompleted work.

Julie is a beautician. She receives payments from clients and tips. She lets the flat above her shop to a friend. Her sales income is calculated as follows:

- Payments from customers including all her tips but excluding VAT.

The rental income is shown separately on her tax form.

Expenses

After calculating your income you need to work out all the deductions you can claim. There are two main types of expense:

- Direct expenses or cost of sales; and
- Overheads.

In addition you can claim a deduction for capital allowances on your equipment (see Chapter 7).

Direct costs

The direct costs are those that you have to incur in order to be able to sell your products or service and they vary according to the business you run. For example:

- A plumber's direct costs will be pipes, fittings, materials and loose tools.
- A builder's direct costs will include materials, equipment hire and payments to sub-contractors and employees.
- A hairdresser's direct costs will be hair products, gowns and towels.
- A gift shop's cost of sales may be purchases of goods for resale, carriage and commission.
- A manufacturer of sunglasses will have a more complex cost of sales that includes components, materials, fixings, discounts given to customers and the wages and associated costs of employees directly concerned with the manufacturing process.
- A PR agency's direct costs include recharged expenses and sums spent on behalf of its clients (disbursements).

Direct costs are always tax-deductible but they must be adjusted for opening and closing stock and work-in-progress (see Problem areas – Stock and work-in-progress). Depreciation of plant and equipment is not tax allowable but you can claim capital allowances instead (see Chapter 7).

Overheads

Overhead expenses are common to many businesses and consist of administrative costs and the costs incurred in selling its goods and services. They are usually tax-deductible provided that they are incurred 'wholly and exclusively' for business purposes.

The following table sets overhead expenses in the order that they appear on the income tax return together with a note of the type of expense which falls into each category, details of whether they are tax allowable and any restrictions on the claim. If you trade as a limited company expenses are deductible on the same basis but with some differences (see Problem areas – Companies).

Tax return entry	Comments
Employee costs	Salaries, wages, bonuses (paid within nine months of the accounting date), pensions, benefits and employer's National Insurance for all non-direct labour employees (permanent, temporary and casual) are tax-deductible. Wages paid to a spouse or civil partner must be justified by the work that they do for the business. Staff welfare costs such as canteen expenses and counselling for redundant employees are tax-deductible, as are recruitment agency fees and sub-contractor costs not included as a direct cost. Payments to yourself such as your own wages, drawings, pension payments or National Insurance must be excluded (see Drawings).
Premises costs	Rent, business and water rates, power, property insurance, security and similar expenses are tax-deductible. Use of home expenses should be included here but not the cost of buying business premises (see Chapter 9).
Repairs	Repairs, renewals and maintenance of business premises and machinery are tax-deductible but not the cost of their alteration, renovation or improvement (see Capital or revenue expense?). Distinguishing between a 'repair' and a 'renovation' can be difficult and many cases end up in the courts. You may require professional help if the costs are significant.
General administrative expenses	Telecoms, Internet, postage, stationery, printing, courier services, and general office expenses, trade or professional press and subscriptions (excluding personal clubs and associations), general insurance (see Chapter 11) and other similar recurring costs are tax-deductible.

Tax return entry	Comments
Motor expenses	Insurance, servicing, repairs, MOT, fuel, hire and leasing charges, parking and breakdown cover are tax-deductible but fines and penalties are not. The costs must exclude travel between home and work and the cost of buying a vehicle, although capital allowances may be due (see Chapter 7).
Travel and subsistence	Rail, air and taxi fares are deductible as are hotels, accommodation costs, reasonable subsistence and similar costs when staying away from home overnight for work purposes (see Subsistence and entertaining).
Advertising, promotion and entertainment	Advertising and promotion of the business through various media including newspapers, mail-shots, trade directories, websites, free samples and loyalty cards are tax-deductible. Entertainment costs (clients, prospective customers and suppliers) are not tax-deductible. Staff entertaining up to £150 per head per year is allowed. Expenditure on gifts is disallowed except promotional items with a conspicuous advert which cost less than £50 each (excluding food, drink, tobacco and vouchers).
Legal and professional costs	Accountancy and bookkeeping fees, legal costs for business, trade and employee matters, surveyors, architects, stock takers and similar professional fees are all tax allowable. Professional indemnity insurance premiums can also be claimed (see Chapter 11). Fines and penalties are not tax-deductible nor is the cost of settling a tax dispute (see Chapter 3 Enquiries). The legal costs of buying property and plant or machinery are not tax-deductible as the expenditure is treated as part of the cost of the asset.

Bad debts	Amounts owed to you at your accounting date but which you consider you will never be able to recover and will have to write-off are bad debts and tax-deductible. The sums must be specific. A provision created just in case a portion of your debtors do not pay is not deductible. Amounts recovered against a previous bad debt should be shown as 'other income'.
Interest	Interest on business loans and overdrafts is allowable but not the capital repayments (see Chapter 4 – Financing the business).
Other finance charges	Bank charges, business credit card charges, hire purchase interest, leasing payments and similar costs including the cost of obtaining the finance are deductible but not the capital repayments.
Depreciation and profit/ loss on sale	Depreciation is calculated to write-off your equipment over its useful life. Losses (or profits) may occur when you sell equipment and other assets. Depreciation and a loss on sale are not tax-deductible expenses but you may be able to claim capital allowances (see Depreciation and capital allowances). A profit on sale does not have to be included as income but you may have a capital gains tax liability (see Chapter 2).
Other expenses	Necessary protective clothing is usually allowable but not ordinary clothing for everyday use. Personal expenditure is not tax-deductible. Contributions to local enterprise agencies, training and enterprise councils and urban regeneration companies can be claimed but donations to charity are not usually allowed, nor are donations to political parties. Illegal payments such as bribes and protection money are not tax-deductible.

Problem areas

As the table on pages 69–71 demonstrates, deciding whether an expense is tax allowable is not always as straightforward. There are a number of further difficulties which bear consideration.

Dual expenses

To be tax-deductible an expense must be incurred 'wholly and necessarily' for business purposes. This would on the face of it appear to deny a tax deduction for many everyday expenses which businesses incur. For example a car will often be used for work and privately and a telephone line may serve for both home and business use. Provided that the expense can be divided into a part relating to the business and a part that is private (for example by reference to miles driven or phone calls made), the business element is tax-deductible. HM Revenue and Customs usually take a pragmatic view of telephone calls and in practice a proportion of both calls and line rental should be tax-deductible. The rules for companies differ (see Companies).

Where a sole trader incurs expenses which have a dual purpose a means has to be found to divide the costs between business and private use. You could keep a record of your business or domestic car mileage, or a log of business telephone calls. There are no hard and fast rules for doing this but some records should be kept even if only for a representative sample period.

Example

Chris is a freelance landscape designer. He has an office but sometimes uses his home phone to make business calls in the evening. He uses his car for both work and private travel and is unsure how to calculate his motor and telephone expenditure.

Telephone: When his phone bill arrives, Chris notes from the itemized list of calls that he spends about £2 per night for four nights a week making calls to clients. He claims a deduction of £8 per week for each week he is working and reviews this claim twice a year to make sure it is still reasonable. He keeps copies of his itemized calls and the phone bills in case HM Revenue and Customs ask to see them.

Car: As his motor expenses are quite considerable, Chris attaches a notepad to his dashboard. When he has finished a business journey he notes the business mileage and the name of the client. Once a week he transfers his business mileage to a spreadsheet and files his back-up notes in an envelope. He uses this information to bill his clients.

At the end of his accounting period Chris checks his milometer and compares it with his mileage reading at the end of the previous year. He finds that he has driven a total of 14,000 miles. His business mileage spreadsheet totals 10,500 miles. Chris therefore claims a tax deduction for 75% (10,500 divided by 14,000) of his total expenditure on fuel, insurance, road tax and servicing. He claims a deduction for all his business parking but he does not claim for a parking fine as this is not tax allowable.

If Chris makes a journey which is partly for business and partly for private purposes, the cost is not strictly deductible but providing that the private part is purely incidental, he can treat the journey as wholly business.

Cars – an alternative

Many sole traders find it burdensome to keep detailed records of their motor expenses. If your business has sales turnover below the VAT registration threshold when you first use the vehicle, you can calculate your motor expenses based on the authorized mileage rate (see Appendix 1) multiplied by your business mileage. The authorized mileage rate includes all your vehicle expenses except tolls, parking and the congestion charge. You may not necessarily be financially better of by doing this if you have a large car or one which is expensive to run.

Capital or revenue expense?

Capital expenditure is not tax-deductible but you may be able to claim capital allowances (see Chapter 7). Most revenue expenses on the other hand are tax-deductible. Distinguishing between capital and revenue expenses takes a bit of practice. One way to differentiate them is to think of capital expenditure as an apple tree (it is fixed and permanent) and the revenue costs as the apples (these come each year). This can be applied to many situations:

- Interest, including arrangement fees is a revenue cost and tax-deductible; the loan, overdraft or hire purchase agreement is capital and the repayments are not deductible.
- Repairs to a building or machine are revenue costs and tax-deductible but the property or asset being repaired is capital.

The cost of improving or altering the asset is capital and not deductible.

- Depreciation of equipment, cars etc. is a revenue cost and although it is not tax-deductible, capital allowances are (see Chapter 7). The cost of buying the equipment or car is capital expenditure and not tax-deductible.

Drawings

Sums that a sole trader or partner takes from the business for their personal expenditure are called drawings. These 'wages' are not a tax-deductible expense of the business rather they are the withdrawal of the business profits. Payments which are drawings include:

- Regular payments to yourself by cash, cheque, transfer, direct debit or standing order;
- Payment of personal bills from the business bank account;
- Tax and Class 4 National Insurance payments;
- Class 2 National Insurance;
- Pension contributions.

It is a common misconception that businesses pay tax on the proprietor's drawings. This is not so. Income tax is paid on the profits made by the business and not your drawings as the following example illustrates.

Example

Helen who has been self-employed for many years made self-employed profits for the year to 31 May 2006 of £25,000. Each month she withdraws £1,200 from the business bank account for her personal living expenses and in the accounting period paid £6,000 to HM Revenue and Customs for tax and National Insurance. Her drawings total £20,400. Helen has not withdrawn all her business profits. She has left £4,600 (£25,000 – £20,400) invested in the business to meet future expenses. Helen is taxed on the £25,000 profit not her drawings of £20,400. Subject to her having the available funds she could increase her monthly drawings or withdraw a lump sum instead of leaving her excess profits invested in the business and still pay the same tax.

If you trade as a limited company, directors' salaries and employer's National Insurance on those salaries are tax-deductible expenses but dividend payments are not. Just as drawings are the withdrawal of a sole trader's profits, dividends are the distribution of a company's profits to its shareholders so no tax deduction can be claimed.

Goods taken for personal use

If you take goods from the business for your personal use you must increase your taxable profit to take into account the market value (not the cost) of these items. For example if you run a fruit and vegetable market stall you must include an adjustment in your tax return for the produce taken to feed your family valued at its market value. If you only eat the items left over at the end of the day with little or no commercial value, then this adjustment may be small but it should still be made.

If your business provides services, your accounts must be adjusted for the cost (not the selling price) of providing free services to yourself or your family and friends. If you are a sole trader with no staff, the cost of providing the service is probably nothing or minimal, because as we have just seen proprietors' drawings are not a cost to the business.

Stock and work-in-progress

Your accounts must include an adjustment for opening and closing stock and work-in-progress valued according to set rules. At your accounting year end, stocks of unsold goods, parts and components must be valued at the lower of:

- their cost; or
- their selling price.

For example a business selling specialist pens would value any unsold pens at its accounting year end at the amount they cost to buy. Only if the items were damaged or otherwise unsaleable for more than their cost price would they be valued at their selling price. In most situations, stock will be valued at cost, since this is usually less than the selling price of the items. A manufacturer or similar business that has work on hand at the end of the accounting period, must also value any work-in-progress at the lower of its cost or selling price.

Service businesses must include the value of any uncompleted contracts at the end of the accounting period in their accounts. You do this by including the portion of the contract that has been completed during the year. For example, a designer is half-way through a design concept for a new product at their year end. The contract when completed will be worth £20,000. The designer must include £10,000 in their accounts to reflect the value of the uncompleted work. If the work is contingent on a future event, for example 'no win, no fee', the accounts do not have to be adjusted.

VAT

If you are not VAT registered, your expenses include VAT and the total cost is tax-deductible.

If you are VAT registered you will reclaim the VAT on most of your expenses through your VAT returns (see Chapter 10). As a result you cannot claim a tax deduction for the VAT unless it is irrecoverable VAT on otherwise allowable expenses. In this case it can be deducted or included in a claim for capital allowances.

Most VAT registered businesses draw up their accounts excluding VAT from their income and expenses i.e. using the net of VAT amounts. You can use the VAT-inclusive figures (this is usual if you use the flat-rate scheme) but you must then make an adjustment to your accounts for the VAT paid to or reclaimed from HM Revenue and Customs. You have to indicate on your tax return whether your accounts are prepared excluding or including VAT.

Companies

Expenses incurred by companies are tax-deductible in a similar way to sole traders and partnerships but with some important differences:

- Expenses cannot be incurred for both business and private purposes (dual expenditure).
- Interest and bad debts which do not relate to the trade have to be accounted for under what is known as the 'loan-relationship rules'.
- Companies can claim tax relief on goodwill and tax credits on research and development and to clean up contaminated land.

Profits

You pay tax on your profits calculated as follows:

- Income *less*
- Deductible expenses *less*
- Capital allowances.

If this calculation gives a positive number, the business has made a taxable profit. If it is negative the business has made a loss (see Chapter 6 for the tax treatment of losses). If the calculation gives a positive figure before capital allowances but a negative one after deducting them, it may be tax effective not to claim the capital allowances (see Chapter 7, Increasing capital allowance claims).

The profits generated by your business may have to be adjusted further as follows:

- Apportioned between tax years depending on your choice of year end date (see Choice of year end);
- Averaged over more than one tax year – creative artists and authors and farmers (see Profit averaging);
- Subject to special treatment – (see Foster carers).

Profit averaging

Artists, authors and farmers often experience fluctuating profits. In some years they earn little or no income whilst in others they make a considerable profit. This means that they can waste their personal allowances and not benefit from the lower rates of tax in a lean year whilst paying tax at the highest rate during a good one. To minimize this disadvantage, artists and authors wholly or mainly creating artistic works or designs, and farmers, are allowed to average their profits over consecutive tax years. Profits for these purposes are calculated after deducting capital allowances but before loss relief (see Chapter 6). Averaging relief can be claimed by sole traders and partners but not if you operate through a limited company. It cannot be claimed in the year in which a trade commences or ceases.

Profit averaging applies if:

- the profits of the lower year are less than 75% of the profits of the higher year; or
- the profits for one (but not both) tax years are nil (this would be the case if you made a loss).

If the profits for one of the years are more than 70% but less than 75% of the profits for the other year, the profit in each year is calculated according to a set formula. The result of the calculation is added to the profit of the lower year and deducted from the profit of the higher year.

Example

Dorinda is a well-known sculptor. Her profits are £3,000 in 2005/06 and £50,000 in 2006/07. She elects to average her profits to £26,500 (£3,000 + £50,000 divided by 2) for both 2005/06 and 2006/07. In doing so she avoids wasting some of her personal allowance in 2005/06 and does not pay tax at higher rates in 2006/07 (see Appendix 1).

The averaging relief is given in Dorinda's 2006/07 self-assessment return, the second of the two years involved and requires two entries to be made on the form. No adjustment is made to the earlier year's return.

- The profit on the self-employed or partnership pages is adjusted to the averaged profit by means of an addition or deduction in Box 3.81 (self-employed) or Box 4.12 (partners).
- A separate entry is required in either Box 18.4 (if it is an increase) or 18.5 (if it is a reduction), to reflect the adjustment to the first year's profits.

The claim must be made by the second 31 January falling after the end of the later tax year, so Dorinda must claim for 2005/06 and 2006/07 by 31 January 2009. If her profits for either year are adjusted for any reason (for example during an enquiry) the averaging claim is treated as if it had never been made, although she could make a new claim if it is still within the above time limit.

If Dorinda did not average her profits for 2004/05 and 2005/06, she cannot go back and average 2004/05 with the now averaged 2005/06. If Dorinda can also average her 2007/8 profit with that for 2006/7, she must make sure that she uses the average profit for 2006/7 in her calculations and not the actual profit.

Making the correct entries on your tax return for averaging relief is quite complicated and you may require professional help to make sure that you receive all the tax relief that you are entitled to. Claiming averaging relief also has other consequences for your return. For example it may no longer be beneficial to claim loss relief or capital allowances, and it may affect the amount of pension contributions you wish to pay (see Chapter 11).

Foster carers

Foster carers looking after children under a foster care agreement are taxed on their profits using special rules. If you have foster care receipts below a set threshold you are exempt from income tax and any profit or loss is treated as nil. If your receipts are above the threshold you can choose to deduct an amount equal to the threshold if you make an election in writing by the second 31 January falling after the end of the tax year. If no election is made you must calculate your profits using the rules outlined earlier in this chapter for working out trading profits.

The threshold and set amount is made up of two parts:

- A fixed amount of £10,000 per residence (this can be a caravan or houseboat) per year. Where more than one person at the same address fosters children, the fixed amount is divided equally between them. If the income period is other than an exact year the fixed amount is apportioned pro rata.
- A weekly amount for each child being fostered depending on their age – £200 a week (or part week) for a child under 11, £250 a week (or part week) for a child aged 11 or over.

Example

Mavis fostered two children aged 8 and 10 for the whole of the tax year to 5 April 2006. Under an agreement with her local authority she is paid £225 per week for the younger child and £285 per week for the 10-year-old. Her total foster care receipts are £26,520. No tax liability arises on Mavis's income because the receipts fall below the relevant threshold. In Mavis's case this is:

- £30,800 (£10,000 plus £200 for two children per week).

If Mavis was paid a further £450 per week by the local authority to foster a baby with special needs her total foster care receipts would be £49,920 and her relevant threshold would rise to:

- £41,200 (£10,000 plus £200 for three children per week).

Mavis can choose between paying tax on £8,720 (receipts of £49,920 less the set amount of £41,200) or she can keep records of all the expenditure she incurs to look after the children as if it were a small business. If she thought that the costs would exceed £41,200 she would be better off being taxed on her 'true' profit. It is however more likely that deducting the set amount will not only save Mavis tax but the inconvenience and difficulty of keeping records. If Mavis chooses this latter option she must elect for it to apply for 2005/06 by 31 January 2008.

How much tax do I owe on my profits?

In Chapter 4 we looked at the payment pattern for income tax payments in the early years of a new business (see Anticipating tax payments). This trend will continue throughout the lifecycle of your enterprise. As described in Chapter 1, ignoring your tax obligations is one of the principal reasons why businesses fail so for your venture to be successful you need to adopt a system to keep track of your tax liabilities as your profits rise and fall over the years. One way to do this is to estimate your tax bill on a regular basis.

Monitoring your tax

Now that you have read this chapter you have the skills to calculate your profits. Using the information in Chapter 2, you should be able to work out the income tax and Class 4 National Insurance charged on those profits if you are a sole trader or partner, or your corporation tax liability if you trade as a limited company. Knowing the amount of your profits and your tax liability will enable you to calculate your tax as a percentage of your profits. You do this by taking your total tax liability for the year and dividing it by your profits. This will give you a percentage that you can apply to future profits to estimate your future tax bills. You could check this figure by reviewing the amount of tax you have paid and profits for the last two years. If the percentage varies, you should consider which figure is more representative of your business for the future. It is important to be realistic. Deluding yourself that your tax bill will be smaller than it actually will be will only cause you problems in the future.

There are disadvantages to estimating your tax in this way because most small businesses only calculate their profits once or twice a year. Estimating your tax bills based on a percentage of sales turnover is more flexible as most businesses review their sales monthly. So to calculate a suitable percentage:

- Review your last tax return and find the figures for your sales and total tax.
- Divide the tax by the sales to come to a percentage.
- Make similar calculations for two previous years and see if they are consistent. If not which percentage seems most realistic to use?
- Apply the percentage to your current sales to provide an estimate of your likely tax.

Example

Wendy runs a clothing shop. Her profits, turnover and tax bills for the last three years were as follows:

Year	Sales	Profit	Tax	Tax:sales	Tax:profit
	£	£	£	%	%
2005/06	200,000	40,000	10,500	5	26
2004/05	160,000	25,000	6,000	4	24
2003/04	155,000	24,000	5,700	4	24

Although Wendy's turnover and profits have increased significantly in the last year as a result of renovating the shop and stocking new ranges of garments, the percentage of tax to sales and profits have remained quite consistent. As she expects her profits to remain at the 2005/06 level she should allocate at least 5% of her sales to tax.

During the accounting year to 31 March 2007, Wendy records her sales on a spreadsheet and keeps a running total of her estimated tax liability. This is shown on page 82.

Month	Sales (£)	Tax estimate (5%)
January	18,000	900
February	10,000	500
March	15,000	750
April	20,000	1,000
May	22,000	1,100
June	16,000	800
July	17,000	850
August	11,000	550
September	19,000	950
October	21,000	1,050
November	16,000	800
December	20,000	1,000
Total	**205,000**	**10,250**

Provided that Wendy allocates at least 5% of her sales turnover each month for income tax, she should always have sufficient funds to pay her tax bills when they fall due on 31 January and 31 July each year.

It is not necessary that she opens a separate bank account as a tax reserve (although some businesses do) because she operates her shop with loans and overdrafts. Wendy should however keep in mind the amount of tax she owes when budgeting for her business.

Recap case study

Matthew is a sole trader manufacturing blinds and awnings. He employs three people and operates from a rented workshop. He has been trading for five years and prepares his accounts to 31 October each year. He keeps his accounting records on a computer package which produces the balances listed below at the end of the year. Matthew is keen to work out his taxable profit for the year to 31 October 2006 so that he knows how much income tax he owes and to enable him to complete his tax return to 5 April 2007.

Year to 31 October 2006	Figures from accounts package
	£
Sales	125,000
Purchases of materials	–40,000
Rent and rates	–10,000
Power and insurance	–3,000
Telephone	–1,800
Staff costs and National Insurance	–40,000
Motor expenses	–1,500
Office and administration costs	–5,000
Bank charges	–500
Advertising	–1,200
Loan interest	–2,500
Drawings	–20,000
Tax payments for self	–8,100
Pension payments for self	–2,500

At 31 October 2006 Matthew works out that three customers owe him a total of £25,000. Last year he was owed £10,000. During the year one client refused to pay for a blind and Matthew does not believe that he will ever recover the £900 he is owed.

Matthew counts his stock of materials on hand at 31 October which comes to £5,000. The previous year it was only £2,000. At the year end he is half-way through making blinds for one customer who will eventually pay him £1,600. He had no partly finished work at 1 November 2005.

Matthew pays most of his bills by monthly standing order or direct debit but he owes a supplier £200 for fixings. Nothing was outstanding at the beginning of the year.

When Matthew goes through his accounting records he finds out that his office administration costs include £150 for a meal for a valued customer. This is entertaining expenditure and is not tax-deductible. Matthew must exclude the cost from his administration expenses because it has been wrongly categorized in his accounting records. It should be included in 'advertising and entertainment' but then shown on his tax return as disallowable expense. Matthew also remembers that he has forgotten to include a subscription to a trade magazine that he buys regularly (total annual cost £50) and the cost of meter parking (averaging £5 per week).

Matthew owns a number of machines which he uses in his business, a computer, office furniture and a car. He calculates that he is entitled to claim capital allowances on these of £2,800 (see Chapter 7).

Matthew should adjust his records as set out in the following table. The layout follows the income tax return self-employment pages.

Tax return 2006/07	£	Comments
Income	140,000	Sales £125,000 + Closing debtors £25,000 – Opening debtors £10,000
Cost of sales	–36,400	Purchase of materials £40,000 + Owed to supplier £200 + Opening stock £2,000 – Closing stock £5,000 – Closing work-in-progress £800
Employee costs	–40,000	
Premises costs	–13,000	Rent and rates £10,000 + Power and insurance £3,000
General administrative expenses	–6,700	Telephone £1,800 + Office and administration costs £5,000 + Subscription £50 – Entertaining £150
Motor expenses	–1,760	Motor expenses £1,500 + Parking £260 (£5 x 52 weeks)
Advertising and entertainment	–1,200	Advertising £1,200 (Entertaining £150 is added but then must be excluded as it is not tax-deductible)

Tax return 2006/07	£	Comments
Bad debts	–900	Owed by customer but not paid
Interest	–2,500	
Finance charges	–500	
Capital allowances	–2,800	
Taxable profit	34,240	Amount on which Matthew pays income tax

Matthew does not deduct the drawings, tax payments or pension contributions when working out his taxable profits (see Drawings).

Matthew could complete the balance sheet pages of the return with details of his equipment, debtors, stock, work-in-progress, creditors, loans and capital but as he is inexperienced in double-entry bookkeeping he chooses not to do so. There is no obligation on him to complete these boxes on the return but HM Revenue and Customs could ask Matthew to prepare a balance sheet if they were to enquire into his return.

Using the information on income tax and Class 4 National Insurance in Chapter 2 and Appendix 1, Matthew now works out the income tax he owes on his taxable profit for 2006/07.

Income tax liability 2006/07	£	£
Profits		34,240
Personal allowance		-5,035
Income subject to income tax		**29,205**
Starting rate: 10%	2,150	215.00
Basic rate: 22%	27,055	5,952.10
	29,205	
Class 4 National Insurance: £29,205 × 8%		2,336.40
		8,503.50

Matthew's tax liability is 6% of his sales turnover (£8,503.50 divided by £140,000) and 25% of his profit (£8,503.50 divided by £34,240). If he has allocated tax on a regular basis he will have sufficient to pay his tax bills when they are due.

Matthew's income tax liability for 2005/06 was £8,100. He will therefore pay the following tax bills for 2006/07 (see Appendix 2):

31 January 2007	£4,050 – Payment on account 2006/07 based on 50% of his 2005/06 tax bill.
31 July 2007	£4,050 – Payment on account 2006/07 based on 50% of his 2005/06 tax bill.
31 January 2008	£403.50 – Balancing payment 2006/07. Matthew owes £8,503.50 less the £8,100 he has paid on account.

On 31 January 2008 Matthew will also pay £4,251.75 on account of his tax for 2007/08 – 50% of his 2006/07 tax bill. He will pay a further £4,251.75 on 31 July 2008.

In this chapter:
- calculating income tax losses
- company losses
- capital losses
- tax relief for business investments that go wrong

In Chapter 5 we looked at how profits are taxed. The reality of the business world is that instead of making profits small ventures often make losses particularly in the first few years. This chapter looks at how you can save tax by claiming loss relief.

Losses are calculated in the same way as profits and arise when business expenses exceed income leaving a negative profit. Losses also occur in other situations and these are examined later in the chapter.

Claiming income tax losses

When a sole trader or partnership makes a trading loss they are treated as if they had made neither a profit nor a loss for the accounting period. You can claim tax relief for the loss in a variety of ways depending on whether it occurs in the early years of a business, when the business ceases to trade or somewhere in between. Claiming losses reduces your tax bill for the year of the claim and you either receive a tax refund or pay less tax. Deciding how to make best use of the loss depends on:

- The rates at which you have paid tax in all the years affected by the claim.
- Whether you will waste your personal allowance and any other tax reliefs that you are entitled to.

You may want to seek professional advice about the best way to use your losses to maximize your tax savings.

Table of possible income tax loss claims

The following table summarizes the possible income tax loss claims you could make.

Loss...	Use...	Claim reference
Claimed against your other sources of income	In the tax year of the loss or the previous year	Section 380
Claimed against any capital gains	In the tax year of the loss or the previous year	Section 72
Carried forward against your future profits	Against the first profits the business makes after the loss-making period	Section 385

Loss...	Use...	Claim reference
Occurring in the first four tax years of a new business	Against your other income of the previous three tax years	Section 381
Occurring in the twelve months to the date your business ceases	In the tax year when the business stops and the three previous tax years	Sections 388–389

We now consider each of the possible loss claims in turn.

Using losses against other income

If you make a loss on your trading activities you can deduct it from any other income you receive in the same tax year. Alternatively you can claim it against your income for the previous tax year. You can claim some of the loss in one year and some in the other if it is a large loss and you have insufficient income in just one year to set it against. Relief for the loss must be claimed by the second 31 January following the end of the tax year in which the loss arose.

Example

Denis, a sole trader, prepares accounts to 31 March. He makes losses in two tax years during which he also receives income from renting a property.

	Loss	Other income
	£	£
31 March 2006 (2005/06 tax year)	5,000	13,000
31 March 2007 (2006/07 tax year)	10,000	9,500

Denis's taxable business profits in 2005/06 and 2006/07 are £0 because he made losses. He makes the following loss claims:

- He uses the £5,000 loss from 2005/06 against his other income for the same tax year. This reduces his rental income to £8,000 (£13,000 – £5,000). His tax bill will be reduced by £1,100 (the £5,000 loss multiplied by tax at 22%) (see Appendix 1).

- He uses £9,500 of the 2006/07 loss against his other income for the same tax year. This reduces his rental income to £0 (£9,500 – £9,500). As Denis has only used £9,500 of his £10,000 loss the remaining £500 can be deducted from his rental income for the previous year. This claim reduces Denis' 2005/06 rental income to £7,500 (£13,000 – £5,000 (2005/06) – £500 (2006/07)).

This example illustrates some of the complexities of loss claims:

- The losses must be used until either the loss or the income against which the loss is claimed has gone. In 2006/07 this wastes Denis' personal allowance. Although his income has been reduced to £0 so he owes no tax, he does not benefit from his personal allowance. Denis cannot claim just a part of the loss so that he does not waste his personal allowance and then use the balance of the loss in a different way, for example by carrying it forward against his future profits.
- Section 380 loss claims can be split between different years. Denis uses £9,500 of his 2006/07 loss against his other income in 2006/07 and the remaining £500 against his income for the previous year. In 2005/06 this means that Denis can deduct losses from two different tax years.
- Instead of using the £500 loss from 2006/07 against his income in 2005/06, Denis could have chosen to carry it forward against any future profits by making a Section 385 claim. If Denis anticipated that he would owe tax at a higher rate in 2007/08 than 2005/06, this would prove a good decision.

In order to make the loss claim, Denis must be carrying on his business on a commercial basis with an expectation of making a profit in the near future. If he continues to make losses HM Revenue and Customs could enquire into his affairs and deny him loss relief.

Problems for specific businesses

There are special rules which restrict some business' loss claims in certain circumstances. If you are a partner in a partnership or your business is involved with farming and market gardening, leasing equipment or film production you should seek help from an accountant if you want to claim loss relief.

Claiming relief against capital gains

If either of the Section 380 loss claims do not work for you because you have insufficient income, any unused losses can be deducted from your capital gains in either the year of the loss or the previous year. Calculating this loss relief can be complicated and you may require professional help.

Carried forward losses

If you do not have any other source of income or gains to set your trading losses against in the current or previous tax year, you can carry them forward to a year in the future when you make a profit. The problem with this loss claim is that you do not know what the future holds for your business and there may be a considerable delay between incurring the loss and obtaining tax relief from it.

To claim this relief you must meet three conditions:

- You must use the loss against your first available profits. This may mean that you waste your personal allowance in that year.
- There must have been no changes in ownership of your business.
- You must officially claim the loss within five years of the 31 January after the end of the tax year in which the loss arose. When you want to use the loss you then receive the tax relief automatically and you do not need to make a further claim.

Example

Christine made a trading loss in 2006/07 of £25,000. She makes a further loss in 2007/08 of £5,000 but a profit in 2008/09 of £40,000. If Christine has no other income against which to relieve her losses she will carry them forward. She will not use the 2006/07 loss in 2007/08 because she makes a further loss. Instead she will use the £30,000 of losses (£25,000 + £5,000) against her 2008/09 profit leaving her with taxable profits of £10,000 (£40,000 – £30,000).

If Christine had made a profit in 2008/09 of £28,000 (instead of £40,000) she will use all of the £25,000 loss from 2006/07 against the profit plus £3,000 of the loss from 2007/08 leaving her with taxable profits of £0. Christine cannot decide to carry the whole of the £5,000 loss from 2007/08 forward to another tax year. She has to use as much of it as possible in the first tax year in which she makes a profit even if it means wasting her personal allowance. Christine will carry forward the remaining £2,000 loss (£5,000 – £3,000) to a later tax year.

Forming a limited company

If you transfer your unincorporated business to a limited company in return for shares but have unused losses, you may be able to claim loss relief against director's fees and dividends paid to you by the new limited company (see Chapter 12).

Losses in the early years of a business

Many unincorporated businesses make losses when they first start trading. There are tax provisions to help you to make the most of them. If you make a loss in any of your first four tax years you can carry the loss back and deduct it from any other source of income you had in the previous three tax years. This enables you to use the loss against income you earned or received before you started the business. There are three conditions you must comply with to claim loss relief in this way:

- You must deduct the loss from the income of the earliest year first. So if the loss was in 2006/07 you must use it against the income of 2003/04 in preference to 2004/05 and against 2004/05 in preference to 2005/06.
- Your business must be carried on commercially with a reasonable expectation that it will make a profit in the near future.
- You must claim the loss by the second 31 January following the end of the tax year in which the loss arose.

Case study

Antonia was a student in 2004/05 and 2005/06 with no taxable income and she was then employed by a nursery school in 2006/07. On 6 April 2007 she starts a business as a children's party entertainer. She prepares her first accounts to 5 April 2008 and they show a trading loss of £10,000. In each subsequent tax year she makes profits. As Antonia had no taxable income in either 2004/05 or 2005/06 she must use the £10,000 loss against her 2006/07 salary. Her tax calculation is as follows:

2006/07	Income £	Tax £
Salary and tax deducted under PAYE (see Chapter 8)	20,000	3,034.30
Less: Loss claimed under Section 381	−10,000	
Less: Personal allowance	−5,035	
Taxable income	**4,965**	
First £2,150 at 10%		215.00
Next £2,815 at 22%		619.30
		834.30
Tax refund due as a result of the loss (£3,034.30 − £834.30)		**2,200.00**

Antonia's tax rebate of £2,200 is equal to 22% tax on a £10,000 loss (£10,000 × 22%). Originally she paid tax on her salary of £3,034.30. As a result of the loss her tax liability falls to £834.30, giving her a tax overpayment of £2,200. Antonia must claim the loss by 31 January 2010.

You may have noticed that Antonia's claim is the same as it would have been if she had claimed tax relief for the loss under Section 380 (see Using losses against other income). If Antonia had earnings in 2004/05 or 2005/06 she would have used the loss against the earliest year's income first.

It is easy to confuse tax years and accounting periods when dealing with loss claims in the early years of a new business.

Example

John starts a small business as a sole trader on 1 November 2002. He prepares his first accounts to 31 October 2003. These show a loss of £15,000. He makes further losses of £12,500 in the year to 31 October 2004, £2,500 to 31 October 2005 and £1,500 to 31 October 2006. The losses are allocated to tax years as follows:

Losses	£
2002/03 (accounts 1.11.02–5.4.03) loss £15,000 × 5 months/12 months	6,250
2003/04 (accounts 1.11.02–31.10.03) loss £15,000 less portion already allocated to 2002/03 – £6,250	8,750
2004/05 (accounts 1.11.03–31.10.04)	12,500
2005/06 (accounts 1.11.04–31.10.05)	2,500
2006/07 (accounts 1.11.05–31.10.06)	1,500

John cannot use the 2006/07 losses under Section 381 because it is the business' fifth tax year even though the profits only cover four accounting periods: 31.10.03, 31.10.04, 31.10.05 and 31.10.06. The 2006/07 loss can be used against John's other income in 2006/07 or 2005/06 under Section 380. Alternatively it can be carried forward against his future profits under Section 385.

Losses when a business ceases

If you make a trading loss in the twelve months to the date that you cease running your business and you have not used the losses in a different claim, relief may be due under the 'terminal' loss provisions. This means that you can use the loss against your trading profits (if you have any) of the tax year when the business stops and the three previous tax years. You must set the loss against the profits of the later years before the earlier years. Overlap relief may be claimed when you cease a business and it will increase or even create a terminal loss (see Chapter 13, Overlap relief).

Terminal loss relief must be claimed within five years of the 31 January after the tax year in which the business stopped trading. For example if a business closes down in 2006/07 the loss claim must be made by 31 January 2013.

Calculating a terminal loss is not straightforward and you may need to ask an accountant to help you with the claim.

Example

Kerry ceased her business on 30 June 2006. She made a profit of £30,000 in her accounting period for the year to 30

September 2005. In the nine months to 30 June 2006 she made a loss of £10,000. Kerry has overlap relief of £5,000. Her terminal loss for her last twelve months of trading is calculated as follows:

Tax year	Accounting period	£	Terminal loss £
2006/07	6.4.06–30.6.06: loss £10,000 × 3 months/ 9 months		3,333
	Overlap relief		5,000
			8,333
2005/06	1.10.05–5.4.06: loss £10,000 × 6 months/ 9 months	6,667	
	1.7.05–30.9.05: profit £30,000 × 3 months/ 12 months	–7,500	
			0
	Terminal loss		**8,333**

In 2005/06 the profit of £7,500 (apportioned from the £30,000 profit for the year to 30 September 2005) cancels out the £6,667 loss which is allocated to the same tax year. As a result nothing further is added to Kerry's terminal loss claim for this period. Her claim for the last twelve months she was in business consists of £3,333 of the £10,000 loss plus overlap relief of £5,000. Kerry can claim the remaining £6,667 (£10,000 – £3,333) of losses under Section 380 if she has any other income to use them against.

Recap

There is often more than one income tax loss claim that you can make. Choosing how to make best use of the loss can be complicated. Seek professional help to ensure that you do not waste your relief.

Company losses

A company may make a number of different losses depending on its sources of income (for example trading, property, overseas or capital losses). This section is concerned only with trading and capital losses.

Trading losses

Trading losses are calculated in the same way as profits. Sometimes a company will deliberately create a loss by paying money into its pension scheme or as directors' bonuses.

Companies claim tax relief for their losses in a similar way to individuals so they can be:

- Deducted from the company's other profits and gains of the same accounting period. Any remaining balance can be carried back and off-set against the profits or gains of the previous year.
- Carried forward to be used against future profits.
- Used when a company ceases to trade. A loss arising in the last twelve months can be carried back against the company's profits for the previous three years, using the later years first.

If the company is a member of a group, its losses can also be relieved against the profits of other members of the group in certain circumstances (and vice versa).

If the company changes hands, alters the nature of its business or the way it operates within a three-year period HMRC may refuse the loss relief claim.

Capital losses

Capital losses can be deducted from a company's capital gains for the same accounting period or carried forward. They cannot be carried back against previous years except in some limited circumstances. Capital losses generated as part of a tax-avoidance scheme will be refused.

Claims

Losses which are to be off-set against the same or previous year must be claimed within two years. No specific claim is required if the losses are carried forward although an entry must be made on the company's corporation tax return. The claim will usually give rise to a tax repayment.

Planning

When deciding how to use company losses you should consider the rate at which the company paid corporation tax in each year affected by the claim (see Appendix 1). In the year to 31 March 2006, a company with £10,000 of profits or less paid no corporation tax unless it paid a dividend when the tax rate was 19%. It will be a waste of a loss to carry it back to a year when the company did not pay corporation tax.

Capital losses

Capital losses arise if you sell a capital asset (for example shares) for less than you bought it for. Both individuals and companies may make capital losses but company losses are dealt with as part of the corporation tax return (see Company losses). This section looks at the position of individuals who make capital losses.

Capital losses are calculated in the same way as gains except that no indexation allowance or taper relief is deducted from a capital loss (see Chapter 2). If you make a capital gain and a loss in the same tax year you deduct the loss from the gain before calculating your entitlement to taper relief. In some circumstances this may mean that you waste some or all of your annual exemption. If you make more than one gain and/or capital loss in the same tax year you can allocate losses to gains in the way that maximizes your entitlement to taper relief. You may want to seek professional advice to help you with this calculation.

Carrying back losses

Unlike income tax losses, capital losses cannot be carried back against the gains of an earlier year. One notable exception is if the loss arises in the year when a sole trader or partner dies when it can be carried back for three tax years.

Carrying forward losses

Any loss you make in excess of your gains for a tax year can be carried forward to be used in a future tax year. When you come to use the loss if you have losses arising in that tax year and losses brought forward from an earlier year, the losses of the year in question are used before the earlier year's losses.

You must tell HM Revenue and Customs about your capital losses by completing the capital gains tax pages of your tax return, or notifying them separately in writing within five years of the 31 January following the end of the tax year.

Maintaining the annual exemption

When a capital loss is carried forward to a future tax year you only need to deduct as much of it as you require to reduce your gain to the level of the annual exemption (see Appendix 1). This prevents some of the carried forward loss from being wasted and any balance can then be carried forward to a subsequent year. Remember that losses are deducted from your gains before claiming taper relief so if the loss reduces the gain to the level of the annual exemption, you have effectively wasted the taper relief.

Example

Colin is a self-employed plumber. He bought a freehold yard and storage unit for use in his business on 1 June 2003 for £50,000. On 1 August 2006 he sells it for £90,000. The gain is eligible for 75% taper relief because it has been a business asset for more than two years (see Appendix 1). On 6 April 2006 Colin has capital losses totalling £4,000 carried forward from a previous tax year from the sale of technology shares.

Colin's capital gains tax calculation for 2006/07 is as follows:

	£	£
1.8.06 Sale of yard	90,000	
1.6.03 Purchase of yard	−50,000	
Gain		40,000
Less: Capital losses brought forward		−4,000
Gain after off-setting losses		36,000
Taper relief: 75% × £36,000		−27,000
Gain after taper relief		9,000
Annual exemption (see Appendix 1)		8,800
Chargeable gain		200

If Colin's losses carried forward were £34,000 instead of £4,000, he would choose to use just £31,200 of them to reduce his gain to £8,800 (the level of the annual exemption in 2006/07). He can carry forward the remaining £2,800 (£34,000 – £31,200) of losses and use them against any capital gains he makes in the future. In this situation Colin's capital gains tax calculation would then be as follows:

	£	£
1.8.06 Sale of yard	90,000	
1.6.03 Purchase of yard	−50,000	
Gain		40,000
Less: Capital losses carried forward		−31,200
Gain after deducting losses		8,800
Annual exemption (see Appendix 1)		8,800
Chargeable gain		0

Colin does not need to claim taper relief as the loss has already reduced his capital gain to the level of the annual exemption.

If Colin had gains on the sale of quoted shares in 2006/07 of £8,000 which did not qualify for taper relief, he would choose to set his losses against the gains on the shares in preference to the gain on the freehold property. By doing so he increases his entitlement to taper relief by £3,000 (£30,000 – £27,000). Assuming his losses to be £4,000 his capital gains tax calculation is now as follows:

	£	£
Gains on shareholding	8,000	
Less: Capital losses carried forward	−4,000	
Gain on shares after off-setting losses		4,000
1.8.06 Sale of freehold	90,000	
1.6.03 Purchase of yard	−50,000	
Gain before taper yard	40,000	
Taper relief: 75% × £40,000	−30,000	
Gain after taper relief		10,000
Total gains		**14,000**
Annual exemption (see Appendix 1)		8,800
Chargeable gains		5,200

Can capital losses be claimed against income?

Capital losses cannot usually be claimed against your business income but if certain business investments fail you can claim income tax relief instead of deducting the loss from a capital gain (see Loss claims for business investments that go wrong). You will want to choose this option if you do not have any chargeable capital gains to use the loss against.

Can income tax losses be deducted from capital gains?

As we saw earlier in this chapter you can use certain income tax losses against your capital gains (see Income tax loss claims – Claiming relief against capital gains).

When a business ceases to trade any expenditure incurred in the seven years after cessation can be deducted from your capital gains if your income is insufficient (see Chapter 13, Income and expenses incurred after the final accounting period).

Loss claims for business investments that go wrong

An individual (but not a company) can claim income tax relief if they invest in shares in an unlisted trading company that fails. If the shares become worthless you calculate a capital gains tax loss in the usual way but instead of deducting it from a capital gain you deduct it from your income.

In order to make this loss claim it is not necessary for you to sell your shares. Instead, under what are known as the 'negligible value' rules, the shares are treated as if you sold them to yourself at their current market value (i.e. for nothing). You must make the claim for the year in which you incurred the loss or the previous year and it takes priority over a Section 380 or 381 loss claim (see Income tax loss claims). It must be claimed in writing on or before the second 31 January occurring after the tax year in which the loss arose.

Making such a loss claim is likely to require professional advice because the shares must be held in 'a qualifying trading company' and you have to meet many detailed conditions.

Recap

If you make a loss you will be keen to recoup some of your money. You can do this by claiming tax relief. Relief is available for most losses provided that you make the claim on time. Calculating losses and working out how they interact with the rest of your tax affairs is complicated. If in doubt seek expert help so that you do not lose out.

In this chapter:
- what equipment can you claim capital allowances on?
- calculating capital allowances
- increasing your capital allowance claims

To operate efficiently most small businesses require tools, equipment and vehicles. As you saw in Chapter 5 you cannot deduct the cost of these items from your income as an expense when calculating your business profits. Instead you must claim capital allowances. This is one of the more tricky aspects of completing your tax return and amongst taxpayers without an accountant one of the main reasons for errors. Failing to recognize that equipment must be treated differently from other business expenses and completing the capital allowance boxes on the tax return incorrectly could result in HM Revenue and Customs enquiring into your affairs.

On which items can you claim capital allowances?

Equipment (or plant and machinery as it is known in the tax legislation) seems an obvious expression but some items of equipment are not eligible for allowances whilst others attract allowances at a higher rate.

For most small businesses the equipment on which capital allowances can most commonly be claimed are:

- Tools (needed to do your work);
- Machinery (including computers and items in a building such as lifts and escalators);
- Furniture (for your workplace); and
- Vehicles (such as cars and vans).

There are no hard and fast rules that define plant and machinery. Machinery is usually fairly easy to identify but 'plant' is not and many cases end up in dispute ultimately to be considered by the courts. To be eligible for capital allowances the asset must be necessary to the functioning of your business not just to create a pleasant setting in which it is conducted. There is a fine (and not always obvious) distinction between the two. When it comes to plant and machinery incorporated in a building the legislation is a little more specific if not always logical. For example central heating qualifies but plumbing and electrical systems do not. Mezzanine floors and moveable partitions do but suspended ceilings and shop fronts do not. If you have purchased a significant number of assets or they are expensive, you will benefit from professional advice to maximize your claim particularly if you are acquiring fixtures with a property (see Chapter 9).

Capital or revenue expenditure?

Capital allowances are claimed on capital items. Broadly this is something that is going to benefit the business over a period of more than twelve months. For example a computer is a capital asset (you expect it to last for more than a year) whereas your monthly broadband connection is a revenue expense, after one month's subscription has expired you will not remain connected to the Internet unless you pay the charges for a further month (see Chapter 5).

Cost

There is no monetary limit that defines capital expenditure. A builder may purchase a £10 hammer that lasts for ten years or a hairdresser may buy scissors costing £20 that last for three years. Whilst both items could be defined as capital equipment since they are of continuing use to the business, it is more usual to treat them as revenue expenditure on the basis that:

- both items cost less than £100 (this is a commonly adopted limit); and
- small items are usually replaced regularly because they frequently get lost or break.

Loose tools costing less than £100 such as the hammer or scissors are therefore usually written off as a revenue expense (see Chapter 5). Equipment purchases that cost more than £100 are usually capital expenditure and you will need to claim capital allowances on them. The £100 limit is not however a hard and fast rule. The size of your business and the frequency with which you replace items may make a £200 limit for example more appropriate.

Length of life

There are special rules relating to assets which have a long life and those with a short life. Those that will last for more than 25 years (for example ships and aeroplanes) are known as 'long-life assets'. You will probably require professional help if you are thinking of buying these assets for your business. Items you expect to last for less than five years are called 'short-life assets'. Your capital allowance claim may be increased by identifying such assets separately (see Increasing your claim).

Financing the purchase

You can claim capital allowances on equipment irrespective of whether you buy the item outright, you finance the purchase with a bank loan or buy the item on hire purchase. If you enter into a leasing agreement, it is the leasing company who gets the allowances not you (see Leasing businesses, at the end of the chapter). If part of the purchase cost is paid for by an insurance company their contribution must be deducted from the cost of the asset (see Chapter 11). This also applies to some (but not all) grants and subsidies.

Types of capital allowance

There are two main types of capital allowance:

- First year allowances, given in the first year that an item of equipment is acquired.
- Writing down allowances, given in the second and subsequent years where a first year allowance is claimed, and in the first year if you do not claim a first year allowance.

First year allowances

The rate at which first year allowances are given varies. For small businesses meeting the size criteria in Table 2, first year allowances are currently 50% of the asset's cost (40% for medium-sized businesses). From 6 April 2007 the rate for both small and medium-sized businesses will be 40% (see Appendix 1) unless the Chancellor announces otherwise in the 2007 Budget. Energy-efficient, environmentally beneficial or water-saving plant qualifies for 100% first year allowances.

Some items do not qualify for first year allowances. The principal ones are:

- Cars; and
- Assets which you owned before starting the trade and introduced into the business at a later date (see Increasing capital allowance claims).

Where no first year allowances are due you can claim writing down allowances.

Writing down allowances

Writing down allowances are 25% of the item's cost in the first year. The allowance is deducted from the initial cost of the asset and in the second and subsequent years you can claim 25% of the balance. The balance reduces annually by the previous year's allowance (see Calculating capital allowances).

Table 1: Capital allowance rates

The following capital allowance rates apply to expenditure incurred between 6 April 2006 and 5 April 2007 (sole traders and partners); 1 April 2006 to 31 March 2007 for companies (see also Appendix 1).

Type of allowance	Rate	Items	Comments
First year	50% for 2006/07 only. Thereafter 40%	New or second-hand plant and machinery but not cars, items already owned or long-life assets	Small businesses (see Table 2)
First year	40%	New or second-hand plant and machinery but not cars, items already owned or long-life assets	Medium-sized businesses (see Table 2)
Writing down	25%	New and second-hand assets including assets already owned. Allowances on cars are limited to £3,000 per year per vehicle (see Cars).	All businesses
Green cars	100%	For a full list see **www.vca.gov.uk**	All businesses to 5 April 2008 only

Type of allowance	Rate	Items	Comments
Energy-efficient, environmentally beneficial or water-saving plant	100%	For a full list of qualifying technologies see **www.eca.gov.uk**	All businesses

Table 2: Size criteria for small and medium-sized businesses

To qualify for first year allowance, a small or medium-sized business (or group of companies) must meet two out of three of the following conditions:

Condition	Small £	Medium £
Sales turnover (below)	5,600,000	22,800,000
Assets (below)	2,800,000	11,400,000
Number of employees (not more than)	50	250

Calculating capital allowances

Having decided whether the item of equipment that you have purchased qualifies for capital allowances and having started to use it in your business it is time to work out your claim. Capital allowances are given for your accounting period not the tax year (although the rates are set for a tax year). If the accounting period is shorter than twelve months you must reduce your claim to writing down allowances proportionately. If it is longer than twelve months they will be increased. In this case you may require help with the calculations. The way in which capital allowances are calculated is illustrated with a series of examples.

First year allowances

Carlos runs a small limited company selling advertising space. He acquires four cars for his inner-city sales force which meet the necessary carbon dioxide emissions standards to qualify for 100% capital allowances. Each car costs £10,000. He will claim

100% capital allowances on each car and deduct £40,000 (£10,000 × 4) from his trading profits in the year in which he acquires the vehicles. There will be no balance to carry forward to the next year.

James sets up in self-employment as a management consultant on 1 May 2006. He qualifies as a small business. On 2 May 2006 he buys computer equipment costing £4,000. He prepares his first accounts to 31 March 2007 and claims first year allowances on the computer equipment as follows: – £4,000 × 50% = £2,000. James will deduct £2,000 from his business profits. The claim will save him income tax and Class 4 National Insurance at the highest tax rate he pays. He will enter details of the capital allowances on his tax return to 5 April 2007. It does not matter that James only started his business on 1 May 2006 and he prepares his accounts for less than twelve months – he can claim the first year allowance in full.

What happens to the £2,000 (£4,000 – £2,000) that James has not been able to claim in his first trading period? This is carried forward to the second year of trading when he will be able to claim writing down allowances on the unused balance. When you are making your own claim it is advisable to keep a note of this figure so that you do not inadvertently forget to claim these allowances in the following tax year. You could note the number in the additional information box on your tax return. Tax practitioners usually keep a running total of claims like this:

Capital allowance computation	Cost	Allowances
Period to 31 March 2007	£	£
2.5.06 bought computer equipment	4,000	
First year allowance: 50% x £4,000	–2,000	**2,000**
Carried forward to next accounting period	**2,000**	
Year to 31 March 2008		
Brought forward from previous period	2,000	
Writing down allowance: 25% x £2,000	–500	**500**
Carried forward to next accounting period	**1,500**	

James will continue claiming a reduced writing down allowance each accounting period until there is no balance left to carry forward to the next year, or as is more likely, he stops using the equipment (see Disposals).

Writing down allowances

Andrea starts work as a freelance potter on 1 July 2006. She already owns a wheel and other tools and equipment which she introduces into her business. She calculates that these have a second-hand value at 1 July 2006 of £500. She prepares her first accounts to 31 March 2007 (a nine-month period) and claims writing down allowances. She cannot claim first year allowances because she already owned the items prior to setting up her business (see Increasing capital allowance claims). Because Andrea started her business on 1 July 2006, her writing down allowance for her first period of trading is restricted to 25% × 9 months divided by 12 months. The following computation shows her claims for the first four accounting periods.

Capital allowance computation	Cost	Allowances
9 month accounting period to 31 March 2007	£	£
1.7.06 introduced wheel and tools	500	
Writing down allowance: 25% × £500 × 9 months/12 months	−94	**94**
Carried forward to next accounting period	**406**	
Year to 31 March 2008		
Brought forward from previous accounting period	406	
Writing down allowance: 25% × £406	−102	**102**
Carried forward to the next accounting period	304	
Year to 31 March 2009		
Brought forward from previous accounting period	304	
Writing down allowance: 25% × £304	−76	**76**

Capital allowance computation	Cost	Allowances
Carried forward to the next accounting period	228	
Year to 31 March 2010		
Brought forward from previous accounting period	228	
Writing down allowance – 25% × £228	–57	**57**
Carried forward to the next accounting period	171	

Multiple acquisitions

Most businesses acquire several items of capital equipment each year. As more items of plant and machinery are added, the calculations get more complicated and it is increasingly important to keep track of which items qualify for first year allowances as well as the brought forward balances on which writing down allowances can be claimed.

Andrea in the above example acquires a kiln costing £3,000 on 1 January 2007, some display shelves at a cost of £400 on 1 June 2007 and a second-hand van on 1 September 2007 for £1,000. Her capital allowance calculations are now as follows:

Capital allowance computation	Cost of assets qualifying for first year allowances	Cost of assets qualifying for writing down allowances (the 'pool')	Allowances
9 month accounting period to 31 March 2007	£	£	£
1.8.06 introduced wheel and tools		500	
1.1.07 bought kiln	3,000		
First year allowance: 50%	–1,500		1,500
Writing down allowance: 25% × £500 × 9 months/12 months		–94	94
Total allowances			**1,594**
Transferred to the pool	–1,500	1,500	

Capital allowance computation	Cost of assets qualifying for first year allowances	Cost of assets qualifying for writing down allowances (the 'pool')	Allowances
Carried forward to next accounting period	**0**	**1,906**	
Year to 31 March 2008			
Brought forward from previous accounting period	0	1,906	
1.6.07 bought shelves	400		
1.9.07 bought van	1,000		
	1,400		
First year allowance: 40% (check Appendix 1)	–560		560
Writing down allowance: 25% × £1,906		–477	477
Total allowances			**1,037**
Transferred to the pool	–840	840	
Carried forward to the next accounting period	**0**	**2,269**	
Year to 31 March 2009			
Brought forward from previous accounting period	0	2,269	
Writing down allowance: 25% £2,269		–567	**567**
Carried forward to the next accounting period	0	**1,702**	
Year to 31 March 2010			
Brought forward from previous accounting period	0	1,702	
Writing down allowance: 25% × £1,702		–426	**426**
Carried forward to the next accounting period	0	**1,276**	

Andrea will be entitled to writing down allowances until there is nothing left to claim on the 'pool' or until she sells or disposes of all her assets.

Disposals

The way in which you calculate the disposal of an asset depends on whether you are claiming allowances on only one asset (see the Example 'James') or whether the pool has a balance that represents the purchase of many assets acquired over a period of time (see the Example 'Andrea').

If James buys new computer equipment on 1 August 2008 for £3,000 and on the same day scraps his old equipment, the capital allowances for the year to 31 March 2009 would be calculated as follows:

Capital allowance computation	Cost	Allowances
Year to 31 March 2009	£	£
Brought forward from previous tax year	1,500	
Equipment scrapped	0	
Balancing allowance	−1,500	1,500
1.8.08 bought computer equipment	3,000	
First year allowance: 40% × £3,000 (see Appendix 1)	−1,200	1,200
Total allowances		2,700
Carried forward to next accounting period	1,800	

James has only claimed capital allowances on one item of computer equipment so when he disposes of it he can claim a balancing allowance. This is equal to the difference between the balance brought forward from the previous tax year and the sales proceeds. In this case as James has scrapped the equipment there is no sales income and a balancing allowance arises. A balancing allowance is an additional capital allowance to ensure that James has received tax relief on the total cost of the equipment spread over his period of ownership. You should note that in the calculation, the disposal of the old computer is dealt with before the acquisition of the new one.

If instead of scrapping the equipment James sells it to another consultant for £2,000, a balancing charge of £500 would arise (£2,000 – £1,500). This reduces his capital allowance claim for the year. A balancing charge is effectively a negative capital allowance and is necessary to limit James' capital allowance claim to the cost of the asset less any income he receives from its sale. James must show the balancing charge separately from his capital allowances when completing his tax return.

Capital allowance computation	Cost	Allowances
Year to 31 March 2009		
Brought forward from previous accounting period	1,500	
Equipment sold	2,000	
Balancing charge	500	–500
1.8.08 bought computer equipment	3,000	
First year allowance: 40% × £3,000 (see Appendix 1)	–1,200	1,200
Total allowances		**700**
Carried forward to next accounting period	**1,800**	

Andrea's capital allowance calculation is different because she has a 'pool' containing more than one asset. On 1 May 2008 Andrea sells her original potter's wheel for £100 and purchases a reconditioned one for £1,000.

Recap

The disposal of the old asset should be dealt with before the acquisition of the new equipment.

Capital allowance computation	Cost of assets qualifying for first year allowances	Cost of assets qualifying for writing down allowances (the 'pool')	Allowances
Year to 31 March 2009	£	£	£
Brought forward from previous accounting period		2,269	
1.5.08 sold wheel		−100	
1.5.08 bought wheel	1,000		
Total on which writing down allowances can be claimed		2,169	
First year allowance: 40% (see Appendix 1)	−400		400
Writing down allowance: 25% × £2,169		−542	542
Total allowances claimed			**942**
Transferred to the pool	−600	600	
Carried forward to the next accounting period	0	**2,227**	
Year to 31 March 2010			
Brought forward from previous accounting period		2,227	
Writing down allowance: 25%		−557	**557**
Carried forward to the next accounting period		**1,670**	

No balancing allowance or charge arises because the assets are 'pooled.' The old wheel less a deduction for the £100 sales proceeds remains in the pool and Andrea continues to claim allowances on it even though the asset is no longer used in her business.

James had a balancing allowance (or charge) because he sold all his assets. The sale of your business is one occasion when a balancing allowance or charge will occur (see Chapter 13). There are three further situations when a balancing allowance or charge will arise:

- You dispose of a car which cost more than £12,000 (see Cars);
- You are self-employed or a partner and use your car, van or another asset partly for work and partly privately (see Cars);
- You purchase computer equipment (or other assets) which you expect to have a short life and make a short-life asset election (see Increasing capital allowance claims).

In each of these situations capital allowances are calculated separately and at no time is any balance transferred to the pool.

Cars

There are special capital allowance rules which currently apply to cars but not vans:

- They are not eligible for first year allowances unless you buy a green car meeting certain conditions (see Table 1).
- Writing down allowances cannot exceed £3,000, so if a car costs more than £12,000 the excess cost does not attract any allowances.
- A car costing less than £12,000 purchased by a company for an employee can be pooled with other items of equipment. Sole traders and partners will only rarely pool a car because if the vehicle is used for private as well as business purposes, the allowances must be calculated separately from your other assets.
- Allowances on a car costing more than £12,000 must be calculated separately from other cars and equipment. When the vehicle is sold a balancing allowance or charge may occur depending on how long the car has been used in the business and the sale proceeds (see Disposals).

Point to note: Car capital allowance claims differ from the calculation of an employee's company car benefit in kind charge (see Chapter 8).

Potential changes

The Government are currently consulting the public on potential reform to the system for calculating capital allowances on cars. Options being considered include a range of first year allowances based on a car's carbon dioxide (CO_2) emissions, a new car pool for all cars, writing down allowances of less than 25% and changes to the treatment of leased cars. If you are completing your tax return after 6 April 2007 you should check HMRC's guidance in case the rules have changed.

Case study

Rashid and his two brothers are directors of Petromax Ltd which operates three fuel stations. In its twelve-month accounting period to 31 December 2006, the company provides each brother with a company car. Rashid's car costs £15,000 and his brothers drive cars that cost £10,000 each. The company's capital allowance computation is as follows assuming that there was no balance brought forward on the pool on 1 January 2006:

Capital allowance computation	Expensive cars (costing more than £12,000)	Pooled cars and equipment	Allowances
Accounting period to 31 December 2006	£	£	£
New cars	15,000	20,000	
Writing down allowance: 25% limited to £3,000	–3,000		3,000
Writing down allowance: 25%		5,000	5,000
Total allowances			**8,000**
Carried forward to next accounting period	**12,000**	**15,000**	

Two years later Petromax Ltd sells Rashid's car for £3,000 and one of the other cars for £2,500. The company's capital allowance computation is as follows:

Capital allowance computation	Expensive cars (costing over £12,000)	Pooled cars and equipment	Allowances
Period to 31 December 2008	£	£	£
Brought forward from previous accounting period	9,000	11,250	
Disposal proceeds	–3,000	–2,500	
Balancing allowance	–6,000		6,000
Total on which allowances are claimed		8,750	
Writing down allowance: 25%		2,188	2,188
Total allowances			8,188
Carried forward to next accounting period	0	6,562	

Rashid's car is not pooled so a significant balancing allowance arises on its sale.

As the cars are owned by a company the allowances do not have to be reduced by a percentage for their private use. Instead the directors each incur a benefit in kind charge on the perk of having a company car (see Chapter 8).

Rashid's sister Farah is a self-employed physiotherapist. In 2007 she decides to acquire a car for her business. She is trying to choose between a model which qualifies as a green car eligible for 100% first year allowances (see Table 1) and a second-hand older model which does not. Both cars cost £10,000 and she expects to use them 50% of the time for work purposes.

Option 1

Capital allowances on environmentally friendly model	Car meeting CO_2 standards (50% private use)	Allowances
First accounting period	£	£
New car	10,000	
First year allowance: 100%	−10,000	10,000
Private use: 50%		−5,000
Total allowance		**5,000**
Carried forward to next accounting period	**0**	

Option 2

Capital allowances on second-hand model	Car (50% private use)	Allowances
First accounting period	£	£
Car purchase	10,000	
Writing down allowance: 25%	−2,500	2,500
Private use: 50%		−1,250
Total allowance		**1,250**
Carried forward to next accounting period	**7,500**	

In the accounting period in which Farah acquires her car she will receive £3,750 more capital allowances by choosing the model qualifying for 100% first year allowances. In subsequent years, she will receive no further allowances on the green model but will do on her alternative choice of car. Assuming that she is a basic rate taxpayer in the year she acquires the car and expects to make similar profits in the future, buying the environmentally friendly car will save her £1,125 in income tax and Class 4 National Insurance in the year she buys it – a significant contribution to the purchase price.

Capital allowance claims

Capital allowances must be claimed on your tax return. If you are a partner you need to claim capital allowances on all your assets on the partnership return. You cannot make a separate claim on your own form for items such as your car or other personally owned assets.

Increasing your claim

Disclaiming allowances

Sometimes you will be better off not claiming all the capital allowances that you are entitled to. This is most likely to occur if your profits are low or you have losses so that you are either not paying tax, or only paying it at the starting rate (see Appendix 1).

You can claim capital allowances on some assets but not others, claim a fixed sum, or disclaim all the allowances for the year (both first year allowances and writing down allowances). You will then carry forward a higher balance to a year when you are a taxpayer and you will save tax then. If you have made a loss and have other income to set the loss against it may be better to claim the capital allowances as they will increase the loss and any tax rebate which you may be entitled to (see Chapter 6). You are likely to require professional advice to maximize your tax savings.

Example

Martin's profits as a piano tuner are £4,250 in his accounting period to 5 April 2007. He is entitled to claim capital allowances on his tools of £200 and on his car of £500 but he decides not to as his profits are below his personal allowance (see Appendix 1). As he has no other taxable income that year, to claim the allowances would waste them. If his profits are £10,000 in the year to 5 April 2008, the unclaimed allowances will save him tax and Class 4 National Insurance of £210 in that year. His capital allowances computation goes like this:

Capital allowance computation	Car (80% business use)	Pooled equipment	Allowances
Year ended 5 April 2007	£	£	£
Brought forward balance from previous accounting period	2,500	800	
Writing down allowance: disclaimed	0	0	0
Carried forward to next accounting period	**2,500**	**800**	
Year ended 5 April 2008			
Brought forward balance from previous accounting period	2,500	800	
Writing down allowance: 25%	625	200	825
Private use of car: 20%			−125
Carried forward to next accounting period	**1,875**	**600**	**700**

Computers and other short-life assets

Another way to increase your capital allowance claim is to elect for assets other than cars (usually computers and other technological equipment) with a limited life-span to be treated as 'short-life' assets. This means that these items are not included in the 'pool' with other equipment so when they are sold or scrapped a balancing allowance arises (see the example of James in Disposals). The assets are treated separately until four years from the end of the accounting period when they were acquired. At this point any remaining balance is transferred to the 'pool'.

In order to qualify for short-life asset treatment you must elect for it to apply. This is done by including separate calculations for each item of equipment with your tax return. Once the election is made you cannot change your mind. If you purchase several assets that you want short-life asset treatment to apply to, the tax authorities will accept that items bought in the same year and qualifying for the same allowances can be combined.

Point to note: You must elect for short-life asset treatment to apply within one year of the 31 January which follows the end of the period of account when you bought the asset if you are an individual. If you are a company the time limit is two years after the end of the relevant accounting period.

Introduced assets

When you commence in self-employment you may own various items that you subsequently start using in your business such as a car, computer, tools and office furniture. You can introduce these into the business at an appropriate value. This is best done by making a list of the items and their values. You should keep details showing how you arrived at the valuation (for example reference to a published car price guide) in case HMRC asks to see it during an enquiry (see Chapter 3).

Recap: You cannot claim first year allowances on introduced items but you can claim writing down allowances (see the example of Andrea in Calculating capital allowances).

Buy equipment before the end of your accounting period

You can accelerate your capital allowance claim by buying any equipment you need before the end of your accounting period rather than shortly afterwards. This means that you can claim a deduction for capital allowances a whole year earlier. You must start using the asset in order to qualify for the allowance so it is no use ordering it before your year end for delivery afterwards.

When considering this tax-saving option, you should only buy equipment you actually need and bear in mind how much tax it will actually save. A trap that people frequently fall into is to believe that buying a £1,000 machine will save them £1,000 in tax. Assuming a first year allowance of 50% and a tax and Class 4 National Insurance rate of 30%, spending £1,000 on equipment will save you just £150 of tax in the year of purchase.

Leasing businesses

Leasing businesses are subject to special rules which restrict their capital allowance claims in some cases. If your business is involved in asset leasing you will require specialist advice.

Recap

- When calculating your tax bill, capital allowances take the place of commercial depreciation. Rather than claiming a tax deduction for depreciation you claim capital allowances instead (see Chapter 5).

- You can claim capital allowances on some industrial buildings (see Chapter 9). Plant and machinery incorporated into a building may be subject to a claim for industrial buildings allowance or a claim for capital allowances.

- The government frequently uses first year allowances to encourage business investment. You should check the current rate of first year allowances before making your claim as they change frequently (see Appendix 1).

08 employees

In this chapter:
- who is an employee?
- operating a PAYE scheme
- taxing perks
- tax-efficient staff benefits
- the construction industry

Taking on staff is a significant event. Few small businesses can function without them and employees' wages will be one of the first major expenses that you will incur. If you have only just taken on staff, how have you been managing until now? Have you been the only person working in the business? In addition to understanding the numerous tax consequences associated with paying your staff, you also need to learn who is and who is not an employee if you are to avoid the additional cost of penalties.

As an employer you are responsible for the following taxes and related functions:

- Ensuring that all employees are paid at a rate equivalent to at least the National Minimum Wage;
- Deducting income tax and Class 1 National Insurance from their wages through the PAYE system;
- Paying employer's Class 1 National Insurance contributions;
- Operating statutory payments – statutory sick pay (SSP), statutory maternity pay (SMP), statutory paternity pay (SPP) and statutory adoption pay (SAP);
- Administering and deducting student loan repayments;
- Notifying HM Revenue and Customs about perks and benefits so that your employees can be correctly taxed on them via their tax code;
- Paying Class 1A or Class 1B National Insurance on certain employee perks;
- Monthly (or quarterly) paying over to HM Revenue and Customs the tax, National Insurance and student loan repayments deducted from your staff less any statutory payments.

You probably feel exhausted already! Dealing with this long list of requirements can be extremely burdensome for new employers and you probably have many other priorities that you would prefer to deal with including getting the business off the ground. Complying with the PAYE rules and regulations is compulsory. It is also essential for good employee relations. No member of staff will be pleased to find that they have been taxed incorrectly so you need to find ways to meet your obligations cost-effectively. HM Revenue and Customs provide a wealth of information on their website to help employers; see **www.hmrc.gov.uk/employers/index.shtml**.

In Chapter 4 you saw how difficult it can be to decide when you are self-employed. It can be equally problematic to know whether someone you engage to help you with your business is an employee. Falling foul of the PAYE rules can be expensive and taking on staff is an occasion when consulting an accountant is advisable.

There are numerous dates to bear in mind when dealing with PAYE. They are set out in the diary in Appendix 2.

Who is an employee?

There is no hard and fast definition of 'employee' but most people who work for you are likely to be employees.

Employed or self-employed?

Having read the list of employer's tax obligations you may think that it would be more cost-effective and less onerous to use people who are self-employed to provide you with services rather than take on employees. In some cases outsourcing work to other small businesses in this way can benefit your business but most people who work for you on your premises are likely to be employed by you. This is the case even if they do not work for you full-time and they do not have a written employment contract. Mistakenly or deliberately failing to operate PAYE on an employee's pay is a serious matter. You may have to pay the tax and National Insurance on the amounts you erroneously paid them at a later date (you will be unlikely to recover this tax from your worker) and you will probably incur a penalty as well.

In deciding whether someone who works for you is an employee, HM Revenue and Customs look at the facts of the case and your relationship with that person. The factors they consider are shown in the following table. For further information see HMRC's Employment Status Indicator (ESI) Tool on **www.hmrc.gov.uk/calcs/esi.htm**.

Even if the worker has their own self-employed business HMRC can still decide that in the particular circumstances of the work that they perform for you they are your employee (see Chapter 4). Resolving whether someone is an employee or self-employed is called an 'employment status dispute'. Should this situation arise, using the services of an accountant or tax adviser will help you to obtain the best outcome.

Table of factors relevant to deciding whether a person is an employee or self-employed

HM Revenue and Customs will examine the following issues to create a complete picture of the relationship between you and the person working for you:

- Control over the worker is a strong pointer to employment. This includes control of what work is done, how, when and where.
- Personal service by the worker indicates employment. Few employment contracts permit a substitute or replacement to be used.
- Provision of major equipment such as a commercial vehicle may indicate self-employment but supplying tools of the trade is not usually persuasive either way. If you provide all the equipment the worker is more likely to be employed.
- Financial risk borne by the worker may indicate self-employment. For example if they make a mistake do they have to correct it in their own time, pay any additional costs or work without pay? Could the worker make a loss undertaking their duties, for example because of the way you pay them?
- Basis of payment – employees are usually paid a fixed monthly or weekly wage or salary and work under a service contract, although some employees are paid by 'the piece'. People who are self-employed supply their services under a contract for services and are paid a fee for a particular piece of work agreed to be undertaken in a specified time.
- Mutuality of obligation – for there to be an employer–employee relationship there must be an obligation by the employer to pay the employee a salary or wage for their work in return for which the employee provides services using their labour or skill.
- Holiday pay, sick pay, maternity or paternity pay and the ability to join the employer's pension scheme usually indicate an employer–employee relationship although the absence of these rights if the employment is short-term does not create a self-employed relationship.
- Being part and parcel of the organization – is the worker an integral part of the organization such that they appear to an outsider to be an employee, for example do they wear a uniform or a badge?
- The length of engagement does not usually determine whether the contract is one of employment or self-employment. An employee may work for an employer for a day, a week or 20

years; a person who is self-employed may also work for an organization for a day, several months or periodically for many years.

- The intention of the parties if genuinely held may be relevant in some borderline cases.

Directors

Company directors are almost always employees and their salaries are taxed under PAYE. There are special rules relating to their National Insurance treatment; see **www.hmrc.gov.uk/nitables/ca44.pdf** and **www.hmrc.gov.uk/calcs/nicd.htm**.

In a few limited circumstances a professional person such as a lawyer or accountant who is also a company director may be able to be treated as self-employed with regard to a modest director's salary.

Family members

Many small businesses rely on help from family members. You will need to decide whether a family member working in your business is your employee, partner or co-director. You may need to seek professional advice to determine the most tax-efficient structure. Family members living in the same household do not need to be paid the National Minimum Wage and it can be cost-effective to pay a family member a small wage between the National Insurance lower threshold and employee's limit (see Employee's National Insurance – Case study).

Yourself

If you are self-employed or a partner any amounts that you pay to yourself or take from the partnership are your drawings. They are not a salary or wages and you are not an employee (see Chapter 5). If you are a director of a limited company the rules are different and sums you take from the company must be either taxed under PAYE or paid to you as dividends (see Chapter 4).

Paying employees

National Minimum Wage

You must pay your employees at a pay rate at least equivalent to the National Minimum Wage (see Appendix 1) and keep records to prove that you have done so. The applicable rate which is enforced by HM Revenue and Customs varies according to whether the worker is an adult, trainee or young person. The National Minimum Wage legislation applies to all employees including agency staff, piece workers, employees with disabilities and those paid by commission. It does not however apply to the following people:

- Those who are self-employed;
- Company directors unless they have an employment contract;
- Some apprentices and trainees; and
- Family members who live in the same household and work in a business together.

Calculating whether an employee's gross pay (before deducting tax and National Insurance) meets the National Minimum Wage is not always straightforward particularly if the employee is paid bonuses, commission, tips, overtime and perks. For further information about the National Minimum Wage refer to **www.hmrc.gov.uk/nmw/** and **www.dti.gov.uk/employment/ pay/national-minimum-wage/index.html.**

What is an employee's pay?

Employees' pay consists of their salary or wages plus overtime, holiday pay, commission and bonuses. This pay before deductions are taken off is known as 'gross pay' and is the sum used to calculate PAYE and National Insurance. Tips and other sums paid through the payroll are also treated as gross pay and so are statutory sick pay and statutory maternity, paternity and adoption pay. If you reward staff with assets such as commodities and shares these also count as taxable income unless the shares are part of an approved share scheme (see Chapter 12). Most perks and benefits are taxed (see Taxing perks). Sometimes they are treated as gross pay but in most cases the employee's tax code is altered to take the benefit into account (see Understanding Tax Codes).

It is sometimes tempting to pay staff a set amount of net pay rather than gross pay. Such arrangements should be avoided as employees' tax codes change for reasons beyond your control which could leave either you or your member of staff out of pocket (see Understanding tax codes).

National Insurance numbers

All your employees must provide you with a National Insurance (NI) number. A valid NI number consist of two letters, followed by six numbers, followed by one letter either A, B, C or D. Temporary NI numbers with the pre-fix TN and based on the employee's date of birth and gender (F for female and M for male) are not acceptable. If an employee does not have a National Insurance number, they should apply to their local Jobcentre Plus office for one. If a NI number has been lost, HMRC will be able to trace it upon submission of form P46 or CA 6855; see **www.hmrc.gov.uk/employers/taking_on.htm**.

Taxing employees

If you have employees you must operate a PAYE scheme so that you can deduct income tax, National Insurance and student loan repayments correctly and pay them statutory sick pay and statutory maternity, paternity and adoption pay when appropriate.

Obtaining a PAYE scheme

PAYE schemes are obtained from HM Revenue and Customs either online on **www.hmrc.gov.uk/employers/new-emp-email-contacts.htm** or by contacting the New Employers' Helpline on 0845 6070143. They will send you a CD-Rom-based starter pack, may suggest that you attend a workshop or offer you a face-to-face meeting with a business support adviser. You can maintain your payroll records manually or on a computer. Many employers may find using a computer program easier than making the calculations themselves and completing the forms by hand, and there are now financial incentives to encourage you to file forms online (see Online filing). There are many payroll packages available but you should choose one which is approved by HMRC. In spite of the help available many small businesses decide that it is more time and cost-effective to use an agency to run their payroll for them.

Running a PAYE scheme

Once you have set up your PAYE you need to learn how to pay and tax your employees. The basic steps are set out in the following Guide to operating a PAYE scheme.

Guide to operating a PAYE scheme

- Each time you pay an employee, the payment falls into a designated month (for monthly-paid staff) or week (for weekly-paid employees).

- Every employee has a tax code (see Understanding tax codes). The code is used in conjunction with PAYE tables (which form part of your computer software) to calculate their income tax deduction (or refund) for the month or week in question.

- National Insurance tables (again part of your payroll software) are used to calculate the Class 1 employee's deduction and the employer's contribution monthly or weekly.

- Additional tables (incorporated in the computer software) are used to calculate statutory additions such as SSP, SMP, SPP and SAP plus student loan repayments.

- Each employee's gross pay, statutory additions, deductions for PAYE, National Insurance and student loans are recorded on an individual form P11 (usually computer-generated). The cumulative pay and PAYE are shown along with the employee's tax coding and National Insurance number.

- Every time that an employee is paid, he or she is given a payslip summarizing the details on their form P11, their net pay and any other employer-specific adjustments such as season-ticket loan repayments and pensions.

- At the end of the month (sometimes quarterly) you have to pay HMRC the amounts deducted from your employees' wages plus your employer's National Insurance contributions less any sums paid out for statutory sick pay, maternity pay etc. Employers whose average monthly payments are less than £1,500 have the option of paying over their PAYE and National Insurance quarterly. The payment dates for both monthly and quarterly options are set out in Appendix 2.

- After the end of the tax year you must give your employees a form P60 summarizing their pay and tax. Staff receiving perks must receive a form P11D (sometimes a form P9D). You also have to complete an end of year return reconciling the amounts that you have paid to HMRC with the details entered on the forms P60 (HMRC's copies of these forms are called P14s). There are incentives for filing the end of year return online (see Online filing). The dates for completion and delivery of these forms are provided in Appendix 2.

Further information: HMRC's 'Paying someone for the first time' (P49 (2005) (2)) – **www.hmrc.gov.uk/forms/p49.pdf** and 'Employer's Help Book E12' – **www.hmrc.gov.uk/helpsheets/e12_2.pdf**.

Online filing

HM Revenue and Customs prefer you to file your employer's returns and make payments via their website. Employers with 50 or more employees already have to file their returns online but small employers have until the return due on 19 May 2010 to begin filing over the Internet. If you want to start filing your PAYE returns electronically before this date HM Revenue and Customs will pay you the following tax-free incentive payments to get you started:

- £150 for 2006/07 (return due by 19 May 2007);
- £100 for 2007/08 (return due by 19 May 2008);
- £75 for 2008/09 (return due by 19 May 2009).

For further details see 'Do it online: Small employers guide to filing PAYE returns' **www.hmrc.gov.uk/employers/onlineguide_smallemp.htm** and 'Do it Online: online filing' on **www.hmrc.gov.uk/employers/onlineindex.htm**. You can register for PAYE Online for employers on **www.hmrc.gov.uk/newemployers/iwt-register-for-paye-online-for-employers.shtml**.

Taking on a member of staff

When a new member of staff joins your business you need to undertake the following steps:

- Ask them for parts 2 and 3 of the form P45. This will have been given to them by their previous employer. If the P45 was issued in the current tax year use the details (including the tax code) to complete a deductions working sheet (form P11) for them. Send part 3 of the P45 to HMRC to notify them that the person is now employed by you. If the appropriate box on the form is marked you should continue to deduct student loan repayments.

- If the employee does not have a form P45, ask them to complete a form P46 and send it to HMRC. The employee will be taxed according to which statement they have ticked on the form (see Understanding tax codes) until such time as HMRC advises you to use a new tax code.
- Check that the employee's National Insurance number appears to be valid (see National Insurance numbers).
- If the employee is entitled to a company car notify HMRC using form P46 (Car).
- Special rules apply if you take on an employee for less than one week.

For further information refer to **www.hmrc.gov.uk/employers/taking_on.htm.**

Forms

The following table summarizes the payroll forms that you may come across. These may be pre-printed manual forms, downloaded from HMRC's website or computer-generated by your payroll software.

Form	Description
P9	Notification of an employee's new tax code. You will not be sent one for all employees.
P9D	Summarizes perks and benefits received by employees earning less than £8,500 a year. You complete it after the end of the tax year.
P11	Deductions working sheet for each employee recording their details for the tax year (including pay, PAYE and National Insurance).
P11D	Summarizes an employee's perks and benefits in kind. You complete it after the end of the tax year.
P11D(b)	Return of employer's Class 1A National Insurance contributions due on benefits in kind.
P14	End of year summary of an employee's pay and deductions for the tax year. It is sent to HMRC with the end of year return (see also P60).
P32	Employer's payment record, recording sums paid over each month to HMRC.

Form	Description
P35	Employer's end of year return.
P38A	Supplementary form to the P35.
P38S	Supplementary form to the P35 recording students' income.
P45	Certificate given to an employee when they leave employment. Parts 2 and 3 of the form are given to you when a new employee starts work.
P46	Completed by a new employee who does not have a form P45 (for example because they were previously self-employed).
P46 (Car)	Form to notify HMRC that an employee or director has a company car.
P60	End of year summary of pay and deductions for the tax year given to an employee (see also P14).

Deductions

Having looked in outline at the operation of a PAYE scheme, we now consider each of the deductions you have to make from gross pay. These are:

- PAYE;
- National Insurance; and
- Student loan repayments.

All the amounts that you deduct are paid over to HM Revenue and Customs monthly or quarterly together with employer's National Insurance (see Employer's National Insurance). Any statutory payments you have to make can be deducted in full or part from your payment (see Statutory pay).

PAYE

PAYE is the means of deducting income tax from an employee's gross pay by using a combination of a tax code, free pay and taxable pay tables (usually incorporated into payroll software). The taxable pay tables apply the various income tax rates (see Appendix 1) to the employee's pay after adjusting it for his or her personal allowance and all the other items included in their tax code (free pay).

Understanding tax codes

An employee's tax code is an integral part of the PAYE system. Many employees will have the same tax code but you will find that some employees will have different tax codes. You will only be told the number you must use not the composition of coding because this is confidential to the employee.

Tax codes may include the following items:

- The employee's personal allowance (see Appendix 1); *plus*
- Any tax-deductible expenses; *plus*
- Higher rate tax relief for gift aid payments and pensions; *less*
- Tax owed for a previous tax year (as long as it is less than £2,000); *less*
- Sums to tax perks; *less*
- Adjustments to collect tax on other sources of income such as investment and property income.

A typical tax code for 2006/07 is 503L. This is also known as the 'emergency tax code'.

- 503 stands for the basic personal allowance (tax-free pay) of £5,035.
- L refers to the fact that the code contains the basic personal allowance. The letter is for administration purposes and does not affect the calculation of the coding.

You may notice that most tax codes include letters. This is what they mean:

- **K at the start** – is used where an amount has been added to an employee's pay so that their deductions are more than their allowances. This would be the case where the employee has significant benefits in kind such as a company car or a tax underpayment from an earlier year. The tax deducted under a K code is restricted to no more than 50% of the employee's pay.
- **P, V and Y at the end** – shows full personal allowances for *those aged over 65 (see Appendix 1).*
- **T at the end** – is used if there are any items HMRC needs to review. It does not mean 'temporary code'.

BR and D0 codes are usually used where the employee has a second source of income and all their tax allowances have been included in a notice of coding applied to the first source of income. BR means basic rate tax; D0 means higher rate tax (see Appendix 1). NT means that no tax is to be deducted.

Tax codes can be cumulative or they can be calculated by reference to the week or month for which pay is operated. This is denoted by the P45 being marked 'week 1' or 'month 1' or you being instructed by HMRC to apply the tax code in this way.

HMRC's website includes an online pay adjustment calculator at **www.hmrc.gov.uk/employers/calc_pay_adjust.htm** which provides an indication of an employee's tax-free pay, or the addition to it if a K code applies.

Operating tax codes

You will obtain information about an employee's tax codes from the following sources:

- Form P45 – for new employees. Provided that the form is for the same tax year you should use the same tax code as the previous employer taking care to operate the coding either cumulatively or on a week 1 or month 1 basis.
- Form P46 – for new employees without a form P45. Depending on which statement your employee ticks, you must choose which tax code to operate, see **www.hmrc.gov.uk/employers/taking_on.htm**.
- P9 – sent by HMRC notifying you of a new tax code for your employee.
- Annual increase – most tax codes apart from BR and D0 change in May each year to reflect the annual increase in personal allowances. You will be sent a notice instructing you to increase all employees' codes of a certain type to a new figure. For example in May 2006 code 489L became 503L.

Employee's National Insurance

An employee's National Insurance contributions are calculated by reference to two main factors:

- Whether they are contracted into or out of the state second pension (S2P); and
- The level of their earnings.

For the applicable rates see Appendix 1.

When an employee's income exceeds the earnings threshold (ET), set at the same level as the basic personal allowance (see Appendix 1) most employees have to pay National Insurance contributions (see Chapter 2 for details of those who do not).

Where an employee's earnings exceed the upper earnings limit (UEL) they pay additional contributions at the rate set out in Appendix 1 on those earnings above the UEL. You will either be provided with National Insurance tables to work out the appropriate contributions by HMRC or they will be incorporated in your payroll software. The lower earnings limit (LEL) is the minimum level of earnings that an employee needs to qualify for state benefits such as retirement pension and jobseeker's allowance. If an employee's earnings reach or exceed the LEL, but do not exceed the earnings threshold (ET), they will not pay any National Insurance contributions. They will however be treated as having paid them when claiming state benefits. Understanding this may help small family businesses to set appropriate pay rates for family members working in the business, enabling them to qualify for benefits but without incurring the cost of employee's (or employer's) contributions. When setting pay rates for other workers the National Minimum Wage will apply (see Paying employees – National Minimum Wage).

Case study

Ray is 19, lives at home with his family and works in his father's import/export business. In 2006/07 he earns £96 per week. This is above the lower earnings limit of £84 per week but below the earnings threshold of £97 per week. As a result he pays no employee's National Insurance but still qualifies for state retirement pension and jobseeker's allowance should he need to claim it. Furthermore his father as his employer does not have to pay employer's contributions. He must however keep records of the sums paid to his son as he would do for any other employee. If this is Ray's only source of income he will not pay any income tax under PAYE as it falls below his personal allowance. As he lives at home with his family and works in a family business the National Minimum Wage rules do not apply to him.

Student loan repayments

HM Revenue and Customs is responsible for collecting repayments of loans made to students by the Student Loans Company. You must deduct repayments from employees earning in excess of the repayment figure set out in Appendix 1 each pay day using the loan deduction tables (usually incorporated into your payroll software). The sums deducted will be paid over to HMRC once a month along with your PAYE and National Insurance.

Further information: Employer's Help Book, E17, 'Collection of Student Loans', www.hmrc.gov.uk/helpsheets/e17.pdf.

137

employees

08

Statutory pay

Employers are not just responsible for deducting sums from their employees. There are four occasions when they must give them statutory payments. These are:

- Statutory Sick Pay (SSP);
- Statutory Maternity Pay (SMP);
- Statutory Paternity Pay (SPP); and
- Statutory Adoption Pay (SAP).

Any statutory payments you make are deducted (in full or part) from the amounts you have to pay over to HM Revenue and Customs for PAYE, National Insurance and student loan repayments. If you pay employees additional sums over the statutory minimum these amounts cannot be recovered from HMRC.

Statutory Sick Pay (SSP)

SSP is paid to employees who are unable to attend work because they are sick or incapacitated and who have average weekly earnings above a certain threshold (see Appendix 1). It is paid for up to a maximum of 28 weeks.

You must pay a sick employee SSP if they are sick for at least four or more days in a row including weekends and bank holidays (this is known as a period of incapacity for work) as long as they have provided you with appropriate evidence of their indisposition.

Calculating SSP can be complicated and you will need to complete additional forms to record the sums paid. The calculations and forms will probably be produced by your payroll software. Alternatively, HMRC have an SSP calculator on their website; see www.hmrc.gov.uk/calcs/ssp.htm.

You can claim back any SSP you have paid over and above a certain percentage of your National Insurance liability for the same tax month in which you pay SSP (see Appendix 1).

Example

Amy pays Class 1 National Insurance before deductions of £1,210.35 in November 2006. She pays total SSP paid in that month to two sick employees of £196.35.

Her recovery percentage is 13% of £1,210.35 = £157.34.

As the total SSP paid (£196.35) is more than the 13% recovery percentage (£157.34) by £39.01 Amy can deduct £39.01 from her National Insurance. Amy should now pay Class 1 National Insurance of £1,171.34 (£1,210.35 – £39.01) to HMRC for November 2006. She has to bear £157.34 of the cost of the SSP herself (£196.35 – £39.01) plus the cost of any sums she pays her staff over and above the statutory minimum.

Small employers face particular problems if members of staff are off work sick. In the case of a business with only one employee it is possible that the business will owe no PAYE, National Insurance or student loan repayments against which to off-set the SSP. If this occurs, you can write to HMRC after the end of the tax month asking them to repay the SSP you have incurred.

Further information: See the Employer's Help Book E14, 'What to do if your employee is sick' on **www.hmrc.gov.uk/ helpsheets/e14.pdf**.

Statutory Maternity Pay (SMP)

SMP is paid to pregnant women employees who have average weekly earnings above a certain threshold (see Appendix 1). It is paid for up to a maximum of 26 weeks. Most mothers are also entitled to a further 26 weeks of unpaid leave.

You must pay an employee SMP if she has been employed by you without a break for at least 26 weeks into the 15th week before the week in which the baby is due. She must give you written evidence of her pregnancy on certificate MAT B1. The earliest that SMP can start is the 11th week before the week in which the baby is due.

There are many detailed rules concerning the payment of SMP and you will need to complete forms to record the sums paid. Once again these will usually be produced by your payroll software. HMRC also have an SMP calculator on their website; see **www.hmrc.gov.uk/calcs/smp.htm**.

The amount of SMP that you can recover from HM Revenue and Customs depends on how much National Insurance you pay them. If your National Insurance bill before deductions for the last complete tax year to the start of the 15th week before the week in which the baby was due was £45,000 or less you are entitled to claim 100% of the SMP you pay plus compensation at the rate of 4.5%. If your annual National Insurance is more than £45,000 you can only claim back 92% of the SMP and you receive no compensation (see Appendix 1). If your contributions are around the £45,000 threshold, HMRC will assist you to calculate your recovery rate. If you pay your employees on maternity leave more than the statutory minimum you cannot recover the excess.

If you only have a small workforce and have insufficient PAYE, National Insurance and student loan repayments to off-set your SMP payments against, HMRC will refund you the payments at the end of each month if you apply to them in writing.

Further information: See Employer's Help Book E15, Pay and time off work for parents on **www.hmrc.gov.uk/ helpsheets/e15.pdf**.

Statutory Paternity Pay (SPP)

SPP is paid to employees of either sex whose spouse or partner gives birth to or adopts a child, provided that they have earnings above a certain threshold (see Appendix 1). It is paid for up to two weeks which must be taken either as one week or one two-week period. It cannot be taken for two separate weeks.

You must pay an employee SPP if the employee has been employed by you without a break for at least 26 weeks into the 15th week before the week in which the baby is due or placed. The earliest that SPP can start is the date of the birth and it must be taken within eight weeks (unless the baby is premature).

There are detailed rules regarding the operation of SPP and once again you will need to complete forms recording the payments. The procedures for recovering SPP are the same as SMP (see Statutory Maternity Pay).

Further information: See Employer's Help Book E15, 'Pay and time off work for parents' on **www.hmrc.gov.uk/ helpsheets/e15.pdf**.

Statutory Adoption Pay (SAP)

SAP is paid to employees (female or male) who are adopting a child (from the UK or abroad) provided that they have earnings above a certain threshold (see Appendix 1). It is paid for up to 26 weeks but the employee may be entitled to a further 26 weeks unpaid leave. The male or female partner of such an employee eligible for SAP may be entitled to Statutory Paternity Pay.

You must pay an employee SAP if they have been employed by you without a break for at least 26 weeks into the week in which the adopter found out from the adoption agency that they had been matched with a child. The earliest that SAP can start is 14 days before the placement. In the event that the employee adopts more than one child only one period of SAP is permitted. Entitlement remains if the placement is disrupted after it has started, or if the child dies after placement with the family.

There are detailed rules regarding the operation of SAP and again forms recording the payments must be completed. The procedures for recovering SAP are the same as SMP (see Statutory Maternity Pay).

Further information: See Employer's Help Book E16, 'Pay and time off work for adoptive parents' on **www.hmrc.gov.uk/helpsheets/2006/e16.pdf**.

Employer's National Insurance

In addition to making deductions from their employee's wages and paying them any statutory entitlements, you also have to pay employer's Class 1 National Insurance (see Appendix 1). This adds significantly to the cost of employing staff and when budgeting for employment costs it must not be overlooked.

Example

Moana runs a delivery business. She employs two members of staff (Jeff and Ken). Jeff earns £1,000 per month and Ken £800 per month. Assuming that the income tax rate is 20% and the employee's National Insurance rate is 11%, she makes the following deductions from their wages paying them net pay of £690 and £552 respectively. If the employer's National Insurance rate is 12.8%, Moana's total employment costs are £2,030 not £1,800 per month – £2,760 a year more than she may have been expecting.

Per month	Jeff	Ken	Total
Staff receive:	£	£	£
Wages	1,000	800	1,800
Less: PAYE	−200	−160	−360
Less: Employee's National Insurance	−110	−88	−198
Net pay	**690**	**552**	**1,242**
Moana's costs:			
Net pay	690	552	1,242
Employee's deductions paid to HMRC (PAYE + Employee's National Insurance)	310	248	558
	1,000	**800**	**1,800**
Employer's Class 1 paid to HMRC	128	102	230
Total cost of employing staff	**1,128**	**902**	**2,030**
Moana pays each month:			
Net pay to Jeff and Ken	690	552	1,242
PAYE and National Insurance to HMRC	438	350	788
Total monthly payments	**1,128**	**902**	**2,030**

In addition to paying Class 1 National Insurance employers also have to pay Class 1A and Class 1B contributions on most perks, benefits in kind and miscellaneous staff payments (see Taxing perks).

Taxing perks

Employers sometimes provide members of staff with perks or benefits in kind instead of pay. If you are a company director you may also be interested in rewarding yourself with a few perks and be wondering how they are taxed. Any reference to 'employee' includes directors. Although perks are more common in larger businesses, many small employers provide their staff with company cars, vans and private medical insurance (see Chapter 11). Others may inadvertently stray into the benefits in kind regime when reimbursing employees' expenses or providing them with a credit card.

Most employees (unless they earn less than £8,500 a year including the value of the perk) are liable to pay income tax on any benefits in kind you provide them with, although some perks are tax-free (see Tax-efficient perks). Before providing any employee with remuneration other than their salary you should consider the tax, National Insurance and administrative implications. It may be simpler and more cost-effective to give your employee a pay rise.

Tax on benefits in kind is usually collected by adjusting an employee's tax code. At the end of each tax year you have to report all benefits in kind (including reimbursed expenses unless there is a dispensation in force) to HM Revenue and Customs on form P11D (occasionally P9D). Copies of the form P11D must also be provided to your employees.

One of the most important things to remember is that if an employee perk is taxed, you usually have to pay Class 1A National Insurance on top which adds significantly to the cost. As this is collected as a lump sum after the end of the tax year, it is easy to overlook when calculating the cost of providing your employees with a benefit in kind.

If you provide employees with perks that cannot easily be divided between them (such as free on-site chiropody) or provide occasional gifts (for example flowers for a sick employee), the tax and Class 1B National Insurance can be paid by you under a PAYE Settlement Agreement (PSA).

If you reimburse staff expenses, give them credit cards or provide minor items such as uniforms you should negotiate a 'dispensation' with HM Revenue and Customs to cover these costs. Once negotiated not only do you no longer have to report the details on form P11D but no Class 1A National Insurance is due (see Applying for a dispensation).

Each different kind of perk that you provide to your employees has its own tax rules. The following sections outline the principal benefits in kind that a small business might be interested in providing to its staff. As there are many detailed rules which affect each benefit in kind, if you want to provide a perk to a member of staff you should read more widely on the subject or seek professional advice. HMRC's website contains an alphabetized guide to the tax and National Insurance treatment of each benefit in kind and the entries to be made on the form P11D; see **www.hmrc.gov.uk/employers/ebik/ ebik2/table-of-contents.htm.**

Cars

Cars are the most popular perk but many are highly taxed. In some cases it may be more tax-effective for your employee to buy their own car and for you to reimburse them tax-free business mileage at the authorized rate (see Appendix 1).

If you provide an employee with a company car, income tax is calculated on it as a percentage of the car's original list price even if you acquire it second-hand. The relevant percentage is assessed according to the level of its carbon dioxide (CO_2) emissions with cleaner cars taxed more favourably (see Appendix 1) but different rules apply to electric, LPG and hybrid cars as well as classic cars and those registered before 1 January 1998. There are many detailed rules which govern the operation of the car benefits regime and you may need to take advice. You must inform HMRC about any employee who has a new company car by completing form P46 (Car).

Example

Liam provides his employee Melanie with a company car costing £15,000. It has CO_2 emissions of 150 grams per kilometre, so in 2007/08 the relevant percentage is 17%. Her scale charge is calculated as £15,000 × 17% = £2,550 (see Appendix 1). If Melanie is a basic rate taxpayer the company car will cost her £561 (£2,550 × 22%) in tax each year. Her tax code will be adjusted to include the scale charge so she pays the tax on it in monthly instalments through the PAYE system. If Melanie is provided with additional accessories for her car she will pay extra tax. Liam will pay Class 1A National Insurance on the car of £326.40 (£2,550 × 12.8%) in a lump sum after the end of the tax year (see Appendix 2).

HM Revenue and Customs website contains a company car and car fuel calculator on **www.hmrc.gov.uk/calcs/cars.htm.**

Free fuel

Providing your employees with free fuel for private journeys attracts a further benefit in kind charge. This is based on a sum set each year by HMRC multiplied by the car's CO_2 percentage (see Appendix 1). In many cases this perk is not worthwhile providing but it depends on how many private miles your employee drives.

Authorized mileage

It is more usual for employers to reimburse their employees for their business journeys. Provided that the payment does not exceed the authorized rate (see Appendix 1), the payment is free of income tax and National Insurance. Your employee should compile a record of their business mileage to justify the claim which you should keep with your payroll records.

Vans

If your employee is a van driver and you let them use the vehicle privately they will pay income tax and you will pay Class 1A National Insurance. From 6 April 2007 the tax and National Insurance could amount to a considerable sum particularly if you also provide fuel for private journeys (see Appendix 1). Pool vans do not give rise to a tax charge and if two employees share a van, the tax charge is reduced.

One way round this tax charge is to restrict your employee's private use of the van to travel between home and work and vice versa (ordinary commuting). This means that there are then no tax implications if your employee takes the van home overnight (but this rule does not apply to cars). Defining a van is not always straightforward. Some vans are cars and some are heavy goods vehicles. In each case different rules apply.

In order for there to be no tax or National Insurance charge on a company van you should make it an employment condition that your employee cannot drive the van on private journeys unless they reimburse the full cost and you must enforce this policy. Insignificant private use is permitted without triggering a charge (for example using the van in an emergency or for an occasional short journey) but HM Revenue and Customs will look closely at the arrangements you have with staff that drive vans and they may question their private use unless your paperwork is in good order.

Travel and subsistence

Reimbursing your employees for necessary business travel does not attract a tax charge provided that the journey is not home to work travel (ordinary commuting). The definition of ordinary commuting is complex particularly if your employee works somewhere else temporarily or is site-based. In this case you may need to consult an accountant to ensure that you complete your end of year returns correctly. For further information see 'Employee travel: A tax and NIC's guide for employers', on **www.hmrc.gov.uk/helpsheets/490.pdf**.

If an employee needs to stay away from home for business reasons reimbursing their hotel bills and the cost of modest meals should not attract a tax charge in most cases. In addition you can pay employees who stay away from home overnight for work reasons up to £5 per night tax-free for personal incidental expenses. Payments above this amount are fully taxable. It is usual to agree a dispensation with HM Revenue and Customs for such payments for staff that travel regularly (see Applying for a dispensation). Your business records should distinguish between subsistence payments and entertaining because subsistence expenditure is tax-deductible whereas entertaining expenditure is not (see Chapter 5, Expenses).

Expense claims

Reimbursing business expenses incurred by your staff (and yourself if you are a company director) is another area where it is possible to inadvertently get into difficulties. You should only reimburse legitimate business expenses for which you have receipts. Round sums, floats or advances could be subject to tax and National Insurance. The best way to avoid problems with your employee's expense claims is to apply for a dispensation.

Applying for a dispensation

A dispensation is a written agreement from HM Revenue and Customs that relieves you from reporting expenses payments and benefits in kind on form P11D where they are satisfied that no tax is payable on them. If you have a dispensation the payments do not count as earnings for National Insurance purposes which may save you a considerable sum.

Expenses typically included in a dispensation are travel, hotel and subsistence expenses (but not business mileage payments) and amounts incurred 'wholly, exclusively and necessarily' in the performance of the duties of the employment such as business entertaining and reimbursements for buying stationery and other sundry items. The dispensation can cover reimbursement made by any means including business expenses paid for by a company credit card. If an employee or director uses a company credit card to buy personal items, this expenditure is either a taxable perk or is treated as income.

Any employer can apply for a dispensation using the form P11DX at **www.hmrc.gov.uk/forms/p11dx.pdf** provided that:

- the expenses are not taxable; and
- the expense claims are independently checked and authorized within the firm and where possible supported by receipts.

Even if you are a one-person company, you can usually obtain a dispensation as long as the expenses are supported by adequate documentation. HMRC will review your dispensation periodically usually as part of a PAYE inspection.

Tax-efficient perks

There are a number of benefits that you can provide to your staff (or their family members) that do not attract a tax or National Insurance charge. These are set out in the table below. Even though the perk listed is not taxable, you should still keep records of the payments to demonstrate to HM Revenue and Customs that any conditions applicable to the provision of the benefit are met. As a small employer, you may decide that the administration involved in providing the perk is not worthwhile.

Table of tax-efficient perks

Perk	Comments
Private use of office equipment. Facilities for disabled employees.	The equipment must be primarily provided for work purposes and private use must be 'insignificant'.
Provision of one mobile phone or similar device.	A second phone is taxable. The tax treatment of landline phones depends on the nature of the contract with the telephone company.
Contribution towards the extra costs of working from home.	Up to £2 per week if the employee works under a home-working agreement.
Office parties.	Not exceeding £150 per head per tax year.
Canteen meals.	In a canteen open to all your staff.

Perk	Comments
Authorized mileage payments for business journeys (car, passengers, motorbike and bike).	Not exceeding the rates in Appendix 1.
Bikes, related safety equipment and cyclists' breakfasts on cycle to work days.	Provided primarily for work and journeys.
Some works bus services.	Mainly for journeys between home and work.
Travel facilities for employees with disabilities.	Between home and work.
Parking spaces at or near work.	For all vehicles including bikes.
Medical checkups and eye tests for employees using computers. Insurance for overseas travel and medical costs incurred whilst travelling abroad.	Medical insurance or treatment in the UK is taxable
Welfare counselling.	Excluding legal and financial advice (but see pensions below). See also Chapter 13.
Work-related training.	Including retraining if made redundant. See also Chapter 13.
University scholarships.	Up to £15,000 per academic year.
Childcare	See Childcare.
Sporting and recreational facilities.	In facilities not available to the general public.
Personal gifts – for example if an employee gets married.	Where the employer is an individual.
Long service awards.	For those with 20 years of service or more up to £50 per year of work.
Cheap or interest-free loans.	Up to £5,000.
Relocation costs.	Up to £8,000.
Pensions and pension advice worth up to £150 per year.	See Chapter 11.
Security facilities.	Where there is a threat to the employee's physical security or safety because of the job.
Directors' and employees' liability insurance.	See Chapter 11.

Childcare

If an employer provides a workplace nursery for its employees' children the places are tax-free. Whilst not many small employers are likely to set up their own childcare facility, you can provide your employees with up to £55 (2006/07) per week in tax-free childcare payments or vouchers. Whilst this may on the face of it seem like a good perk for certain employees, it can reduce the value of an employee's tax credits so may not be suitable for all members of staff with children.

Construction industry

If you are a contractor or sub-contractor in the construction industry you are affected by special tax rules known as the Construction Industry Scheme (CIS). Even if your business is not in the construction industry you may be affected by CIS because a 'contractor' includes any business undertaking construction work of more than £1 million per year.

Contractors and sub-contractors must register with HM Revenue and Customs. If you are a contractor you must ensure that any sub-contractor you engage is not really your employee by following the guidance set out in 'Who is an employee?' See also 'Are your workers employed or self-employed?' on **www.hmrc.gov.uk/pdfs/ir148.htm**. Anyone who is employed by you should be taxed under PAYE.

The current CIS rules are outlined below. The rules are expected to change in April 2007. For details of the proposed new CIS see 'New Scheme'.

Sub-contractors

Registered sub-contractors will either hold a registration card (CIS4) in which case you must deduct 18% of the amount they charge you for their labour (not materials), or a sub-contractor's tax certificate (CIS5 or CIS6 – there are different versions depending on whether they operate as a sole trader, partnership or limited company). In this situation you can pay the holder gross without deducting either income tax or National Insurance.

When paying a sub-contractor you should:

- Check that the registration card or tax certificate is valid and belongs to the person presenting it.

- Complete vouchers each month for the payments you make to them (CIS23 for holders of CIS5; CIS24 for holders of CIS6 and CIS25 for holders of CIS4). Details of how to complete the vouchers can be found on **www.hmrc.gov.uk/cis/section3g.htm**.
- Complete end of year returns CIS36 after 5 April each year.

Your own business may require a sub-contractor's tax certificate so that you can receive gross payments from contractors you work for. To qualify you must meet three stringently applied conditions:

- Have sufficient sales turnover for a continuous three-year period of £30,000 per year if you are a sole trader or £30,000 a year per partner or director (if the company is controlled by five or fewer directors). Alternatively, if you trade as a partnership or company your turnover must be at least £200,000 per annum. Different rules apply to new businesses and if you meet the test for two but not three years; see **www.hmrc.gov.uk/cis/section3b.htm**.
- Have a need for a certificate, keep good accounting records and operate through a business bank account.
- Have kept your tax affairs up to date for the three years immediately preceding the application including filing returns and making tax payments on time.

New scheme

A new construction industry scheme was announced in 2003. Its introduction has been deferred twice but it will probably come into effect in April 2007. Under the new arrangements sub-contractors will register with HMRC by calling into a local office, electronically or by phone. They will be told whether they should receive payments gross or net but will no longer be issued with a card or certificate. As you will no longer have these documents to look at when you engage a sub-contractor you must contact HMRC to confirm two matters:

- That the contract is one of self-employment – see CIS 349 'Employment Status Factsheet'; and
- To ascertain whether the sub-contractor should be paid net or gross.

You will have to submit a monthly return to HMRC on form CIS 300 showing the sums you have paid to sub-contractors and the deductions you have made together with a signed declaration confirming that none of your sub-contractors are your employees. You will be liable for a penalty for a false declaration.

There are two other important changes under the new rules:

- You will be able to pay an unregistered sub-contractor subject to a higher tax deduction.
- The three-year rule for subcontractors' gross payment certificates will be reduced to one year.

Further information: HMRC's Business Support Teams provide training for contractors and sub-contractors. They can be contacted on 0845 6070143.

Recap

- If you have employees you must operate a PAYE scheme. You can do this yourself but there is a considerable amount of work involved in administering employees' salaries. With compulsory Internet filing for all employers irrespective of size from 2010, you may find it more efficient to use a payroll agency.
- Deciding whether a worker is your employee is not always straightforward. You may require expert advice particularly if you work in the construction industry.
- Remember to apply for a dispensation for staff expenses – it will make your paperwork easier and may save you Class 1A National Insurance.
- HM Revenue and Customs visit all employers periodically to check that they are operating their PAYE schemes correctly so make sure that you keep your records in good order.
- Details of penalties and interest for late returns and payments are set out in Chapter 3.
- There are numerous dates to bear in mind when dealing with PAYE. You will find them in the diary in Appendix 2.

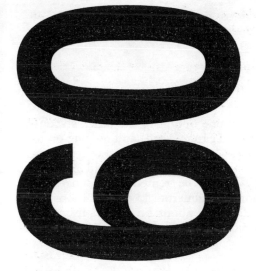

09

premises

In this chapter:
- working from home
- renting premises
- business rates and council tax
- buying and selling business property

All small businesses need to operate from some form of premises. There are three main choices depending on the nature of your business:

- Working from home;
- Renting; and
- Buying.

Many ventures progress from one option to the other, starting from a spare room (or even the garden shed) and moving on to rented premises as the business expands. At some stage you may decide to purchase your own leasehold or freehold business premises and in turn these may be rented to a tenant or eventually sold. Each option has numerous tax implications for your business. If you are thinking about investing substantial sums in property you should always take expert advice about the tax consequences.

Working from home

Increasing numbers of self-employed people now work from home. Being home-based covers a wide range of possibilities from working on a corner of the dining room table to having a self-contained office. If you trade as a limited company claiming a deduction for your home costs is fraught with difficulties and you should seek advice first.

You can claim a tax deduction for some of your home costs but in doing so you must exercise care. There are many grey areas, little Revenue guidance and overlapping tax implications.

Before you claim any expenses you need to:

- Note how much space your business occupies. You could calculate this based on the number of rooms in your home or in square metres.
- Ascertain whether the space your business takes up is used exclusively for work purposes (as might be the case with a purpose built garden office) or whether the room has mixed business and domestic use (such as a study which also doubles as a guest bedroom).

Running costs

Home running costs such as heating bills usually relate to the whole property. If you use your home partly for business purposes, in order to claim a tax deduction you need to divide the costs between business and domestic use.

Costs relating to the building such as heat and light, council tax, water rates and rent can be apportioned based on the area used for business purposes. Landline telephone costs are better allocated using a call log and Internet connections can be based on your business as opposed to private use of the service. If you have a separate business phone line all the costs are tax-deductible. Home insurance covering your office or other business equipment could be allocated according to the value of the items insured.

Other home costs which you may incur and which may be tax-deductible include a proportion of security costs (such as alarm maintenance), cleaning (but be aware that a cleaner may be your employee – see Chapter 8) and repairs and renewals (such as redecorating).

Example

Jenny is a full-time freelance illustrator who has a home studio. She rents a two-bedroom flat with three other rooms so that she can work from home. Her rent is £650 per month (£7,800 a year) and her other home bills (utilities, council tax etc.) total £2,000 a year. Based on room numbers her studio represents one-fifth of rooms in the flat. Jenny works full-time so she claims one-fifth (or 20%) of her total domestic costs (£9,800). Her tax deduction is £1,960 (£9,800 × 20%).

As Jenny rents her flat she will have no problems with capital gains tax.

Mortgage interest

If you use part of your home exclusively for work purposes a proportion of any mortgage interest may be tax deductible. You cannot however claim a deduction for the capital repayments or payments into an endowment policy (see Chapter 11). You need to be careful if you claim a deduction for mortgage interest because if you use a room exclusively for business purposes you could incur a capital gains tax charge when you come to sell the property (see Selling a home you have worked from). You may also have to pay business rates (see Business rates). If you are considering claiming a proportion of your mortgage interest as a business expense, you should take advice before doing so.

Use of home allowance

If you are a self-employed homeowner one way to avoid the issue of capital gains tax is not to claim a tax deduction for a proportion of any domestic expenses but rather to claim a 'use of home allowance'. Deducting a set amount per week or month has no legal basis but a modest claim (a few pounds per week) should be acceptable. You should provide details of the amount deducted in the additional information box on your tax form. You may need to take advice from an accountant as to a suitable sum to claim.

Business rates

If you use a room in your home exclusively for business purposes you may be liable to pay business rates. If you do you can deduct the whole cost as a business expense.

You are most likely to be liable to business rates if you have modified your home to accommodate your business. For example:

• Converting a garage into an office;
• Turning a downstairs room into a surgery, practice room or office where members of the public come to see you;
• Modifying a driveway to accommodate clients' cars.

Further information about business rates can be obtained from your local authority.

Capital costs

The costs of altering, improving or expanding your home to enable you to work there is capital expenditure and no income tax deduction is permitted. Repairs are tax-deductible but as it can be difficult to distinguish 'repairs' from 'improvements' you may require advice if you are making a substantial claim for repairs in your accounts.

Even though it is not deductible for income tax purposes, capital expenditure can be deducted from a future capital gain, so you should keep a note of any conversion costs in case you incur a capital gain when selling your home in the future.

Selling a home you have worked from

When you sell your home there is usually no capital gains tax to pay but if you have used any part of it exclusively for business purposes a capital gains tax charge could arise. You will be able to reduce the gain by deducting any capital costs relating to your business use and claiming business asset taper relief (see Appendix 1). You may also be entitled to claim rollover relief (see Selling business property). Calculating the gain and any tax liability will be complicated and you will need professional advice.

Remember: If you have *not* used any part of your home exclusively for business purposes, no capital gains tax liability will arise.

Renting premises

Renting business premises is perhaps the simplest option as far as tax consequences are concerned. You will be entitled to a tax deduction for all the premises costs you incur including:

- Rent;
- Business rates;
- Water rates;
- Heat and power;
- Insurance;
- Repairs;
- Legal and professional fees.

If you rent business premises with a residential flat attached to it in which you live, for example a flat above a shop or a pub, you will need to apportion the expenses between the business premises on a sensible basis (such as floor area). You should provide details of how you have divided the expenses between business and private use on your tax return.

Buying business property

At some stage if your business expands you may decide to purchase freehold or leasehold premises (feu in Scotland). As purchasing property is an expensive decision, you will need expert advice to make sure that you understand all the tax consequences of the transaction.

Stamp duty land tax

All purchases of commercial land and buildings costing more than £150,000 incur a stamp duty land tax (SDLT) charge at one of three rates depending on the purchase price (see Appendix 1). SDLT is charged on the whole purchase cost including VAT if it is charged.

Example

Dave buys a freehold workshop for use in his joinery business which costs £200,000. He pays stamp duty land tax of £2,000 (£200,000 × 1%) (see Appendix 1).

Financing the purchase

Most small business people require a mortgage or loan, or the Islamic equivalent to purchase business premises as few can afford to buy outright. There are two aspects to a mortgage and each is treated differently for tax purposes:

- *Interest charged on the sum advanced.* The interest on the mortgage or loan is fully tax-deductible against your accounting profits. If you have taken an interest-only loan there is nothing further to consider.
- *Funding the repayment of the sum borrowed.* Many lending institutions require you to repay the sum you have borrowed over a set period of years through a repayment mortgage, endowment policy, pension or other means of saving such as an Individual Savings Account (ISA). Repaying the sum borrowed or saving up a sum to repay the mortgage is not a tax-deductible business expense as it is the repayment of capital. Funding the repayments with a pension mortgage can be tax-effective for some people as the premiums attract tax relief (see Chapter 11).

Can I claim tax relief on my property purchase?

As we have seen, you receive no tax relief when you repay money borrowed to finance the purchase of business premises as it is a capital transaction. The same rules apply to the purchase price of the property or a building's construction costs. In many cases there is no tax relief you can claim against your business profits for these costs (but see Allowances). You do however receive tax relief when you come to sell the property. At this time the amount you paid for the property reduces your capital gain (see Selling business premises).

Example

Shadi buys the freehold of a café for £230,000. She finances the purchase with a repayment mortgage and spends £30,000 having the building improved and converted to suit her business.

Shadi can deduct the interest on the repayment mortgage from her trading profits. She will not obtain any income tax relief for the mortgage repayments, the £230,000 purchase price or the £30,000 spent on alterations.

When Shadi comes to sell the property she will owe capital gains tax if she sells the café for more than she paid for it. She should keep records of the purchase price, the building work and the date of acquisition so that she can deduct these costs from the eventual sale proceeds, thereby reducing her capital gains tax liability (see Selling business property).

Allowances

Having said that no income tax relief is available on the purchase of property, some buildings qualify for allowances which reduce trading profits in a similar way to capital allowances on equipment (see Chapter 7). The potential claims you could make are set out in the table below.

Type of building	Allowance	Buildings on which the allowance can be claimed	Excluded buildings	Allowance
Industrial building	Industrial Buildings Allowance	Buildings used by trades manufacturing or processing goods or materials, for example a factory.	Offices, shops, warehouses and repair shops (with some exceptions).	4% of the, construction costs a year (Note 1).
Agricultural building	Agricultural Buildings Allowance	Farm buildings, shops, houses, fences, roads and services.	Not more than one-third of the cost of a farmhouse. Some restrictions on shops.	4% writing down allowances a year over a 25-year period.

Type of building	Allowance	Buildings on which the allowance can be claimed	Excluded buildings	Allowance
Hotel	Industrial Buildings Allowance	Hotels with 10 letting bedrooms open for four months April–October.	Hotels which do not meet the qualifying conditions.	4% of the construction costs a year (the building or an extension to an existing hotel).
Space above a shop	Flat conversion allowances	Conversion of unused space above shops into residential flats.	Subject to many detailed conditions.	Initial allowance of up to 100% of the cost with a 25% writing down allowance if the initial allowance is not claimed in full.
Building in an Enterprise Zone	Industrial Buildings Allowance	Any building in a designated enterprise zone.	Residential property	Initial allowance of up to 100% of the cost with a 25% writing down allowance if the initial allowance is not claimed in full.

Note 1: If you purchase an industrial building from someone who has previously claimed industrial buildings allowances on it, your allowance will take into account their original cost and date of acquisition. The availability of allowances may affect the amount you are prepared to pay for the building.

Each allowance has many detailed rules about which buildings or trades qualify for the allowance. HM Revenue and Customs are likely to question all but the most clear-cut of claims and cases regularly end up in court because of the large sums of money involved.

Apportionment

When you buy an existing property the purchase price may have to be apportioned between the building and its fixtures. Some fixtures form part of the building. Depending on the type of building involved you may be able to claim industrial or agricultural buildings allowance on them. Other fixtures can be subject to a claim for plant and machinery capital allowances (see Chapter 7). You will require professional advice to help you agree a favourable division of costs and to assess which allowances you can claim.

Leases

If you purchase leasehold business premises you are sometimes asked to pay an extra up-front payment known as a lease premium to the landlord or outgoing tenant. If the lease is for less than 50 years you may be able to claim a deduction against your trading profits for part of the premium each year.

Sometimes a landlord will persuade you to take a lease of business premises by paying you a lump sum. This is known as a reverse premium and is usually treated as your taxable income. As the terms of each lease are different you should seek professional advice to confirm the tax treatment.

VAT

VAT on the purchase of land and buildings is complicated and different rates of VAT apply to different types of property. New freehold commercial and industrial buildings and those which are less than three years old are liable to VAT at the standard rate (see Appendix 1). Land and the sale and lease of commercial buildings which are more than three years old are exempt from VAT unless the person selling the building has exercised an option to charge it. VAT on commercial property can amount to a considerable sum, so before purchasing land or buildings for your business you need to find out whether VAT will be charged on the price and if so whether you can reclaim it in full or part.

Selling business property

At a future date you may decide to sell your business premises. This could be because you are moving to a new building or because you are disposing of the whole business (see Chapter 14). The most significant tax issue when you sell property used in your business is calculating your capital gains tax liability.

Capital gains tax

Sales of any business real estate can give rise to a capital gain if you sell the land or the building for more than you originally paid for it. If the sales proceeds are less than you paid to acquire the property you will have made a capital loss which can be deducted from any future capital gains you make (see Chapter 6, Capital losses). An Example showing a capital gain tax calculation for the disposal of shop premises is included in Chapter 2.

When working out the capital gain on the disposal of business premises there are two important points to remember:

- If you trade as a limited company the gain will be reduced by indexation allowance and not taper relief. It will form part of the company's corporation tax liability.
- If you are a sole trader or a partner, you may be able to claim indexation allowance and your gain will be reduced by taper relief. If the property has been used throughout the time you have owned it by you for your trade, you should be entitled to business asset taper relief (see Appendix 1). If the property has only been partly used by you for business purposes, or you have had periods of time when the whole property has not been used in the business, you may only be entitled to the lower rate of non-business asset taper relief on part of the gain (see Appendix 1).

Taper relief is complex with many detailed rules and you are likely to need assistance with the calculation if you want to minimize your tax bill.

Deferring your capital gain

If selling your business premises has resulted in a capital gain you may be able to reduce it by deducting any capital losses you have made previously on the disposal of other assets (see Chapter 6). There are also two ways of deferring capital gains tax:

- *Rollover relief.* You can claim this relief if you invest in another qualifying asset one year before the sale or up to three years afterwards. The new asset does not have to be used in the same business. You do not have to buy replacement land and buildings but this is the most likely investment you will make because the other qualifying assets are fixed plant and machinery, ships, aircraft, hovercraft, satellites, space stations and spacecraft, goodwill, milk and potato quotas, fish quota, farming payment entitlement under the single payment scheme and Lloyd's syndicate rights! If you trade as a limited company you cannot rollover your gain into goodwill or quotas.
- *Enterprise Investment Scheme deferral relief.* You can claim this relief if you invest in shares in a company qualifying for the Enterprise Investment Scheme one year before the disposal of your premises and up to three years afterwards.

There are many detailed rules relating to both reliefs and you are likely to require advice from an accountant to make the claim, undertake the calculations and understand tax implications for the new property.

Effect on allowances

Capital gains tax is not the only tax you need to be concerned about if you dispose of your business premises. If you have claimed industrial or agricultural buildings allowances you have to consider the effect of the sale on the allowances you have claimed unless the premises are sold after you have claimed them all (see Allowances). You are likely to require advice.

Renting out unwanted property

Instead of selling your business premises you may decide to let all or part of the property to a tenant. Any rents you receive are taxable income and liable to income tax if you trade as a sole trader or partner, or corporation tax if you operate as a limited company. You will be able to deduct any expenses you incur in connection with the letting when working out your taxable profits. Tax-deductible expenses include mortgage or loan interest, repairs, insurance, legal costs, and if you pay them rather than the tenant, business and water rates and utilities. You will need to maintain records of the rental income received and expenses incurred so that you can enter the details on the land and property pages of your tax return.

Recap

- Businesses often start off based at the proprietor's home and later progress to rented or purchased business premises. Each option has tax consequences.

- If you own your home and base your self-employed business there you should be careful which expenses you claim as you could have to pay capital gains tax when you sell the property. It may be simpler to claim a 'use of home allowance'.

- If you work from home you may be liable for business rates if members of the public visit you there or if you have altered part of the premises to accommodate your business.

- When you purchase business premises remember that you cannot claim an income tax or corporation tax deduction for the cost of purchasing the building unless you qualify for an allowance.

- When considering the purchase of property you need to take into account all the costs including stamp duty land tax and VAT.

- When you sell business property you are likely to owe capital gains tax. Your tax liability can be reduced by deducting taper relief and claiming loss relief (if applicable). Your tax bill may be deferred by making a suitable alternative investment.

10

VAT

In this chapter:
- what is VAT?
- when do I need to register?
- cars
- the different VAT schemes
- trading overseas

Most small businesses find that VAT (short for Value Added Tax) is the principal tax that they have to deal with on a daily basis. A VAT registered enterprise must account for VAT on its transactions, include entries for it in its accounting records and use this information to make regular returns of VAT collected and paid out to HM Revenue and Customs. If you are not yet VAT registered you must monitor your sales in case you have to register for VAT in the future. Failing to register on time can be very expensive.

Many business people learn how to account for VAT and prepare their own returns but if you undertake more complex transactions you may require professional advice. These include the purchase of property, vehicles and businesses, and trading overseas. Knowing when to seek advice will prevent you making potentially costly mistakes.

For further information about VAT see VAT Notice 700 available on HMRC's website –follow the links from 'VAT'.

What is VAT?

VAT is a tax on consumer expenditure. It is charged by VAT registered businesses on the goods and services that they sell in the UK. Other business transactions such as imports and acquisitions from EU countries also attract VAT and these are dealt with under special rules (see Complications). In return for collecting VAT, businesses are rewarded by being able to deduct the VAT they pay to others. This means that they pay less VAT to HM Revenue and Customs as a result. It is the private consumer who bears the full cost of VAT because they are not VAT registered. This is illustrated in the following case study.

Case study

Melissa's business makes machine parts. She sells £10,000 worth to Nathan. As she is VAT registered she adds VAT at 17.5% to the sales price and invoices Nathan £11,750. Melissa will pay HM Revenue and Customs VAT of £1,750.

Nathan makes air-coolers. He is also VAT registered. He sells £30,000 worth of coolers to Omega, a supermarket chain. He adds VAT of £5,250 (£30,000 × 17.5%) to the sale and charges his client £35,250. Nathan will pay HM Revenue and Customs £5,250 less the £1,750 that he paid to Mandy for the parts, making his net payment £3,500.

Omega is VAT registered. It sells the air-coolers in its stores for £50 each including VAT on each one of £7.45 (£50 × 17.5/117.5). It will pay HM Revenue and Customs £7.45 for each unit it sells after deducting the £5,250 it paid to Nathan.

Pat is a member of the public. She visits her local Omega store and purchases an air-cooler for £50. Included in the price is £7.45 of VAT. As she is not a VAT registered business she cannot recover the £7.45 from anyone.

Rita also purchases a machine. She is a self-employed therapist and buys the cooler to use in her practice room. She is not VAT registered and as a result cannot reclaim the £7.45 she pays.

Simon buys a machine too. He runs the village store and needs a cooler for his shop. He is VAT registered and as a result can reclaim the £7.45 he pays in VAT on the machine when he completes his next VAT return.

This case study illustrates a number of important issues about VAT.

- VAT is charged on some goods at 17.5%. There are two other VAT rates, 5% and 0% (see What is the rate of VAT?).
- VAT registered traders have to charge VAT on their sales. They do this by adding VAT to the cost of the goods or services. If the VAT rate is 17.5%, an item which is sold for £100 will cost the buyer £117.50 when VAT is added (£100 × 1.175%). The £100 before VAT is added is called the amount 'net' of VAT. The VAT is £17.50 and the total price inclusive of VAT (£117.50) is known as the 'gross' amount.
- Retail goods are sold at a VAT inclusive price (for example the coolers at £50) so you will frequently need to work out how much VAT is included in these items. It is tempting to think that you do this by multiplying £50 by 17.5%. This is not the case as the £50 is the VAT inclusive sum. You work out the VAT on a 'gross' figure by multiplying the total price by 17.5 and dividing it by 117.5. You can also multiply the total by 7 and divide the answer by 47 which will give you the same result. Check that you understand this calculation and practise these sums on your calculator. For example if you purchase an item which costs £1,000, the VAT included in the price is £148.93 (£1,000 × 7/47). If you purchase something which costs £1,175, the VAT is £175 (£1,175 × 17.5/117.5).

- VAT charged on sales of goods and services is known as 'Output' VAT. The VAT you can recover on the goods and services you buy in, is known as 'Input' VAT (see Records and VAT returns).

If you are not VAT registered, VAT will have only a small impact on your business. You will not add any VAT to your sales and you do not need to separately identify the VAT on your expenditure (see Chapter 5, Problem areas – VAT). There is no VAT to pay to HM Revenue and Customs. If you are VAT registered the situation, as we have already seen, is entirely different.

When do I need to register for VAT?

You can register for VAT in two circumstances:

- When your sales (known as 'taxable supplies') reach a certain threshold (see Appendix 1). This is called 'compulsory' registration.
- If your sales are less than the registration threshold in Appendix 1, you can register voluntarily if you are running a commercial venture. This is known as 'voluntary' registration.

For further details see VAT Notice 700/1 – 'Should I be registered for VAT?'

Compulsory registration

If the value of your sales at the end of any period of twelve months (or shorter period) exceed the registration threshold, you must register for VAT within 30 days of exceeding the limit unless one of the exceptions applies to you. If you expect your sales in the next 30 days to exceed the limit, you must also register. When working out your 'sales' for the purpose of VAT registration, you ignore any exempt supplies (see What is the rate of VAT?) and in some cases sales of any capital assets (equipment, cars etc.). Different rules apply if you carry out all or part of your business overseas or if you dispose of land or buildings. In these situations you may need to seek professional advice to determine the correct time to register.

If you fail to register on time you will be liable to a penalty. This varies according to the length of time you delayed registering but it can be up to 15% of the net VAT due. In addition you will have to account for VAT on all the sales you have made since exceeding the threshold. In some cases you may not be able to recover the VAT from your customers or will be too embarrassed to ask them for it. This could be financially ruinous, so it is very important to keep a close eye on your sales income particularly if you know that you are trading close to the registration threshold. This limit increases each April.

Example

Bernadette is a freelance computer trainer. She starts in business on 1 June 2005 but does not want to register for VAT voluntarily. Her sales for the 17 months to 30 October 2006 are as follows:

Month	Sales (£)	Cumulative sales for the previous 12 months (£)
June 2005	6,000	6,000
July 2005	5,000	11,000
August 2005	4,000	15,000
September 2005	10,000	25,000
October 2005	5,000	30,000
November 2005	7,000	37,000
December 2005	4,000	41,000
January 2006	5,000	46,000
February 2006	3,000	49,000
March 2006	3,500	52,500
April 2006	2,000	54,500
May 2006	4,000	58,500
June 2006	4,000	56,500
July 2006	10,000	61,500
August 2006	9,000	66,500
September 2006	8,000	64,500
October 2006	12,000	71,500

Bernadette's sales for the twelve months to 31 July 2006 exceed the VAT registration threshold (see Appendix 1). As a result she must notify HMRC that she needs to VAT register by 31 August 2006 and start adding VAT to her sales from 1 September 2006. She cannot claim exception from registration (see Exceptions) as all her sales are standard-rated (see What is the rate of VAT?) and her sales turnover looks set to remain above the VAT deregistration limit (see Appendix 1). If Bernadette does not realize that she needs to register until 30 September 2006 she will incur a late registration penalty.

If you are not VAT registered it is a good idea to add a cumulative sales column to your accounting records as Bernadette has done so that you can keep track of the sales for the previous twelve months. In this way you will know when the time has come to register.

Remember: VAT registration applies to any twelve-month period (calculated to the end of the month). It has nothing to do with the tax year or your accounting period.

Exceptions

There are some circumstances where even if your taxable supplies exceed the VAT registration threshold you may not necessarily have to register for VAT:

- Your sales are wholly or mainly zero-rated (see What is the rate of VAT?);
- You expect your future sales to be below the VAT deregistration limit (see Appendix 1). In this circumstance, you must still notify HMRC that you have exceeded the limit.

If all your supplies are exempt (see What is the rate of VAT?) you cannot register for VAT (although there are exceptions to this rule mainly connected with supplies of land and buildings and financial services).

Business splitting

It is not possible to avoid compulsory VAT registration by dividing your business into several parts and claiming that each is an autonomous business, for example that a dry-cleaning chain consisting of three shops is really three separate businesses. Many people have tried this and it usually fails.

Voluntary registration

If you have only recently started to trade and your sales have not yet reached the VAT registration threshold, you can register for VAT voluntarily. If you have yet to make any sales, HMRC will want to see evidence that you are in business, such as copies of contracts, details of purchases, planning permission etc.

Reasons why you might want to register voluntarily include:

- So that you can recover VAT on the goods and services you purchase. These costs may be significant in the early days of your business.
- PR – it makes your business seem more established and significant.

If you sell direct to final consumers (usually members of the public) who cannot recover the VAT on the goods or services they buy from you, you should think carefully before registering for VAT voluntarily as you may have to pay the VAT out of your selling price and could be worse off by registering.

Example

Trevor starts in business as a self-employed hairdresser. He is not VAT registered and charges £40 for a cut and blow-dry. Two years later he exceeds the VAT registration threshold and must compulsorily register for VAT. He has two options, either he can still charge his customers £40 and account for VAT of £5.96 (£40 × 7/47) out of each cut giving him £34.04 instead of his previous £40, or he can raise his prices and charge customers £47 for the same service (£40 × 1.175). Trevor still gets £40 per cut with HMRC taking £7. Whether Trevor can do this depends on the local competition.

Once he is VAT registered Trevor can off-set the VAT he pays to his suppliers and on the other goods and services he buys against the VAT that he has to pay over to HM Revenue and Customs. This is unlikely to fully compensate him if he is unable to increase his prices and he may be worse off being VAT registered. Trevor needs to understand how VAT works when he is planning his business so that he can price his services realistically taking into account all the taxes he might have to pay over the first few years of the business. He should seek advice about VAT registration at an early stage.

Forms

To register for VAT you need to complete form VAT 1 plus a VAT 2 if you are a partnership. You will need to complete different forms if you operate wholly or partly overseas. VAT registration forms can be requested from HMRC. Alternatively, the VAT 1 can be completed online.

HMRC will usually notify you that you have been VAT registered within three weeks. You will then receive a VAT number which must be included on all your sales documentation such as invoices and bills (see VAT invoices).

Once registered, there are a number of schemes which you may have to or will want to take advantage of (see Special schemes).

Claiming back VAT before registration

You can reclaim VAT on items purchased for your business in the three years before registration if you have proof of the VAT you paid (for example an invoice or receipt with a VAT number) and you keep a list of the items and the VAT claimed with your VAT account (see Records and VAT returns). The items must still be in existence at the date of registration so you cannot reclaim the VAT on consumables such as fuel, utilities or phone bills.

What is the rate of VAT?

One area that VAT-registered businesses often find difficult to understand are the different rates of VAT and how they are applied to individual goods and services.

There are currently three VAT rates (see Appendix 1):

- Standard rate: 17.5%;
- Reduced rate: 5%; and
- Zero rate: 0%.

In addition some goods and services have no VAT on them because they are:

- Exempt from VAT;
- Not supplied by a VAT registered person;
- Supplied overseas.

The law which sets out which items are subject to which rate of VAT is contained in Schedules 7A, 8 and 9 of the Value Added Tax Act 1994.

- Schedule 7A sets out the reduced rate supplies;
- Schedule 8 shows zero-rated supplies; and
- Schedule 9 lists those items which are exempt from VAT in the UK.

A full list of items is shown in VAT Notice 701/39.

The following table summarizes the main items which are charged to VAT at 0%, the reduced rate, or are VAT-exempt. Everything else is standard-rated, i.e. VAT is charged on it at 17.5%. The list below is only intended as a general guide. For each item listed there are many detailed conditions, exceptions set down in the legislation and aspects which have been considered by the courts. For example to take the apparently simple statement 'food' listed as being zero-rated. Food does not include (amongst others) confectionery, crisps, hot take-away meals or food consumed in restaurants all of which is liable to standard-rate VAT. Over the years, the courts have had to consider the VAT treatment of very specific food items including jaffa cakes, tea cakes and different types of crisp!

Reduced rate	Zero rate	Exempt
Domestic fuel or power	Food	Land
Installation of energy-saving materials	Sewerage and water	Insurance
Grant-funded installation of heating equipment, security goods or gas supply	Books	Postal services
Women's sanitary products	Talking books for the blind	Betting, gaming and lotteries
Children's car seats	Construction of buildings	Finance
Certain residential conversions	Protected buildings	Education
Certain residential renovations and alterations	International services	Health and welfare

Reduced rate	Zero rate	Exempt
Contraceptives	Transport	Burial and cremation
	Caravans and houseboats	Subscriptions to trade unions, professional and other public interest bodies
	Gold	Sports, sporting competitions and physical education
	Bank notes	Disposal of works of art and antiques from historic houses
	Drugs, medicines and aids for handicapped persons	Fund raising events by charities and other bodies
	Imports and exports	Cultural services such as admissions
	Tax-free shops	Supplies of goods where input tax cannot be recovered
	Children's clothing and shoes, certain protective clothing such as cycle helmets	Investment gold and gold coins

Further help and advice on the rates of VAT can be obtained from the National Advice Service on 0845 010 9000 between 8.00 am and 8.00 pm, Monday to Friday.

It is important to understand the difference between zero-rated VAT and exempt from VAT. In the case of zero-rated supplies, you charge VAT to your customers at 0% which entitles you to recover any VAT you have been charged by your suppliers from HM Customs and Excise. If you make exempt supplies you cannot register for VAT and therefore cannot recover VAT on your purchases from HM Revenue and Customs. Sometimes you will sell something that consists of two elements which are treated differently for VAT purposes. Here you have to decide whether what you are supplying consists of clearly identifiable parts or whether it is one supply. You will probably require advice to be sure and may also need to confirm your treatment with HM Revenue and Customs. If you supply some goods or services which are exempt and some which are taxable, you will be able to recover some of your input VAT from HM Revenue and Customs but it is likely to be restricted under what are known as the partial exemption rules (see Complications).

Records and VAT returns

Once you are VAT registered you have to complete regular VAT returns to calculate the VAT that you need to pay over to HM Revenue and Customs. VAT returns are completed every three months (quarterly) unless you use the annual accounting scheme (see Special schemes) or you regularly receive VAT refunds because you sell zero-rated goods or services. Different businesses have different VAT return dates. If you have a preference for a particular series of dates you should advise HM Revenue and Customs when you register.

VAT returns must be submitted within 30 days of the return date together with any payment due. If you pay your VAT electronically you have an extra seven days' credit. If you are late sending in the form (or paying over the VAT) twice or more within a year you will be fined (surcharged) unless you have a reasonable excuse for making a late payment. If you have a turnover of £150,000 or less, HM Revenue and Customs will offer you help to complete your returns on time and only if you continue to file late returns will they then penalize you. The amount of the surcharge depends on how many times you have been late. If the fine is below a minimum set by HM Revenue and Customs they do not collect it. For further information see HMRC Notice 700/50.

To complete the VAT return form, you need to keep records of the VAT on your income and your expenses. For details of how to maintain suitable accounting records see VAT Notice 700/21 and *Teach Yourself Small Businesses Accounting*. It does not matter whether your records are computerized or kept manually provided that they show the information that HM Revenue and Customs require (see Chapter 3). In addition to your usual accounting records you must also keep a VAT account showing how you have worked out the entries on your VAT return and it is advisable to retain a copy of the completed VAT form. If you bill your clients electronically, HM Revenue and Customs must be informed. You must keep your accounting records safely for at least six years. Failure to comply with any of these requirements could cost you a penalty.

VAT invoices

It is important to raise accurate VAT invoices once you are VAT registered. These have to show specific information as detailed in the following chart.

Information to be shown on a VAT invoice

- Your name and address;
- Your VAT registration number;
- Customer/client's name and address;
- Date the invoice was issued and 'tax point' if different (see Complications);
- Unique reference number (for example the bill number);
- Description of the goods sold or services provided;
- For each type of goods the quantity supplied;
- The unit price of the goods or services;
- The rate of VAT;
- The amount excluding VAT, the VAT and the total invoice value.
- Details of any cash discount offered.

If you are a retailer you may provide a less detailed invoice for sales of less than £250 (including VAT).

VAT returns

The VAT form (VAT 100) which you can complete manually or electronically, requires you to enter the VAT on your sales (outputs) and deduct VAT on your purchases (inputs) to arrive at the VAT you owe HM Revenue and Customs. If your input VAT exceeds your output VAT, you will receive a VAT repayment.

You also have to enter the total of your sales (net of VAT) and the total of your purchases (net of VAT) on the form. HM Revenue and Customs use these figures to check the accuracy of your return and for statistical purposes. The output VAT when divided by your net sales should not exceed the maximum VAT rate (17.5%). You can also use this simple sum to check the accuracy of your return. In many cases the output VAT divided by net sales should come to exactly 17.5%. If not you should consider the reason why. Maybe you have made exempt or zero-rated sales or sales to another EU country? Is this usual and if so are you confident that no VAT should have been charged on the sale?

The same calculation applies to your input VAT. The input VAT when divided by your net purchases and expenses should not be more than 17.5%. The resulting calculation is likely to be less than 17.5% because some items you buy will not have VAT on them (see What is the rate of VAT?) or you may also be partially exempt (see Complications). It is worthwhile doing this calculation each time you complete a return because it can save you making an innocent error and may avoid a VAT inspection.

Finally, the VAT return requires you to enter details of EU sales and purchases (see Trading with the European Union).

Further information about completing your VAT return can be found in HM Revenue and Customs' Notice 700/12.

Output VAT

Recording the output VAT on your income is relatively straightforward. You usually do this by keeping a list of your sales invoices or till totals together with the output VAT. You have a choice as to whether to draw up this list based on actual sales (invoices) or on a cash basis (see Special schemes). Most small businesses will pay over their VAT on a cash basis. It is important to remember that even though you use the cash basis for your VAT returns, your accounts cannot be prepared in this way. They must be drawn up using generally accepted accounting principles which means including all your invoices (whether paid or not) and the value of any uncompleted work (see Chapter 5). This disparity of treatment means that you will need to adjust your accounting records to arrive at the correct figures for your VAT returns if you use the cash accounting scheme. You will need to find a convenient way to do this, so that you do not omit any entries.

In addition to adding VAT onto your sales, you have to charge VAT on all your taxable supplies. This includes the sale of equipment (not necessarily cars) and private fuel (see Complications – Cars).

Input VAT

Your accounting records must include a separate column for VAT on your expenditure. When you prepare your VAT return you will either take into account the VAT on bills you have paid or on bills you have received depending on whether or not you use the cash accounting scheme (see Special schemes).

You can reclaim input VAT on your expenditure including direct costs, overheads and purchases of equipment provided that:

- The expense is not zero-rated or exempt from VAT (see What is the rate of VAT?).
- The supplier is VAT registered.
- You obtain a valid VAT receipt.
- The expense is not one where there are special rules, for example if you are partially exempt (see Complications).

Dealing with HM Revenue and Customs

If you make a mistake involving VAT of less than £2,000 when completing a VAT return but you correct it voluntarily on a subsequent return, you will not be penalized and no interest will be charged. Errors involving VAT of more than £2,000 must be notified to HM Revenue and Customs (use form 652). No penalty will be charged if you tell them voluntarily although interest will be. For further information see HM Revenue and Customs' VAT Notice 700/45 'How to correct errors and make adjustments'.

If you fail to make a VAT return, HM Revenue and Customs will issue an estimated assessment of your liability.

Periodically HM Revenue and Customs will want to inspect your VAT records. They do this by assessing the risk that you have underpaid VAT based on your previous records, your VAT returns and the business sector you are in. Sometimes HMRC carry out combined inspections to check other aspects of your affairs at the same time, for example PAYE or corporation tax but they will usually inform you in advance that they are going to do this.

If you disagree with HM Revenue and Customs on any matter, you can appeal to the VAT Tribunal.

Complications

When dealing with your VAT affairs there are any number of potential complications that you may encounter. This section highlights the principle ones. The VAT implications for business premises are dealt with in Chapter 9 and the sale of businesses in Chapter 14. As a general rule if you have not encountered a particular transaction before, you should always check what you have to do, either with HM Revenue and Customs or your adviser.

Cars

You cannot recover VAT on the purchase of a car in most circumstances, although you can reclaim it on the cost of a van. You can reclaim the VAT on a car if you run a taxi, driving school, car hire business, retail motor outlet or leasing business. If you lease a car for use in your business, you can usually only reclaim 50% of the VAT on the leasing charges.

When you sell a car you do not have to charge VAT on the sale if you did not claim back any VAT when you bought the vehicle. If you did reclaim VAT, you have to charge or account for output VAT on the sale proceeds. If you deal in second-hand cars you will probably account for VAT in accordance with the Second-hand scheme (see Special schemes).

Private fuel also causes complications. If you are a sole trader or a partner who drives a car, you have to disallow part of the input VAT by using the private scale charges set out in Appendix 1. If your mileage is low, it may not be worthwhile claiming back any of the VAT but you have to adopt this treatment for all business vehicles. In most cases you will reclaim the VAT on your fuel in full but include as output VAT the appropriate scale charge. If you drive a van, you should disallow VAT on the private use of the vehicle by reference to the percentage of your private mileage compared to the total miles you have driven.

As far as other motor expenses are concerned, you can reclaim VAT on repairs and maintenance but insurance is exempt from VAT and no VAT is charged on car tax.

Entertaining

You cannot recover VAT on business expenditure although you can reclaim it on staff welfare and necessary subsistence.

Bad debts

If you do not use the cash accounting scheme and a customer does not pay you for the goods or services you have supplied, you can reclaim the output VAT you have paid over to the HM Revenue and Customs once the debt is six months old. For most small businesses it is preferable to use the cash accounting scheme (see Special schemes) because you automatically obtain relief for any bad debts.

If you fail to pay a supplier for any reason you should not claim back the VAT, or if you do you should repay it to HM Revenue and Customs within six months.

Substantial capital expenditure

If you spend £50,000 or more on computer equipment (excluding VAT) or £250,000 (excluding VAT) or more on land, buildings, civil engineering works or refurbishments, you have to account for VAT on these items in accordance with the 'capital goods scheme'. This means that you cannot claim all the VAT at once; instead, the VAT is recovered over five years (computers and leases of less than ten years) or over a ten-year period.

Partial exemption

Partial exemption means that you sell some goods or services which are exempt and some which are not. If your input VAT on the expenditure relating to your exempt sales is less than 50% of your total input VAT and it is also £625 or less a month on average, you can claim back all your input VAT. If you do not meet these conditions your input VAT is restricted by special rules. If you are a partially exempt trader you are likely to require help with your VAT returns to ensure that you recover the correct amount of VAT from HM Revenue and Customs.

Date of supply

The date on which you supply goods or services is known as the 'tax point'. You need to identify it so that you can include the date on your invoices (see VAT invoices) and to enable you to account for VAT if you do not use the cash accounting scheme. The date of supply is usually the earliest date of these three points in time:

- when goods are supplied or the services performed; or
- the date of the invoice; or
- the date of payment.

If you bill your customers within 14 days of supplying goods or services then this later date is the tax point unless the customer pays you beforehand. If your services are supplied continuously, the tax point is the date of the invoice, or if earlier the date that your customer pays you.

Imports and exports

Imported goods from outside the European Union (EU) are liable to VAT at the time of import. When you prepare your VAT return, you can claim a credit for the VAT you have already paid. If you regularly import goods from outside the EU, you can join a deferment scheme which enables you to pay customs duty and VAT on a monthly basis.

If you export goods to a country outside the EU you can zero-rate the sale if you have sufficient proof that the goods have left the country, for example evidence from Customs' control. You will probably use an agent to handle your overseas freight. If you are not sure where the goods are going to, you must charge VAT.

Trading with the European Union (EU)

If you import goods from a European Union country the rules differ from those relating to imports and exports from other countries. Firstly purchases and sales of goods between EU member states are not treated as imports and exports but as 'acquisitions' and 'supplies'.

If you sell goods to a VAT-registered EU customer, the goods are zero-rated (but special rules apply to new transport including cars). You must state the customer's VAT number on your invoice and you also have to complete and submit an EC sales list to HM Revenue and Customs each quarter. For further details refer to HM Revenue and Customs 'EU VAT registration checker' by following the links from 'VAT'.

The principal difficulty with EU exports is obtaining proof that the goods have left the UK because within the EU there are no Customs barriers. HM Revenue and Customs advise that you should retain some or all of the following documents as proof that goods have been transported abroad:

- Orders and correspondence with your customer;
- Sales invoice and shipping note;
- Details of freight charges and insurance;
- Confirmation of receipt and evidence of payment; and
- Transportation documents.

If you make supplies or acquisitions above £225,000 a year you also have to complete a monthly statistical declaration called an Intrastat return.

If you sell goods to any other EU customer you must add UK VAT as usual unless you are selling by mail order when you have to comply with the 'distance-selling' rules. These require that when your mail order sales in another EU country reach a specified threshold (about £70,000 but it depends on the country), you must register for VAT in that country and charge its rate of VAT to your customers instead of UK VAT. You will require professional help and a tax representative in the relevant country if you sell by mail order.

If you buy goods (make acquisitions) from other EU countries costing more than the VAT registration threshold (see Appendix 1), you have to register for VAT, regardless of whether or not you would otherwise have to do so. When you come to complete your VAT return you must account for output VAT on your acquisitions but you can deduct an equal amount as input tax. Even though there is no additional VAT cost to you, you cannot just ignore these transactions.

Providing services overseas

If you provide services rather than goods overseas, you will require professional help to work out the VAT treatment as this depends on the nature of the services you supply and where you supply them. The rules do not just affect whether or not you charge VAT on your invoices but also how much VAT you can recover. The rules are extremely complicated and they are not the same as those for goods. Making a mistake here could be expensive.

Special schemes

There are a number of special VAT schemes. Three are general schemes and you do not have to be in a specific line of business to use them. You will however need to meet a number of other conditions. These schemes are the:

- Cash accounting scheme;
- Annual accounting scheme; and
- Flat-rate scheme.

For further information see HM Revenue and Customs' 'Choose the right VAT scheme for your business' and 'VAT schemes wizard' by following the links from 'VAT' on their website.

Cash accounting scheme

The most important of the special schemes as far as small businesses are concerned is the cash accounting scheme. Under cash accounting you pay over the VAT on your invoices when you are paid by your customers (giving you automatic bad debt relief if a customer does not pay you). You reclaim VAT when you pay your suppliers.

To join the scheme your sales turnover (excluding VAT) must be no more than £660,000 a year. You must also be up to date with your VAT returns and payments. You cannot use cash accounting for hire purchase and similar transactions where payment is either deferred or in advance. You have to leave the scheme if your annual turnover exceeds £825,000. For further information see HM Revenue and Customs' VAT Notice 731.

Annual accounting scheme

You can apply to complete just one VAT return a year under the annual accounting scheme (form VAT 600AA). You cannot however pay your VAT once a year. You have to agree a provisional liability with HM Revenue and Customs which you pay by monthly direct debit over ten months. The first payment starts four months after the beginning of the year. A balancing payment is made with the tenth instalment and it and your annual return has to be submitted within two months of the annual accounting scheme year end. You also have the option to pay quarterly if it suits your business better. Annual accounting is not suitable if you receive regular VAT refunds.

You can join the annual accounting scheme if your turnover (excluding VAT) is £1,350,000 or less. You have to leave when your turnover reaches £1,600,000 (excluding VAT). You can use the annual accounting scheme in conjunction with other schemes except the flat-rate scheme. For further information see HM Revenue and Customs' VAT Notice 732.

Flat-rate scheme

This scheme offers you an entirely different way of accounting for VAT than this chapter has so far described. Instead of calculating your output and input VAT and paying over the difference to HM Revenue and Customs, you apply a flat-rate percentage (depending on your business sector) to the VAT-inclusive value of all your sales (including those that are exempt, zero-rated or charged at a reduced rate). The only exception is if you buy equipment costing more than £2,000 when you can claim back the VAT in the usual way.

To join the scheme you must have an annual turnover of up to £150,000 (excluding VAT); £187,500 (including VAT). Having joined, if your turnover exceeds £225,000 you must usually leave the scheme. You cannot use the scheme if you also use the second-hand scheme or capital goods scheme and you cannot account on a cash-basis when using this scheme. For further information see VAT Notice 733.

There are also specific schemes for businesses in certain trade sectors including retailers, dealers in second-hand goods and tour operators.

Retailers

If you are a retailer you have to account for your VAT under one of HM Revenue and Customs' retail schemes, see HM Revenue and Customs' VAT Notice 727.

Second-hand goods

If you buy and sell second-hand goods such as antiques, collectables, works of art, cars, caravans etc., you only have to account for output VAT on your profit margin, that is the difference between what you sell the item for and your purchase costs. Where you use this scheme, your invoices must not show any VAT and as a result your customers cannot reclaim any VAT.

If you are charged VAT when you buy an item, you can recover input VAT in the usual way but you must then charge VAT on the full sales price.

Tour operators

If your business buys-in and resells travel and accommodation you can use the tour operator's margin scheme (TOMS for short). The scheme enables VAT to be accounted for on travel supplies without you having to register and account for VAT in each EU country where the services and goods are enjoyed. The rules are complicated and you are likely to require specialist advice if you operate in this field. For further information see VAT Notice 709/5.

Cancelling your VAT registration

You can cease being VAT registered if your turnover falls below a set threshold (see Appendix 1). This is set slightly lower than the registration threshold. You can however remain registered if you want to and you are trading commercially.

If you want to de-register, you must tell HM Revenue and Customs within 30 days of the date you want your VAT registration to stop. You will need to complete a VAT return to the date you have chosen and pay over any outstanding VAT.

There are special rules regarding any business equipment or assets you own at the date of de-registration. If their value is more than £6,714 (£1,000 worth of VAT) and you claimed VAT on them when you purchased the items, you have to pay VAT on their value unless you are de-registering because you are transferring your business to someone else as a going concern.

Recap

- One of the most expensive mistakes that businesses make is failing to register for VAT at the appropriate time. This is usually the end of any month in which the turnover from all your business activities in the previous twelve months exceeds the VAT registration threshold (see Appendix 1).

- Most small businesses will want to use the cash accounting scheme. This means that you only pay over VAT when you have received the money from your customers and when you have paid your suppliers. This differs from the way in which you prepare your accounts for income tax purposes.

- If you use the cash accounting, annual accounting or flat-rate schemes, they do not affect the amount of VAT you charge your customers.

- If you offer customers a cash discount, you should only charge VAT on the discounted amount.

- You should familiarize yourself with the rules for claiming input VAT on cars to avoid making mistakes.

- If you trade overseas you should learn which countries are in the European Union and those which are not as the rules differ. You also need to understand that the rules for goods and services are not the same. In most cases if there is an international dimension to your business you will require professional help.

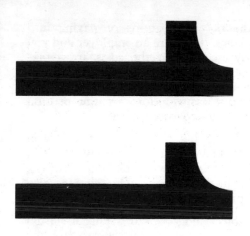

pensions and insurance

In this chapter:
- paying pension contributions
- employers
- maintaining your state pension entitlement
- different types of insurance policy

This chapter looks at the tax implications of paying into pensions and insurance policies. If you are an employer and you contribute to your employees' pensions the costs are a tax-deductible business expense. If you pay into your own pension the premiums are not a tax-deductible business expense but you are given tax relief on your contributions by the pension company or by claiming relief in your tax return.

Saving for your retirement through a pension scheme is largely a matter of personal preference but as paying pension contributions is one of the principal ways of reducing your tax bill we consider the rules in some detail. This chapter also considers how you can improve your state pension.

Pensions are a complex subject and you will require impartial advice from an independent financial adviser regulated by the Financial Services Authority (see Appendix 4).

Before 6 April 2006 there were eight different sets of rules relating to pensions (including personal and stakeholder pensions, occupational and company schemes and retirement annuities). These have now been consolidated into one set of requirements for all pensions under what is known as pension simplification.

Paying into your own pension

Many business people decide to save for their retirement by paying regular sums into a pension. This section looks at the rules governing tax relief on pension contributions and the tax consequences on retirement. It also highlights ways of making your contributions more tax-effective and indicates how pensions can assist you to finance the purchase of business property.

How much can I pay into a pension?

Unless you are an exceptionally high earner, you can contribute as much as you like to a pension and the premiums will qualify for tax relief. Tax relief on contributions is restricted by two factors:

- A lifetime allowance capping the value of contributions you make throughout your life (see Appendix 1); and
- An annual allowance restricting the amount you can contribute to a pension each year (see Appendix 1).

How much tax relief do I qualify for?

You can get tax relief on sums you contribute to your pension up to the following limits:

- £3,600 a year (if your annual profits are between £0 and £3,600);
- 100% of your income (if your annual profits exceed £3,600) until your income reaches the annual allowance (see Appendix 1).

Sums paid in excess of the annual allowance attract a tax charge.

All contributions are paid to the pension company after deducting basic rate tax relief (see Appendix 1). This means that if you agree to pay £200 per month into a pension you will actually pay the pension company £156 per month (£200 less basic rate tax relief). The pension company will recover basic rate tax of £44 per month from HM Revenue and Customs and invest it in your fund. If you do not pay tax at the higher rate this is the end of the story.

If you pay tax at the higher rate you are entitled to a further tax saving. This is calculated on the difference between the highest rate of tax (currently 40%) and the basic tax rate (currently 22%). You must claim this tax relief through your self-assessment tax return, or if you are employed through your tax coding.

Claiming higher rate tax relief

One mistake that people make when claiming higher rate tax relief on their pension contributions is to claim it on the wrong amount. The following example illustrates how you should claim.

Example

Gordon makes self-employed profits as a marketing consultant of £50,000 a year and pays tax at the highest rate. He decides to pay pension contributions of £4,200 a year (£350 per month). Each month he pays the pension company £273 (which is £350 less a deduction for basic rate tax relief). When he comes to complete his self-assessment return he is unsure whether to claim the additional relief on £350 per month or £273.

Gordon should claim higher rate relief on the amount he pays before deducting tax relief (i.e. on £4,200 a year or £350 a month). This is known as the gross amount. He will be entitled to a tax saving in his return of £756 (£4,200 × 18%). 18% is the difference between 40% (higher rate tax) and 22% (basic rate tax). If Gordon only enters £273 per month on his return he will miss out on £166 of tax relief per month.

You can check your tax relief in the following way:

- If you pay tax at the highest rate you are entitled to tax relief on your pension contributions of 40%.
- This means that a contribution of £100 per month attracts relief of £40 and costs you £60.
- You pay the pension company £78 (£100 less £22 basic tax relief).
- You claim higher rate relief through your self-assessment return which saves you a further £18 per month.
- The total tax saved on a contribution of £100 is therefore £40 (£22 + £18).

Recap

If you pay tax at anything other than the higher rate you have already received all the tax relief that you are entitled to and there is nothing further to claim on your tax return. Nevertheless HM Revenue and Customs still require you to enter details of all your pension contributions on the form.

Low earners

If you make low profits or losses and pay little or no tax you may wonder why you receive tax relief on your pension contributions. The good news is that even if you are a non-taxpayer, or you only pay tax at the starting or lower rates (see Appendix 1), you are still entitled to basic rate tax relief deducted at source on your contributions. This makes paying into a pension tax-effective for lower earners – if you can afford the premiums.

Paying a pension for someone else

If you cannot afford to make pension contributions someone else could pay them on your behalf. If they do you are still entitled to receive basic rate tax relief on the contributions.

If your business is doing well you may be able to afford to pay pension premiums for other members of your family such as a non-working spouse, partner or your children. Contributions receive basic rate tax relief irrespective of your income or theirs as long as they fall within the limits set out in 'How much tax relief do I qualify for?'

The following examples illustrate the tax treatment of pension contributions for business people on different levels of income.

Examples

Andy is a successful businessman paying higher rate tax. He contributes £3,600 a year into a pension policy for his 10-year-old grandson Sean. Sean is entitled to basic rate tax relief, so Andy only has to pay £2,808 to the pension company. The pension company reclaims tax of £792 from HM Revenue and Customs and invests it in Sean's policy. Even though Andy pays 40% tax, he can not claim any further tax relief.

Betty is a self-employed counsellor making annual profits of around £3,000 a year. As her income is less than her personal allowance she is a non-taxpayer. Betty can pay pension contributions of up to £3,600 and obtain basic rate tax relief on the payments.

Clare is a self-employed film and television producer. Her profits are £50,000 a year, she pays 40% tax and pension contributions of £5,000 a year. Clare pays the pension company £3,900 net of basic rate tax relief and they reclaim £1,100 from HM Revenue and Customs. She claims higher rate relief in her tax return of £900. Clare's total tax relief is £2,000 and the pension costs her £3,000.

David is a solicitor approaching retirement. His profits (net relevant earnings) are £80,000. He pays a one-off pension contribution of £80,000. He is entitled to basic rate tax relief at source on the payment plus higher rate relief claimed through his tax return, provided that the contribution and all the other pension contributions that he has made in his life do not exceed the lifetime allowance (see Appendix 1).

Evelyn is a well-known self-employed actress. She earns £250,000 a year and pays a one-off pension contribution in 2006/07 of £230,000. Her tax relief is restricted by the annual allowance so only £215,000 of the £230,000 she has contributed attracts tax relief. Evelyn has to pay higher rate tax through her self-assessment return on the extra £15,000 she pays into her pension scheme.

Director/shareholders

The amount you can pay into a pension and receive tax relief on depends on your income (net relevant earnings), the annual allowance and the lifetime allowance. Net relevant earnings and income are not the same. In particular share dividends are excluded from net relevant earnings. This means that if you are a shareholder/director remunerated partly by a salary and partly by dividends, you need to calculate how much salary you require each year to make your desired level of pension contributions.

Financing your pension with higher rate tax relief

If you have an established business making profits above the higher rate tax threshold (see Appendix 1) you can fund your pension more tax-effectively by limiting your pension premiums to those which obtain higher rate tax relief.

Case study

Edgar runs an electrical retail outlet. His annual profits are usually in the range £40,000–£50,000. His aim is to pay annual pension premiums to reduce his profits to the basic rate tax threshold. As a result he obtains higher rate relief on all the sums he invests in his pension.

The following table illustrates how much Edgar should pay into his pension in 2005/06 and 2006/07 to optimize his tax savings.

Year	Profits (A)	Higher rate threshold (B)	Personal allowance (C)	Amount above which higher rate tax is due B + C (D)	Optimum pension premium A–D (E)	Tax relief (E × 40%)
	(£)	(£)	(£)	(£)	(£)	(£)
2005/06	41,000	32,400	4,895	37,295	3,705	1,482
2006/07	45,000	33,300	5,035	38,335	6,665	2,666
Total					10,370	4,148

Edgar should restrict his pension contributions to £3,705 in 2005/06 or £6,665 in 2006/07 because any additional sums will only receive basic rate tax relief and not higher rate tax relief.

Over two years Edgar invests £10,370 in his pension. As he has obtained higher rate tax relief on the entire sum contributed it has only cost him £6,222 (£10,370 – £4,148) to obtain £10,370 of pension benefits (60% of the sum invested). If he had paid £10,370 into his pension in either 2005/06 or 2006/07, he would only have obtained basic rate tax relief on the 'excess' £6,665 or £3,705, so making the same contribution would have cost him either £1,200 or £667 more than arranging his contributions in this way.

It is almost impossible to calculate a pension premium to this degree of accuracy but if you maintain good business records, you (or your adviser) should be able to estimate a suitable one-off premium towards the end of the tax year which will more or less maximize your tax relief. In the past it used to be possible to carry back pension contributions paid in a later tax year against the profits of an earlier year so accurate figures could be calculated. From 6 April 2006 you can no longer do this.

Self-administered pension schemes

If you have an established business and you would like a greater degree of control over where your pension fund is invested, you might consider a self-invested scheme such as a Small Self-Administered Scheme (SSAS) or a Self-Invested Personal Pension (SIPP). The range of investments attracting tax relief excludes residential property and items such as classic cars, art and antiques. Self-administered schemes can be tax-effective if you are considering the purchase of commercial property for your business or if you want to transfer ownership of an already-owned commercial property to a pension scheme. There are many detailed rules which must be followed and restrictions on how much the scheme can borrow to finance the purchase of property. You will require specialist advise if you want to explore this option further.

Pension mortgages

If you are purchasing a property for use in your business or domestically, you could consider a pension mortgage. The sum borrowed will eventually be repaid by the tax-free lump sum from the policy (see Retirement below). For this to be a viable option you need to have a sufficiently high and stable level of income, preferably be a higher rate taxpayer and be prepared to sacrifice some of your income in retirement to repay the mortgage. You will require professional advice to determine whether this is a suitable means of financing the purchase.

Retirement

Even though retirement is probably a long way off it is important to understand what you will get for your pension contributions and when.

By 2010 the minimum age at which you can draw your pension rises from 50 to 55 although if you suffer from ill-health it may be possible to retire sooner. The later you decide to retire the more your pension will be worth as the contributions will be invested longer. The date you choose to receive your pension does not have to coincide with the date you receive your state retirement pension and you can continue to run your business and receive a pension at the same time. If you are paying into a pension for children, you should note that the earliest the fund can be accessed is when they reach age 55.

Up to 25% of your pension fund can be taken as a tax-free lump sum. The sum is restricted to a maximum of 25% of the lifetime allowance (see Appendix 1). Alternatively you have the option of taking no lump sum and a higher pension.

Between the ages of 55 and 75 most people choose to take their pension (which is taxed under PAYE). If you do not want to take your pension, for example because annuity rates are low, you have the option to draw income from the fund instead. There are also various types of pension that you can take depending on your health and family circumstances and you will probably require advice.

By age 75 most people will have taken their pension but even at this age it is possible not to take an annuity but rather to choose an 'alternatively secured pension' instead. Once again each option has tax consequences and you should seek professional advice.

Death benefits

When taking out a pension it is possible to use the policy to provide for your dependents if you die. Subject to various limits they could receive a lump sum or a pension. As the contributions receive basic and higher rate relief (depending on your income), this is more tax-effective than taking out separate term life assurance (see Insurances).

Employers and pensions

If you employ five or more people in your business (including any company directors) you need to offer them access to a registered pension scheme but you do not have to contribute to their pensions. You will require advice about the options available. If you decide to set up your own pension scheme you must contribute to it in order for it to be registered with HM Revenue and Customs and qualify for favourable tax treatment.

Contributions

Contributing to your employees' pensions is usually a good way to incentivize your staff as well as being tax-effective for the following reasons:

- There are no tax or National Insurance consequences for your staff or directors as the payments do not count as a perk (see Chapter 8).
- The contributions reduce your business profits so you receive tax relief on the contributions.
- You may be able to eliminate your taxable profits by paying additional pension contributions. If the contributions turn a profit into a loss, you can claim loss relief (see Chapter 6). Tax relief for irregular contributions of more than £500,000 however has to be spread over up to four years.

Life insurance

Insuring the lives of your employees in case they die whilst they are working for you can be arranged through a pension scheme. Lump sums paid out in the event of a death up to the value of the lifetime allowance are tax-free.

State pension

In spite of what has been said in the previous sections about the need to provide your own pension or a pension for your employees, the state pension is still a significant source of income in retirement.

To be entitled to a state pension you (or your spouse/civil partner) need to have paid sufficient National Insurance contributions (or received credits) during your working life. When you receive it, the state pension is taxable income.

If you want to know how much state pension you will be entitled to you should ask the Pensions Service (part of the Department for Work and Pensions (DWP)) for a pension forecast; see **www.thepensionservice.gov.uk/atoz/atozdetailed/ rpforecast.asp.**

Improving your state pension

You can improve your state pension particularly in the years coming up to retirement in the following ways:

- Pay any missing National Insurance contributions. The Contributions Agency usually contacts you if your contributions in any year do not meet the minimum requirements. Alternatively if you know that your contribution record is erratic you should contact them; see **www.hmrc.gov.uk/faqs/vol-conts.htm.** Paying missing contributions does not benefit everyone so you should take advice.
- If you have a period of time when you do not run your business or work because you are caring for children or a disabled person, you should apply for home responsibilities protection (use form CF411).
- Consider deferring the date when you start to receive your state pension. As a reward for deferring for at least twelve months, your weekly pension is increased or you can choose to receive a one-off taxable lump sum instead. This can be claimed in the year when you first receive your pension, or in the following year.

State second pension

The State Second Pension or S2P replaced the State Earnings Related Pension or SERPS in 2002. If you are an employee or director, S2P and SERPS increase your state pension by an earnings-related addition. You can contract out of S2P and make your own provision or your employer may arrange for you to be contracted-out as part of a company scheme. Whether contracting-out is a good idea depends on how much you earn and your age. You may need to seek advice about whether this is a good idea for you.

Insurances

This section reviews the tax treatment of a range of different insurance policies. Not all insurance premiums are tax-deductible and in some cases even where a deduction could be claimed, it may be advisable not to. Some types of insurance taken out to cover your staff are treated as a perk whilst others are not. In other words before taking out any kind of insurance, you should consider the tax consequences for your business and staff.

General insurance

Insurance premiums paid to cover loss, theft or damage are tax-deductible against your business profits on the following types of policy (amongst others):

- Buildings and contents insurance;
- Stock loss and goods in transit;
- Motor insurance;
- Employee and public liability insurance;
- Loss of profits;
- Professional indemnity;
- Other business risks such as libel or breach of copyright.

Fee protection insurance to cover accountancy costs in the event of an enquiry by HMRC is not tax allowable (see Chapter 3).

Sums you receive from an insurance company for a claim may be taxable trading receipts (for example claims for lost stock or loss of profits). In some cases they will be capital (for example to replace a vehicle) and will affect a claim for capital allowance (see Chapter 7). In other circumstances the insurance pay-out may result in a capital gain (for example where a building is destroyed).

Sickness insurance

If you take out a policy to provide an income or a lump sum in the event that you are injured or fall ill, you may claim a tax deduction for the premiums in your business accounts but if you do, any sums paid under the policy whilst you are sick become taxable income. If you do not claim a tax deduction for the premiums, sums paid out do not count as taxable income. Similar rules apply to policies taken out to insure against periods of unemployment.

Group sickness policies taken out to insure against staff illness do not usually give rise to a benefit in kind charge.

Medical insurance

There is no tax relief available on your own private medical insurance premiums. If you provide this perk for your staff they will pay income tax on the cost of the premiums and the business will incur a Class 1A National Insurance charge (see Appendix 1). You can claim a tax deduction in your accounts for the cost of providing the private medical cover and the associated National Insurance.

No benefit in kind or National Insurance charge arises on medical insurance taken out to cover employees on business trips overseas.

Mortgage endowment policies

If you are financing the purchase of a commercial or domestic property with an endowment policy, you cannot claim a deduction for the premiums in your business accounts. This is because in most cases the sum paid out when the policy matures is tax-free. If you redeem an endowment policy before the expiry of its term and you are a higher rate taxpayer you may face an unexpected tax charge. If you are considering cashing in a policy early you should seek professional advice as keeping it going may be more tax-effective.

Key employee/director insurance

You can insure for loss of profits arising from the death or illness of a key employee or director. The premiums are usually tax-deductible. Any sums paid under the policy are treated as taxable income.

Directors' liability insurance

If you are a company director, no benefit in kind tax or National Insurance charge arises if the company takes out directors' liability insurance for you. This is the case whilst you are employed and for up to six years after you leave the company. The company can claim a deduction in its accounts for the cost of the premiums. If you have to pay your own directors' liability insurance, you can claim an income tax deduction in your tax return.

Life insurance

There is no tax relief on policies taken out to insure your own life (except for some policies taken out before 14 March 1984). Lump sums paid out under a term assurance policy are usually tax free. If you include term assurance in a pension policy tax relief is given on the premiums. Death benefits for your staff in case they die whilst they are working for you can also be included in a pension scheme.

12
incorporating a business

In this chapter:
- changing from being self-employed to a limited company
- transferring the business tax-effectively
- the advantages of running a business with share capital

Many people start a business as a sole trader (or a partnership) but as it grows they wonder if they should change it into a limited company. Sometimes this will be because of government incentives, for example companies being taxed at a lower rate than individuals. In other cases becoming a limited company (incorporation) is desirable because the business has expanded, greater risk is involved or external investment is required. It is worthwhile revisiting parts of Chapter 4 before reading this chapter so that you understand the tax differences between unincorporated businesses and limited companies.

When incorporating a business, the assets and liabilities belonging to the sole trader are transferred to a limited company. There are three main stages to the transfer and each has tax implications:

- Closing down the self-employment – see Chapter 13.
- Starting up a new limited company – this is dealt with in Chapter 4.
- Structuring the transfer to minimize capital gains tax – we look at this in detail here.

The tax legislation recognizes that incorporating an existing self-employment does not create an entirely new business; instead the original business continues in a different form. As a result you are permitted to transfer assets, losses, capital allowances and your VAT registration between the two entities as long as you meet various conditions.

Incorporation is complicated and unless your business is very small with minimal assets, you are likely to require professional advice so that you do not pay tax unnecessarily.

When is the best time to incorporate?

You need to select a suitable date to incorporate. From an income tax point of view there is little benefit in one date over another because there is no scope to manipulate your self-employed profits so that some of them are not taxed. It could however be beneficial from a capital gains tax point of view to incorporate in a year when you have all your capital gains tax annual exemption available (see Appendix 1) but unless the end of the tax year is approaching and delaying incorporation for a month or two is convenient, commercial reasons should usually govern your choice of date.

Closing down your self-employment

When you started your self-employment there were four tax-related things that you had to do:

- Register to pay Class 2 National Insurance.
- Advise HM Revenue and Customs that you were in business.
- Set up a PAYE scheme for your employees.
- VAT register (if appropriate).

As you are now ceasing to be self-employed and incorporating your business, you have to reverse these registrations or modify them.

National Insurance

From your chosen incorporation date, you must notify the National Insurance Contributions Office (NICO) that you are no longer self-employed and liable to pay Class 2 National Insurance. You should also contact your bank and cancel your direct debit.

As a company director you will now pay employee's Class 1 contributions and the company will pay employer's Class 1 contributions on your salary, bonuses and perks but not dividends (see Chapter 2).

Income tax

You must inform the tax office that deals with your affairs that you are no longer self-employed (the address and phone number will be on your tax form or other correspondence). You will then complete your accounts to the date that you cease the self-employment. You can claim overlap relief against your final profits if your original accounting year end was any date other than 31 March or 5 April (see Chapter 13). You must also follow special rules when valuing your stock, claiming losses and calculating capital allowances.

You must make sure that you have sufficient personal resources to be able to pay your final income tax bills. Once the company is formed you cannot withdraw money from it unless you have funds available on your director's loan account or you are paid a salary, bonus or dividend.

When you incorporate a business one of the key decisions you have to make is to decide how much of the value of your self-employment to treat as share capital in the new company and how much to leave available as a director's loan account (see Minimizing your capital gains tax). In making this decision you should take into account any tax owed on your former self-employment so that you do not lock too much money into the company as share capital only to find yourself in a difficult financial position because you cannot pay your income tax.

After the end of the tax year in which your final self-employed accounting period falls, you will no longer complete the self-employed (or partnership) pages of the tax return. You will in future complete the employment pages because you are now a company director.

PAYE scheme

You must inform the tax office dealing with your PAYE scheme about the transfer of your old business to the limited company. They will arrange to transfer your scheme to the company if you comply with various conditions.

VAT registration

You can ask HM Revenue and Customs to transfer your VAT registration (including the VAT registration number) from your self-employment to the company. You do this by completing form VAT 68, application form VAT 1 and agreeing to certain conditions. Alternatively, you can cancel your existing VAT registration by completing form VAT 7 and apply for a new registration number by completing form VAT 1.

Three aspects of your affairs have special rules on incorporation. These are:

- Stock (see Chapter 5);
- Losses (see Chapter 6); and
- Capital allowances (see Chapter 7).

Stock

Any stock you have on hand at the date of incorporation will be transferred to the company. You can choose the value at which this transfer takes place. You could use market value. This will usually create a larger profit in your final self-employed accounts and a smaller one in the company. Alternatively, you can elect within two years of incorporation for the stock to be transferred at its cost, or the amount paid by the company for the items if this is more. This will usually give you a lower profit in your self-employed accounts and a higher one in the company. The value that you choose to use will depend on the profit profile of the business, whether there are unused losses and the respective tax rates applying to the company and your self-employment.

Losses

If you have trading losses accumulated during your self-employment which you were carrying forward to use against future trading profits, you will now have to re-think what happens to them. You have three possible options:

- To use them against the year of the loss or the previous year (if you are in time to make this claim and you have income against which the losses can be used);
- To use them in a terminal loss claim;
- To carry them forward against your director's fees and dividends from the company. In order for the losses to be used in this way you must transfer your self-employed business to the company in return for shares (not cash or a director's loan account) which you must still own when you claim the loss relief. You cannot deduct the loss from the company's profits.

Capital allowances

You cannot claim writing down allowances or first year allowances in your final self-employed accounts. The company can claim writing down allowances on the value of the assets transferred to it but not first year allowances. These restrictions on your capital allowance claims mean that where possible the company should buy any assets on which you can claim first year allowances, particularly where allowances can be claimed at the 100% rate (see Appendix 1).

When a business ceases a balancing allowance or charge may arise when the assets are disposed of (see Chapters 7 and 13). When you incorporate, you have the option of transferring the assets to the company at their tax written down value. As a result there will be no balancing allowance or charge in your final self-employed accounts. You have to elect for this treatment to apply within two years of the transfer.

Starting a limited company

Some aspects of incorporating an existing self-employment are just as they would be if you had started trading as a limited company from the outset. This means that:

- You must notify HM Revenue and Customs about the formation of the company and pay corporation tax on your profits (see Chapter 4, Notification process).
- You are required to operate PAYE on your directors' and employees' salaries. If you have asked your tax office to transfer your existing PAYE scheme to the company you have satisfied this requirement (see Closing down your self-employment). If you do not have a PAYE scheme, you will need one now even if you are the company's only employee/director as you must operate PAYE and National Insurance on your salary and perks.
- You need to register for VAT. If you have transferred your VAT registration from the unincorporated business you will have complied with your VAT obligations (see Closing down your self-employment). If you are not VAT registered, you should reconsider whether you need to register (see Chapter 10).

Minimizing capital gains tax

You learned in Chapter 2 that capital gains tax is charged on the profit you make when you sell or otherwise dispose of your capital assets. When you incorporate a self-employed business or partnership this is what you are doing. You are disposing of personally owned capital assets by transferring them to a limited company. You may have to pay capital gains tax as a result.

Fortunately capital gains tax is not charged on all your assets. It only applies to the transfer of freehold or leasehold business premises, plant and machinery attached to the building and goodwill (see Goodwill). Stock, debtors, money in the bank and other investments, and liabilities such as creditors, loans and overdrafts are not liable to capital gains tax. Equipment on which you have claimed capital allowances is not liable to capital gains tax provided that the individual items are valued at less than £6,000.

Goodwill

Goodwill can cause complications on incorporation. Basically goodwill is the difference between what your business is worth and the value of its identifiable assets such as buildings, equipment and stock. The amount it is worth depends on the type of business you run, your turnover and profits, clients, brands, reputation and the skills and management abilities of yourself and your staff. HM Revenue and Customs distinguish between personal and business goodwill but are often of the opinion that a sole trader supplying their own services with few staff has no goodwill associated with the business. This is a mixed blessing. On the plus side if there is no goodwill you cannot owe capital gains tax on it. On the negative side, you cannot use the goodwill to create a director's loan account in the company and you will not be able to claim corporation tax relief on it. HM Revenue and Customs review goodwill calculations carefully, so you should always have your business professionally valued.

Case study

Monty, a higher rate taxpayer, started a security business on 1 November 2002 as a sole trader. He decides to incorporate the business on 31 October 2006. The business is valued at £500,000 made up as follows:

	£
Freehold office (acquired 1 November 2002 for £175,000)	350,000
Equipment (no items worth more than £6,000)	50,000
Goodwill	75,000
Stock	50,000
Debtors	40,000
Bank balance	35,000
Loans	−100,000
	500,000

Monty does not have to pay capital gains tax on the transfer of the equipment, stock, debtors and cash and loan to the company but capital gains tax will be due on the value of the freehold office and goodwill. The loan cannot be deducted from this value even if it is used to finance the purchase of the building. Monty has no costs to deduct from the goodwill as he started the business from scratch.

The capital gains tax calculation goes like this:

	£
Freehold office – value 31.10.06	350,000
Freehold office – cost 1 November 2002	–175,000
	175,000
Goodwill	75,000
Gains before taper relief	250,000
Taper relief – assuming the 75% rate applies (see Appendix 1)	–187,500
Chargeable gains	62,500
Annual exemption assuming Monty has no other gains	–8,800
Taxable gain	53,700
Capital gains tax at 40%	21,480

It will cost Monty £21,480 to transfer the assets from his self-employment to a limited company. This liability would be higher if he had not owned the building and been in business for at least two years so that he qualifies for the maximum amount of business asset taper relief. If you are in this situation, it could be worthwhile deferring incorporation until the two-year period has elapsed, assuming that it makes commercial sense to delay.

There are several other things that Monty could do to reduce his capital gains tax liability.

Do not transfer the office
Monty could retain ownership of the office and either rent it to the company or let it use it free of charge. If he charges the company rent he will pay income tax at his highest rate on the

rental income but not National Insurance. He could reduce the income tax charge by taking out a mortgage on the property. The interest on the loan is deducted from the rental income along with any other property expenses he incurs before income tax is calculated.

There are further reasons for Monty to keep hold of the property. If he transfers the office to the company he will also have to pay stamp duty land tax on the transfer. This will amount to a further £10,500 (£350,000 × 3%). The transfer of the office building may also have VAT implications.

If Monty does not transfer the office to the company, he will only owe capital gains tax on the goodwill. This amounts to £3,980 and is calculated as follows.

	£
Goodwill	75,000
Taper relief – assuming the 75% rate applies (see Appendix 1)	−56,250
Chargeable gain	18,750
Annual exemption assuming he has no other gains	−8,800
Taxable gain	9,950
Capital gains tax at 40%	3,980

Monty may be happy to pay the capital gains tax of £3,980 because doing so will enable him to credit £75,000 (the value of the goodwill) to his director's loan account with the company – at a tax rate of only 5.3% (£3,980 divided by £75,000). This is explained in more detail later in the chapter (see Director's loan account).

If Monty does not want to pay this amount of capital gains tax he has further options available to him.

Claim gifts relief on the goodwill
The gain on the goodwill cannot be cancelled but it can be deferred (completely or partially) by claiming 'gifts relief'.

If Monty wants to defer the whole of the gain on the goodwill he should charge the company £35,200 for it. This means that he has 'gifted' the company £39,800 (£75,000 – £35,200) by charging it less than the goodwill is worth. The disadvantage is that he only has £35,200 credited to his loan account rather than the full £75,000.

The sum of £39,800 is the exact amount required to reduce Monty's chargeable gains to the level of the annual exemption in 2006/07. Assuming he has not made any other gains that year he will have no capital gains tax to pay as a result. If Monty was to incorporate the business in another tax year, the gift required to achieve the same result would differ. Monty must claim gifts relief in his tax return.

The calculation with gifts relief is as follows:

	£
Goodwill	75,000
Gifts relief	–39,800
Paid by the company for the goodwill	35,200
Taper relief – assuming the 75% rate applies (see Appendix 1)	–26,400
Chargeable gains	8,800
Annual exemption	–8,800
Taxable gain	0
Capital gains tax at 40%	0

The company can claim corporation tax relief when it writes off the £35,200 of goodwill over its useful life. If the company was to sell the goodwill at a future date, capital gains tax will be calculated using £35,200 (and not £75,000) as the cost.

Monty could also transfer the goodwill to the company for any other amount between £35,200 and £75,000. Providing that he has the full capital gains tax annual exemption available to him there is no benefit to charging less than £35,200. For example, if Monty was to charge the company £50,000 for the goodwill, claiming gifts relief of £25,000 (£75,000 – £50,000), his chargeable gain would only be £1,480 and he would have £50,000 credited to his director's loan account. To recap this has two advantages:

- It gives Monty a bigger credit to his director's loan account (or payment) for the work he has put into the business up to the point of incorporation; and
- The company has a higher value of goodwill on which to claim corporation tax relief and a greater value to off-set against any future capital gains.

Director's loan account

It is unlikely that the company will have the resources to pay Monty for the goodwill at the date he incorporates. As a result the amount owed by the company is usually credited to a director's loan account. Creating a loan account enables Monty to withdraw the equivalent of his salary against it each month until the balance has been used up (but he must not overdraw it). This means that he should not need to take a salary during this period, saving the company employer's National Insurance and himself higher rate income tax depending on the amount of money that he needs to live on.

Claim incorporation rollover relief

Monty also has the option of deferring the gain on the property and goodwill through incorporation rollover relief. You should be familiar with the expression 'rollover relief' from Chapters 2 and 9. Where you meet the relevant conditions this relief is given automatically. In other words you do not need to claim it as long as you qualify for it.

To be eligible for rollover relief, you must transfer *all* the assets from your self-employment to the company (you can exclude any bank balances). All other assets such as cars, equipment, stock and debtors must be transferred. In return you will receive shares in the company.

Returning to Monty's original gains on the office building and goodwill; in exchange for transferring all his assets (excluding the bank balance) to the company, he receives 465,000 £1 shares in the company. He no longer has a capital gains tax liability because the gains are 'rolled over'.

	£
Value of business	500,000
Cash	–35,000
Shares: 465,000 £1 shares	465,000
Gains on office and goodwill before taper relief (see page 205)	–250,000
Cost of 465,000 £1 shares for capital gains tax	215,000

When Monty comes to sell his shares, instead of deducting £465,000 from the sale proceeds, he can only deduct less than half this value, i.e. £215,000. He will therefore have a higher gain because he did not pay any capital gains tax when he incorporated the company. He may however be able to defer the gain again.

Pitfalls

There are three pitfalls which can jeopardize your entitlement to incorporation rollover relief.

1 All the assets (apart from the bank balances) must be transferred to the company including your car. Many people prefer to own their cars privately rather than transfer them into the company to avoid a benefit in kind charge (see Chapter 8, Taxing perks). You cannot do this without losing rollover relief. One way round this difficulty is to take the car out of the business well before you incorporate.

2 Your investment in the company is locked up as share capital. You may want a greater degree of flexibility than this provides with some of the value of your business credited to a director's loan account so that you can draw against it when the company has the available resources. For example, instead of receiving 465,000 shares Monty might choose to receive 279,000 £1 shares and have £186,000 credited to his loan account. This means that only 60% (£279,000 divided by £465,000) of the £250,000 gain can be rolled over. This will result in a capital gains tax liability on the remaining 40%. Monty may consider that the capital gains tax is worth paying for the benefit of having access to £186,000. Alternatively, he may decide to allocate the balance between shares and his loan account so that the resulting gain is covered by his capital gains tax annual exemption.

3 If Monty keeps the shares for two or more years he should be entitled to the higher rate of business asset taper relief when he sells them, assuming that the shares qualify as business assets. If he sells the shares within two years of incorporation, his gain will be significantly increased. Should this circumstance apply, he has the option of cancelling his claim for rollover relief and reverting to his original capital gains tax position if it would save him tax.

Enterprise investment scheme deferral relief

There is a further option for deferring a gain on incorporation. Whether or not you can take advantage of it depends on the nature of your business. The Enterprise Investment Scheme (EIS) gives income tax and capital gains tax relief for certain investments by some people in suitable companies. There are a myriad of conditions for the investment, the investor and the company to comply with. You will require specialist advice if you are considering deferring a gain in this way.

The advantage of running a business with share capital

However you structure the transfer of your self-employment to the company, some of the investment you have accumulated in the business will become share capital in the company. Running a business with a share capital gives you new options to attract investment and reward yourself and your staff.

1 You can pay dividends to shareholders. Dividends are not liable to any sort of National Insurance but if you pay income tax at the highest rate you may have additional tax to pay (see Chapter 2 and Appendix 1). If your company provides just your services or those of your spouse or partner, paying a large dividend and a small salary may not be tax effective. HM Revenue and Customs can block any tax advantage by rules known as 'IR35' (see Chapter 4).

2 Your spouse or civil partner, or other family members can own shares in the business and receive dividends on them. If you pay dividends to divert income which is really yours to someone else, usually a spouse, partner or child under 18 because they pay tax at a lower rate than you do, the income may be treated as if it still belonged to you and you could be taxed on it under what is known as the 'settlements legislation' (see Chapter 4).

3 External investors are more likely to want to invest in your business if they can become shareholders and as a result have a say in the business affairs under company law. Depending on the nature of your business, you may be able to structure it so that you are a 'qualifying company' for the purposes of the Enterprise Investment Scheme. This means that investors may be able to obtain income tax and capital gains relief on their investment as long as various conditions relating to the company, the investor and the shares are met. You will need professional advice.

4 Trading through a limited company enables you to reward your staff with shares, or options to buy shares in the company. If these are awarded through a scheme approved by HM Revenue and Customs, the shares receive favourable tax treatment. The approved schemes are:

- Share incentive plans (SIPs);
- Enterprise management incentives (EMI);
- Save As You Earn (SAYE) schemes;
- Company share option plans (CSOP).

Each scheme has many detailed rules about the organization and structure of the company, the employees that can participate and the nature and extent of the shares or options involved. Directors can only participate if they own or control (including with other people such as a spouse or civil partner) less than 25% (in some cases 30%) of the company's shares.

If you are interested in these arrangements you will need professional help to set up the scheme. You should be aware that all the share schemes will involve you in additional administration.

Recap

- There is no easy way to tell whether or not you will save tax by trading as a limited company rather than a sole trader or partner. It all depends on the profits of the business, how much you retain in the business as working capital and the amount you pay yourself as salary and dividends. Your adviser could prepare comparative calculations to ascertain which option will minimize your tax bill but as your profits and the tax rates change annually, the best option in one year will not necessarily be so in another. Transferring your business to a limited company should usually be because of commercial factors, for example increased risk or the need for external investment.

- When you incorporate, you have to close down your self-employment (or partnership) and start up a new company. You will transfer assets, registrations, losses and capital allowances from one to the other.
- The legislation is designed to minimize the tax cost of incorporation. Freehold and leasehold land and buildings and goodwill are the most likely assets to give rise to a capital gains tax liability when you incorporate.
- One way to eliminate a gain on land or a building is not to transfer it to the company. However owing it personally prevents gains on other assets such as goodwill from being rolled over.
- The value of assets transferred to a limited company can be credited to your director's loan account, paid to you in cash, or formed into share capital. The advantage of share capital is that the business has a stronger balance sheet. The disadvantage is that you cannot easily get your hands on the money (selling private company shares depends on you finding an independent investor willing to buy them). You cannot draw money from the company against the value of your shares but you can withdraw a loan account as long as the business has the resources to enable you to do so. Your bank and other financiers will sometimes stipulate that your investment must be tied up in the business as share capital.
- The advantage of claiming gifts relief to defer a capital gain is that the capital transferred does not have to be treated as share capital which it does if you claim incorporation rollover relief. The amount credited to your loan account is however reduced.
- Gifts relief must be claimed on your tax return (use Helpsheet IR295). Rollover relief is given automatically without the need for you to make a claim.
- If you claim rollover relief, the issue of shares on incorporation must be reported to HM Revenue and Customs on form 42 by 7 July following the tax year in which the shares are issued. This form may also need to be completed at other times if you make changes to your shares, for example if you issue new ones. You will require help to complete it.
- If you have more than one business you could defer some of your gains by claiming rollover relief against an investment in assets in that venture rather than the new company (see Chapters 9 and 14). You could also defer the gain by investing in a furnished holiday let.
- Remember – forming a limited company is straightforward but running and getting rid of one is not.

13
closing a business

In this chapter:
- closing down your self-employment
- closing down a company
- VAT de-registration
- redundancy payments

In Chapter 4 we looked at the tax consequences of starting up your business. We now consider what happens when you close it down. There are many reasons why a business closes such as retirement, failure to make a profit and personal reasons. A business may also be shut down because it is incorporated (see Chapter 12) or sold to a third party (see Chapter 14).

The closure process depends on whether you have been running an unincorporated business (sole trader or partnership) or a limited company. Closing down the former is relatively straightforward. Closing a company is more complicated because unless it is solvent and its affairs very simple, it can only be closed by a formal liquidation.

Closing down an unincorporated business

In Chapter 12 you learned that to close down a self-employment or partnership, you have to tell HM Revenue and Customs that the business has ceased for the purposes of income tax, PAYE, VAT and Class 2 National Insurance. This section looks at how your business is taxed in the final years.

Cessation date

The first thing to decide is a date for the business to cease. Over the lifetime of your business all your profits are taxed so you cannot reduce your taxable profits by choosing one date over another; however, depending on your profits, future intentions and other sources of income, you may benefit by closing down the business in one tax year rather than another. This is particularly relevant if the cessation date is to be shortly before or shortly after 5 April.

Allocating profits to tax years

In Chapter 5, you learned that there are special rules for taxing business profits when a business starts. There are also special rules for taxing profits when a business ceases. The way in which they operate depends on the date you stop trading and your last accounting year end. Sometimes the rules for the opening and closing years overlap if you are only self-employed for a short period.

Examples

Cora, who has been self-employed for many years, retires on 30 September 2006. Her accounting year end was previously 31 March. Her 2006/07 self-assessment will be for the period 1 April 2006 to 30 September 2006.

Derek has been self-employed for ten years preparing accounts to 31 October each year. He stops being self-employed on 31 December 2006. When he drew up his first accounts, he was taxed twice on the same profits because his year end is a date other than 31 March or 5 April. This created overlap profits of £5,000. His trading profits are as follows:

- Year to 31 October 2005   £30,000
- 1 November 2005–31 December 2006   £25,000
  (14 months)

His taxable profits are:

Tax year	Accounting period	Profits £
2005/06	Year to 31 October 2005	**30,000**
2006/07	1 November 2005–31 December 2006 (14 months)	25,000
	Less: Overlap relief	–5,000
	Taxable profit	**20,000**

Note: The profits taxed in the final tax year may exceed twelve months.

Edwardo prepares accounts to 31 May and has overlap profits of £2,000. He ceases self-employment on 31 December 2006. His trading profits as are follows:

- Year to 31 May 2005   £15,000
- Year to 31 May 2006   £10,000
- 1 June 2006–31 December 2006 (7 months)   £ 5,000

His taxable profits are:

Tax year	Accounting period	Profits £
2005/06	Year to 31 May 2005	**15,000**
2006/07	Year to 31 May 2006 (12 months)	10,000
	1 June 2006–31 December 2006 (7 months)	5,000
	Less: Overlap relief	–2,000
	Taxable profit	**13,000**

If Edwardo's overlap profits had been £20,000 instead of £2,000 he would have made a loss of £5,000 (see Losses).

Flo prepares accounts to 31 August and ceases self-employment on 30 April 2007. She has overlap profits of £10,000. Her trading profits as are follows:

- Year to 31 August 2005 £ 20,000
- 1 September 2005–30 April 2007 (20 months) £ 15,000

Her taxable profits are:

Tax year	Accounting period	Profits £
2005/06	Year to 31 August 2005	**20,000**
2006/07	Year to 31 August 2006 (12 months) £15,000 × 12 months/20 months	**9,000**
2007/08	1 September 2006–30 April 2007 (8 months) £15,000 × 8 months/20 months	6,000
	Less: Overlap relief	–10,000
	Loss	**–4,000**

As Flo has no accounting date ending in 2006/07, a year's worth of profits from her final accounts are taxed in that year. The balance of eight months is taxed in 2007/08. There is no choice about when Flo can deduct the overlap relief – it can only be deducted from the final tax year. Flo has various options for using her loss, (see Chapter 6, Losses when a business ceases).

Overlap relief

Overlap profits were created when you first started to be self-employed because you chose to prepare your accounts to a date other than 31 March or 5 April (see Chapter 5). You may have already used some of your overlap profits if you changed your year end. Any overlap relief that is left over can be deducted from your taxable profits in your final year of being self-employed (or a partner). You will know how much your overlap profits are because each year you have to enter them on the self-employment pages of your tax form. If you have a year end other than 31 March or 5 April and no overlap profits, this is probably because you made a loss in your first accounting period.

Stock

When you stop being self-employed, you may have left-over stock. You cannot ignore it for tax purposes and must value it accurately. If you take it from the business for your own use, you must value it at market price. If you sell it to someone connected to you (a spouse, civil partner or relative) it must usually be valued at its sale price or its cost, whichever is the highest amount.

Capital allowances

You cannot claim capital allowances in the year that you cease your business. Instead you dispose of the assets (even if only to yourself) and calculate a balancing allowance or charge (see Chapter 7, Calculating capital allowances – Disposals). It is quite probable that you will take some assets out of the business for your private use, for example cars, computers, office furniture etc. These must be taken out of the capital allowance calculation at their market value (not tax written down value). The same rule applies if you sell the assets to someone connected with you such as your spouse, civil partner or relation.

Losses

If you make a loss in your final year it is calculated in the usual way. It may be increased by overlap relief giving you a bigger loss to claim if you are a sole trader or a partner (see Overlap relief). Loss claims when you cease in business are covered in detail in Chapter 6.

Income and expenses incurred after the final accounting period

After you have closed down your business, you may unexpectedly receive income or incur expenses relating to the business. For example you may receive payment for a debt that you had previously written off in your accounts as a bad debt. These items cannot be ignored. 'Post-cessation receipts' (as such income is called) are either treated as taxable income in the year you receive them, or if you are a sole trader or partner and you receive the income within six years of ceasing the business, you can ask for it to be treated as the income of the year when you stopped trading. You will want to do this if it results in you paying less tax, for example because you had unused losses in that year or a lower income than the current year. To opt for this treatment you must enter the income on the tax return (at Question 13 not on the Self-employment pages) in the year you receive it and file the form on time. You do not need to alter the tax form for the year you ceased in business but you will need to know the details of your taxable income for that year so you can work out how much tax you would have owed on the post-cessation receipt had you received it in the year you stopped being in business.

If you incur certain expenses (known as 'post-cessation expenses') in the seven years after ceasing your business, you can deduct them from:

- post-cessation receipts (if you have any); or
- your other income and gains for the year in which they arise.

To obtain a tax deduction for post-cessation expenses you must claim them (by making an entry in Box 15.8 and not on the Self-employment pages of the tax return) by the second 31 January filing date following the tax year in which you incurred the expense. The type of expenses that you can claim as post-cessation expenses are:

- The costs of remedying defective work;
- Damages;
- Associated legal and insurance costs;
- Bad debts and debt recovery costs;
- Professional indemnity insurance.

Closing down a limited company

The tax consequences of closing down a company are more complicated than shutting down a self-employment or partnership. The degree of complexity depends on whether the company is solvent, in administration or liquidation. Administration and liquidation are formal arrangements under company law for winding up a company.

Striking-off a company

The simplest way to get rid of a limited company that you no longer need is to have it 'struck-off' the register of companies. You can only do this if you obtain HM Revenue and Customs approval. Their consent will usually be given if you have filed the company's final accounts and returns and settled the outstanding corporation tax, PAYE and VAT (or provide an undertaking to do so). For a small company with no outstanding debts, apart from to director/shareholders, the tax authorities will usually agree to the company distributing any remaining funds to the shareholders without income tax consequences if only a small sum is involved. It is usual to have paid out the majority of any remaining profits by way of a dividend before applying to HM Revenue and Customs to strike the company off the register. A capital gain could arise on the final profit distribution but it depends on the original cost of the shares, the amount of the payment and the availability of the annual exemption.

Formal arrangements

If your company is insolvent (or has complicated affairs) you will only be able to close it down by a formal liquidation. In this case dealing with the tax authorities on company matters is taken out of your hands as they are dealt with by the liquidator (or administrator).

The principal concern for you as a shareholder is with regard to capital gains tax. Your entitlement to business asset taper relief may be jeopardized by a liquidation. If you make a gain on a capital sum paid out on liquidation you will need to take advice.

VAT de-registration

If you cease your business you have to de-register for VAT from the date you stop trading by completing form VAT 7. You will then be sent a final VAT return to complete.

In your final return you may have to account for VAT on any unsold stock and on assets such as equipment, vans (but not most cars), computers, furniture etc. You should normally value the items at the price you would expect to pay for them in their present condition. If their value is £6,714 or less you do not have to account for VAT (the official limit is £1,000 or more of VAT). You must keep a list of all these items irrespective of whether you have to pay VAT on them. If you use a VAT scheme you may have to follow additional procedures, and barristers have to account for their outstanding fees in accordance with special rules. Approximately three weeks after applying for de-registration you will receive official confirmation of de-registration on form VAT 35. HM Revenue and Customs may inspect your records before finalizing your de-registration application.

From the date that you de-register you must not charge VAT. In some limited circumstances however you can reclaim VAT for up to three years after de-registration on:

• Bad debts (if you did not use the cash accounting scheme).
• Professional invoices, for example from your solicitor or accountant provided that the services relate to the period when you were VAT registered.

To reclaim this VAT you must complete form VAT 427 and send it together with the original invoices to HM Revenue and Customs Accounting Adjustments (VAT 427 team).

For further information on VAT de-registration see VAT Notice 700/11.

Closing down your PAYE scheme

In addition to notifying the HM Revenue and Customs department handling your PAYE scheme that you have ceased trading, you will need to undertake the following:

• Pay employees up to their leaving date including any entitlement to holiday pay;

- Issue employees with a form P45 (see Chapter 8);
- Pay redundancy pay (see Redundancy payments);
- Complete all outstanding returns P35, P11Ds etc. (see Chapter 8);
- Pay all outstanding PAYE and National Insurance, including Class 1A and Class 1B contributions.

HM Revenue and Customs may conduct a final PAYE inspection prior to closing the PAYE scheme.

Redundancy payments

If you lay-off your staff because you are closing down your business you will be liable to pay them statutory redundancy (paid at a set rate) if they have been employed by you for two or more years since the age of 18. If you are self-employed or a partner you are not entitled to receive redundancy if you close the business but if you are a company director working under an employment contract you may be eligible for it. For further information about redundancy refer to the DTI's website (see Appendix 4).

Redundancy payments are not liable to income tax or Class 1 National Insurance but unpaid wages, bonuses and holiday pay are taxed under PAYE in the usual way. If you provide counselling services and retraining for redundant employees this perk is tax-exempt (see Chapter 8).

Should you decide to pay your employees a termination payment of more than the statutory minimum, they will not have to pay income tax and employee's Class 1 National Insurance on it, and you will not have to pay employer's Class 1 National Insurance as long as they had no contractual entitlement to the payment and the package you give them is £30,000 or less. You will require professional advice, particularly if you want to pay a termination payment to a company director.

Recap checklist

When you close down an unincorporated business you should:

- Select a cessation date;
- Cancel your Class 2 National Insurance;
- De-register for VAT by completing a final VAT return remembering to account for VAT on stock and assets if they are worth more than £6,714;
- Pay your employees redundancy and outstanding pay;
- Complete outstanding forms and close down your PAYE scheme;
- Prepare accounts to the date you stop;
- Make sure that you account for stock correctly.

14

selling a business

In this chapter:
- what are you selling?
- case study – selling shares or assets?
- will you receive cash or shares for the business?
- reducing capital gains tax
- recap checklist

In the last two chapters we looked at the tax consequences of the disposal of your business by:

- transferring it to a limited company; and
- cosing it down or liquidation.

In this chapter we consider the tax consequences of the ultimate disposal – sale to a third party. Selling a business is complicated and this is a time when you will need professional help.

What are you selling?

When you come to sell your business, the first thing to ask yourself is 'what are you selling?' The answer depends on whether you are self-employed, in partnership or a limited company. The tax consequences for sole traders and partners are relatively straightforward. Selling a limited company is more complicated because you can sell either the individual assets or the entire company by selling its shares.

Sole traders

If you operate as a sole trader you cannot sell the 'business' because legally there is nothing to sell as there is with a limited company. You can however sell all the individual business assets such as land, buildings, equipment, goodwill (such as your client list) and stock. In some situations you might decide to incorporate your self-employment in order to sell it (see Chapter 12). You need to plan ahead if you are doing this because you will minimize your capital gains tax liability if you are incorporated for two or more years before the sale (see Reducing capital gains tax).

The tax consequences of selling your self-employed assets are as follows:

- Land, buildings, plant fixed to a building, goodwill and intangible assets such as patents, licenses, rights and designs are all liable to capital gains tax (see Chapter 12). You have to work out the gain on each item individually, deduct the cost of acquiring the asset and any purchase and sale costs, indexation allowance if appropriate and then deduct business asset taper relief (see Chapter 2 for an example of the calculation).
- Equipment on which you have claimed capital allowances is not liable to capital gains tax unless the selling price for an individual item is £6,000 or more. 'Chattels' relief will reduce

any gain that does arise. You will include the proceeds from the sale of equipment in your final capital allowance calculation which will give you either a balancing allowance or a balancing charge (see Chapter 7, Calculating capital allowances – Disposals). The balancing allowance or charge will decrease or increase your final accounting profit and in consequence your income tax bill.

- Income from the sale of stock will be included in your final trading accounts and is liable to income tax.

- If you sell your debts there is no capital gains tax to pay. If you receive less than the debts are worth you will include a deduction for bad debts in your final trading accounts.

- If you are not selling the business as a going concern you may have to charge VAT on some of the assets (see Company).

Once you have sold the assets to a third party, you will close down your business along the lines described in Chapter 13. Any assets you keep for yourself such as a car, computer or office equipment must be valued at their market value and included as a disposal in the final capital allowance calculation.

The sale agreement

Balancing your requirements with those of the buyer can be difficult. As the seller you will probably want an agreement which allocates a greater proportion of the sale proceeds to those assets which are liable to capital gains tax (principally property) rather than those that have income tax consequences. Although there is little difference between the rates of capital gains tax and the income tax rates, you will save tax by having gains rather than income because you can reduce these by claiming business asset taper relief and the annual exemption. In some circumstances you can also defer paying tax on your gain (see Reducing capital gains tax).

On the other hand the buyer will prefer to allocate higher values to goodwill (if they trade as a limited company), equipment and stock rather than property because they can obtain tax relief on these items in the first accounting period after the purchase. They will not receive tax relief on the sums they invest in land and buildings until they sell the property.

HM Revenue and Customs may challenge the division of the sales proceeds between the various assets. You will require professional help to agree the allocation of the sales price so that it is acceptable to you, the purchaser and the tax authorities.

Partners

A partnership may sell its assets or the individual partners may sell their share in the partnership. If a partnership sells its assets to a third party, the tax consequences are the same as they are for a sole trader, with each partner being liable for capital gains tax on their share of the partnership property and goodwill. Any payment received for the sale of stock and work-in-progress is adjusted in the final partnership accounts and the disposal of equipment is included in the final capital allowances computation. The partnership is then closed down (see Chapter 13).

It is more usual for a partner (or partners) to sell all or part of their partnership share to the existing partners or a new partner joining the partnership. The tax consequences are then as follows:

- If you leave a partnership and the partnership continues in business without you, the withdrawal of your investment in the partnership (your capital account) has no capital gains tax consequences unless the partnership assets such as land, buildings and goodwill are revalued and you are given a share of the profit resulting from that revaluation.

- If you continue as a partner but you reduce your profit share by selling it to an existing or new partner, you will have a capital gains tax liability if land, buildings and goodwill are revalued. Capital gains tax is due irrespective of whether you withdraw the revaluation profit or the new partner's contribution, or whether it remains invested in your capital account.

Company

If a company wants to sell its business it has two options:

- to sell its assets (as would be the case where a sole trader sells up); or
- for all the shareholders to agree to sell their shares (here the purchaser takes over all the company's assets and liabilities including the tax liabilities).

Once again the vendor (seller) and the purchaser (buyer) may have different objectives in the sale negotiations and what will be tax advantageous to one party is likely to be to the detriment of the other. These differences will need to be reconciled if a successful sale is to result.

The vendor will probably prefer to sell shares because this minimizes their capital gains tax liability (see Case study).

The purchaser often prefers to buy assets because it is usually more straightforward without the risk of taking on all the company's liabilities. An asset sale has the following tax advantages for them:

- Capital allowances can be claimed (see Chapter 7);
- A tax deduction can be claimed on the write-off of the goodwill (assuming that the purchaser is a company);
- The assets may be a suitable reinvestment in a claim for rollover relief (see Reducing capital gains tax).

If however the purchaser can be persuaded to buy shares, they will obtain two tax advantages:

- Stamp duty on the acquisition of shares is less than the cost of stamp duty land tax on the purchase of land and buildings.
- No VAT is charged on the sale of shares.

In some circumstances the vendor may prefer to sell assets instead of shares where:

- It has trading losses which can be off-set against the gains (see Chapter 6);
- It can claim rollover relief.

VAT

VAT on the sale of a business is notoriously complex. If you sell a company as a going concern (i.e. a new owner takes it over and operates it without major changes), you do not have to charge VAT on the sale. If the business is not sold as a going concern, you must charge VAT on the assets, including goodwill, stock and equipment and some cars. As far as property is concerned, sometimes you must charge VAT even if you are selling the business as a going concern. HM Revenue and Customs' view of whether you have sold a business as a going concern may differ from your own and many cases end up being considered by the VAT tribunals. It is essential to take professional advice because if you get it wrong the amount you receive for selling the company could be significantly reduced if you have to pay VAT out of the proceeds.

Case study – shares or assets?

The following case study illustrates the tax that will be saved where a company sells shares rather than assets.

FF Ltd has been trading since March 2002. It owns freehold premises included in its accounts at £300,000 and has net current assets of £200,000. Its share capital is £50,000 and it has reserves of £450,000.

GG Ltd, a competitor, wants to buy the business and offered FF Ltd £750,000 for it in March 2006. This sum is divided as follows: property and goodwill £550,000 and net current assets £200,000. FF Ltd wants to know how much tax it will owe depending on whether it sells shares or its assets.

Shares

	£
Offer by GG Ltd to buy the shares from the shareholders of FF Ltd	750,000
Cost of shares	–50,000
Gain before taper relief	**700,000**
Taper relief: 75% assuming that the shares have always qualified as business assets	–525,000
Gains after taper relief	175,000
Capital gains tax at 40% (assuming no further reliefs available)	70,000
Amount received by shareholders of FF Ltd (£750,000 – £70,000)	680,000

Assets

	£	£
Assets in accounts		500,000
Increase in value of property and goodwill	250,000	250,000
Indexation on the £300,000 cost of property (approximately)	−35,000	
Gain	215,000	
Corporation tax on gain (assumed) rate 23.25%	−50,000	−50,000
Distributed to the shareholders when the company ceases trading		700,000
Cost of shares		−50,000
Gain before taper relief		650,000
Taper relief: 75% assuming that the shares have always qualified as business assets		−487,500
Gains after taper relief		162,500
Capital gains tax at 40% (assuming no further reliefs available)		65,000
Amount received by shareholders of FF Ltd (£700,000 − £65,000)		635,000

If FF Ltd sells its assets and is then liquidated, the shareholders receive £45,000 less than they would do if the company sold its shares without selling the assets first. This is because on an asset sale capital gains tax is charged twice:

1 On the increase in value of the premises (as corporation tax); and

2 On the shareholders when the company makes a capital distribution (as capital gains tax).

If GG Ltd is aware of the comparative tax advantage to FF Ltd of a share sale, it may use this information to negotiate a reduced price for the shares. Alternatively, if GG Ltd only wants to buy the assets, it may be persuaded to pay a higher price to cover FF Ltd's extra tax costs. Insofar as the sales proceeds are allocated to goodwill and equipment, GG Ltd will be able to claim corporation tax relief on the write-off of the goodwill and capital allowances on the equipment (see Selling assets) and these tax savings may go some way to off-setting the higher price that FF Ltd will expect from an asset sale.

Will you receive cash or shares?

When you sell a company you need to agree what you will receive in return and when you will receive it. The most straightforward option is for the purchaser of the company to pay you in 'cash'. This means that you receive payment on the agreed sale date and that is the end of the matter. Your tax liability is calculated as shown in the Case study according to whether you have sold shares or assets. If you sell your business for cash to be paid in the future, conditional on the company's ongoing business performance, you will still have to pay capital gains tax. Working out when this liability arises and valuing the sales proceeds in this case is more complicated.

If you agree to sell the shares in your company to another company there is an alternative to being paid in cash – you can trade your shares for shares in the purchasing company. This is called a share for share arrangement or a paper exchange. You can also exchange shares for loan stock. The advantage of agreeing to a paper exchange is that you do not dispose of your shares for capital gains tax purposes until you sell the new shares. When you come to sell the new shares at a future date you will deduct the amount you originally paid for the old shares. You can claim taper relief from the date you originally purchased the shares and not from the date you exchanged them. If you exchange your shares for loan stock, your entitlement to taper relief depends on the nature of the stock.

Most people selling a business prefer to receive cash for it straight away and usually consider shares to be a risky option (unless they are quoted on the stock exchange). A compromise deal is often reached to sell shares partly in exchange for cash and partly for shares. The part you receive in cash is liable to capital gains tax whilst the gain on the paper exchange is deferred until the new shares are sold.

Example

Hannah the director/shareholder of HH Ltd agrees to sell the company to II Ltd. She receives cash of £1,000,000 and shares in II Ltd valued at £1,000,000 in return for her shares in HH Ltd which originally cost £100,000 four years ago. Her capital gains tax position is as follows:

	Cash (£)	Shares (£)
Sales proceeds	1,000,000	1,000,000
Cost of shares – divided 50:50	–50,000	50,000
Gain before taper relief	950,000	–
Taper relief – assuming 75% relief applies	–712,500	–
Gain after taper relief	237,500	–

Hannah has no capital gains tax liability on the £1 million she is paid in shares in II Ltd. She will however have to pay capital gains tax when she sells these shares. At that point she can deduct £50,000 as the cost of the shares in II Ltd. This is half the original cost of £100,000 and not the £1 million that they were worth at the date of exchange.

If as part of the sale agreement you are to have a continuing involvement in the business, you may not receive all the shares straight away. Some of them may be held back and only transferred to you if the company's performance meets expectation. This is called an 'earn-out'. The value of the earn-out is treated as part of the shares being exchanged so once again no capital gains tax is due until the new shares are sold. If the arrangement with the purchaser is that you will receive shares for personal performance they will be liable to income tax and National Insurance as employment earnings.

Reducing capital gains tax

If the sale of your business results in a capital gains tax liability, there are several ways to reduce or defer it.

Do not jeopardize business asset taper relief

You will save tax if you qualify for business asset taper relief rather than the non-business variety (see Appendix 1). In the scenarios outlined in this chapter there should not usually be a difficulty in obtaining business asset taper relief. The higher rate of taper relief can be jeopardized where a company sells its assets, ceases trading and only later distributes capital to its shareholders. Ensuring that the company makes a capital distribution before it ceases trading is therefore important.

Claim rollover relief

Rollover relief works like a rolled over lottery jackpot but instead of the prize being deferred, the date when you have to pay capital gains tax is rolled over to a future date. To qualify you must reinvest in new assets. The assets you sell and the replacement assets must be 'qualifying assets' and you must make the reinvestment during the year before the sale or up to three years afterwards. You do not need to use the new assets in the same business and you can sell one type of asset and reinvest in another. The usual qualifying assets are land, buildings and fixed plant and machinery (for a full list see Chapter 9). Goodwill is a qualifying asset if you are a sole trader or partner. If you only reinvest part of the proceeds, the gain may be only partly rolled over, or not rolled over at all as the following Example illustrates.

Example

When Jamie sells his business, he disposes of all his assets including retail premises for £350,000, making a gain on the property of £200,000. A year after selling his business he invests £375,000 in a freehold restaurant building and goodwill.

	£
Gain on retail premises	200,000
Rollover relief (no restriction because all the sales proceeds are reinvested)	–200,000
Immediately chargeable gain	–
Cost of restaurant premises and goodwill	375,000
Rolled over amount	–200,000
Revised cost of restaurant and goodwill for capital gains tax	**175,000**

When Jamie comes to sell the restaurant his gain will include the gain from the retail premises but he may be entitled to rollover that gain too.

If Jamie only reinvests £300,000 in the restaurant the calculation goes like this:

	£
Gain on retail premises	200,000
Rollover relief (restricted because £50,000 of the sales proceeds are not reinvested)	−150,000
Immediately chargeable gain before taper relief	50,000
Taper relief – assuming the 75% business asset rate applies	−37,500
Chargeable gain after taper relief	**12,500**
Cost of restaurant premises and goodwill	300,000
Rolled over amount	−150,000
Revised cost of restaurant and goodwill for capital gains tax	**150,000**

If Jamie only reinvests £100,000 in the restaurant, he has not reinvested any of the gain.

	£
Gain on retail premises	200,000
Rollover relief (restricted because £250,000 of the sales proceeds are not reinvested)	–
Immediately chargeable gain before taper relief	200,000
Taper relief – assuming the 75% business asset rate applies	−150,000
Chargeable gain after taper relief	**50,000**
Cost of restaurant and goodwill for capital gains tax	**100,000**

Where there is a chargeable gain, Jamie will claim taper relief. Where there is no immediately chargeable gain he cannot claim taper relief. Jamie needs to own the replacement asset for two or more years before being entitled to business asset taper relief at the highest rate.

Claim Enterprise Investment Scheme deferral relief

You can claim Enterprise Investment Scheme deferral relief if you invest in shares in a company qualifying for the Enterprise Investment Scheme one year before the disposal of your premises and up to three years afterwards. There are many detailed rules relating to this relief and you are likely to require professional advice.

An alternative course of action

If you are unsure about selling your company but need to because you do not have the resources to develop its potential, an alternative course of action is to seek a larger company to invest in the business. A company may be encouraged to invest in your business if they can obtain tax relief on their investment through the Corporate Venturing Scheme (available until 1 April 2010). There are many detailed conditions that must be met and you will need professional advice if you want to consider this option further.

Recap checklist

Selling a company is complex and you will need to engage experienced advisers to help you. You will usually need both an accountant and a solicitor. They will usually undertake the following for you:

- Assist you to negotiate the sale agreement with the purchaser.
- Determine your future role (if you are to have one).
- Calculate your capital gains tax liabilities and tell you when they are due to be paid.
- Suggest ways to minimize your capital gains tax liability.
- Advise whether or not you should charge VAT on the sale.

- On a share sale, provide the purchaser with financial information so that they can check out the company's liabilities (including to all the various taxes). This is called the 'due diligence' process.
- On a share sale, negotiate with the purchaser regarding the indemnities and warranties they require concerning the company's tax liabilities.
- Draw up the sale document.
- Make the necessary conveyances of land and buildings and deal with the stamp duty land tax.
- Liaise with HM Revenue and Customs regarding any contentious issues.

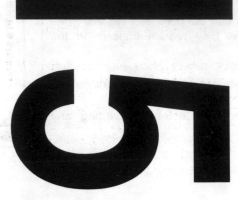

15

passing on a business

In this chapter:
- giving away your business
- what happens to my business when I die?
- making a will

We have already looked at two ways of disposing of your business – closing it down and selling it. In this chapter we consider a third option – passing it on to someone else such as your children or other relatives. We also consider the tax consequences for your business when you die and look at the inheritance tax reliefs available for business and agricultural property.

When you die your executors have to pay inheritance tax on the value of your estate above a certain threshold including the value of your business (see Appendix 1). If however you are entitled to business or agricultural property relief there may be no inheritance tax to pay on the business or farm. If you are unsure whether inheritance tax will be charged on your estate you should refer to Chapter 2 bearing in mind that inheritance tax depends on the nature of your assets and who you decide to leave them to.

Irrespective of whether you want to hand over the reins while you are still alive or continue working until you die, you will need professional advice to minimize the inheritance tax on your estate.

Giving away your business

At some stage in your life you may decide that you want to retire from your business and pass it over to someone else, usually your children or someone from the next generation. Although this transaction has both capital gains tax and inheritance tax consequences, in most cases there will be no immediate capital gains tax charge because of 'gifts relief' (see Gifts relief) and there will be no inheritance tax to pay if you are entitled to business or agricultural property relief (see Inheritance tax).

When you transfer your business to your children or other relatives, it has to be commercially valued because it is being transferred to a 'connected' person (see Appendix 3). Valuing small businesses is subjective and it is possible that the amount you think the business is worth and the value that HM Revenue and Customs place on it could differ significantly. If you claim gifts relief they will usually accept your valuation without protracted negotiations but may query it if the person you give the business to later sells it. As this may be many years down the line, it is important to keep a record of the gift and the valuation.

Different rules apply if you transfer your business to your spouse or civil partner. In this case the business is transferred for capital gains tax purposes at its cost plus any indexation allowance so there is no gain and no loss. For inheritance tax, the business is usually transferred to a spouse or civil partner at its commercial value but there will be no inheritance tax to pay provided that they are from the UK (domiciled). If they are not UK domiciled you can only transfer assets worth £55,000 to them free of inheritance tax (see Chapter 2).

Gifts relief

Although you need to value your business, most gifts of business assets do not attract an immediate capital gains tax charge because you can claim gifts relief to defer the gain until the recipient sells the business. Details of how gifts relief is calculated can be found in Chapter 12.

The principal assets eligible for gifts relief are:

- Business assets (including agricultural property) used in a self-employment or partnership.
- Shares in or assets used by a trading company in which you own at least 5% of the shares.

You have to claim gifts relief in your tax return (see Help sheet IR 295).

Inheritance tax

Providing that you live for seven or more years after transferring your business, there will be no inheritance tax to pay. This kind of transfer made during your lifetime is called a 'potentially exempt transfer' because there potentially may be tax to pay but it all depends on a number of factors.

If you die within seven years of transferring your business, inheritance tax may be due on the transfer depending on its value, any other gifts you have made in the seven-year period and the value of the nil rate band (see Appendix 1). If you are entitled to 100% business or agricultural property relief no inheritance tax will be charged on the potentially exempt transfer (see What happens to your business when you die?). This relief can be jeopardized if the person you give the property to disposes of it before you die or the property ceases to meet the conditions to qualify for the relief. If you are not entitled to 100% business or agricultural property relief, any inheritance tax due on the transfer will be reduced if you live for three or more years after making the gift. If you claimed gifts relief, inheritance tax which becomes due on the gift can be taken into account in working out the gain on an eventual sale of the business.

There are other tax consequences to giving away your business while you are alive depending on whether you operate as a sole trader, partner or company.

- **Sole trader:** If you give away a business you have previously run as a sole trader you will simply pass over some or all of the business assets (including property, equipment, goodwill and stock) and then close down your self-employment. All the income tax considerations relevant to closing down a self-employment will apply to you (see Chapter 13).
- **Partner:** If a partner gives away his or her partnership share and/or capital account, the partnership will continue without needing to be closed down. Where just one partner remains they will operate from then on as a sole trader.
- **Company:** If you are a director/shareholder of a small limited company, you will usually pass control of your business to your heirs by giving away your shares. The company will continue trading.

What happens to my business when I die?

Dying 'in-the-saddle' is something that few business people want to think about but it is vital to plan in advance to minimize inheritance tax and so that your business passes to your chosen successor. This means that you need to make a will (see Making a will).

Dying without a will

If you die intestate (without making a will) your estate will go to your dependants and relatives in accordance with strict rules. This may jeopardize the smooth running of your business and may mean that it has to be sold. It is possible to 'vary' the intestacy within two years of your death by a formal variation (see Appendix 3) so that the estate passes in a different way but everyone who would inherit under the intestacy must agree to it. This is not always easy to achieve.

Running the business until it can be passed on

If you are a sole trader or the sole director/shareholder of a company, when you die there may be no one to run your business. You need to plan for this in advance by appointing suitable executors in your will such as the eventual beneficiary and a solicitor or accountant. If the business has a viable existence without you, the executors will run the business from the date of your death to the date when probate is obtained so that the business can either be sold or passed on in accordance with the instructions in your will. If the business cannot continue without you, the executors will close it down. Either way if you are a sole trader, the business ceases on your death (see Chapter 13). If you are a partner or a director in a larger company, the business will probably continue after you die without the involvement of the executors. They will however need to liaise with the partnership or company to arrange for your capital account or director's loan account to be repaid to your estate. Depending on what is stipulated in any shareholder agreement, they will either sell or retain your shares. The executors are responsible for preparing estate accounts and tax returns for the administration period.

If you have insured your own life the executors will claim on the policy and pass the proceeds to the nominated beneficiaries. If the policy forms part of your estate the proceeds are liable to inheritance tax. If the policy is written in trust, there may be no inheritance tax to pay. If you have an insurance policy written in trust you should review the terms as there have been recent changes in the trusts legislation which could result in unexpected inheritance tax charges. If your spouse, civil partner or business partner has insured your life or your company has 'key-man' insurance, they will also make claims. The tax consequences are covered in Chapter 11.

Capital gains tax

Your business, partnership share or shareholdings have to be valued when you die but this is for the purposes of inheritance tax, not capital gains tax as there is no capital gains tax to pay when you die.

Inheritance tax

If you bequeath everything to your spouse or civil partner (assuming that they are domiciled in the UK) there will be no inheritance tax to pay on your estate. Such a course of action is ineffective for inheritance tax purposes because it does not make use of the nil rate band (see Appendix 1). It is often more tax-efficient to leave a sum equal to the inheritance tax nil rate band to other beneficiaries such as your children and leave everything exceeding the inheritance tax nil rate band to your spouse or civil partner. This course of action also results in there being no inheritance charge but it is not always easy to achieve unless you have suitable assets to give away. In some instances a trust will be advantageous but you will need professional advice.

There will be no inheritance tax to pay on your business and agricultural assets if you are entitled to business property relief or agricultural property relief. If you qualify for these reliefs, you will waste them in most cases if you give or bequeath the business or farm to your spouse or civil partner. It will save inheritance tax to leave it to someone else.

Business property relief

Your self-employed business, a partnership share or shares in an unquoted company may qualify for 100% business property relief. Bequests of partnership assets (property, equipment, goodwill etc.) or assets used by a company which you control, are eligible for 50% business property relief, as are shares in a quoted company which you control.

To qualify for business property relief:

- you must have owned the business, shares or assets throughout the previous two-year period; and
- your business must not be principally concerned with holding investments or dealing in property or shares.

The second prohibition is wider than you may first expect. For example the courts have denied business property relief to some caravan parks and those involved in letting commercial property.

Agricultural property relief

Most agricultural property (including the farmhouse) is entitled to 100% agricultural property relief. The courts sometimes deny relief if they consider that the land is not used for 'agriculture' for example where the farm has diversified. Where agricultural property relief does not apply, business property relief may be due instead.

To qualify for agricultural property relief:

- you must have occupied the property for the purposes of agriculture throughout the previous two years; or
- you must have owned the property for seven years with either you or someone else farming it throughout that period.

Making a will

If you have a business of any kind you should make a will. You will need the services of a solicitor to draft a will which is effective for inheritance tax. Writing your own could result in costly mistakes which your dependants will have to try to resolve at a difficult time in their lives. Having made a will you must then review it at least every couple of years (in case there have been changes in legislation or your business operations) and re-make it if you marry, form a civil partnership or divorce. Should your will turn out to be unsuitable or tax-ineffective for any reason, it can be changed by a formal variation within two years of your death provided that all the beneficiaries agree to the changes (see Appendix 3).

Recap

- Planning for your succession is an emotive subject but many businesses fold because the proprietor has devoted insufficient time to planning their succession and ensuring that the business qualifies for business or agricultural property relief.
- A regularly reviewed will and professional advice are essential.

16

putting it all together

In this chapter:
- tax in the early years of a new business
- important dates and forms
- avoiding pitfalls

You have now looked at all the different taxes that affect a small business from formation to closure and you should have an understanding of how the UK tax system operates. If you are planning a new venture, you should appreciate that your tax will differ depending on whether you trade as a sole trader or limited company. If you are already running a small business, you will have considered the tax consequences of major investments such as buying equipment and taking on employees.

This chapter brings together many of the themes in the book as a case study. It highlights how tax affects a small business as it develops, which forms have to be completed and how to avoid costly mistakes.

Nina's Kitchen

Meet Nina, she used to work as a PR consultant but left her job 18 months ago when she had her first baby. She is a keen cook and enjoys making chutneys and pickles which she gives away to friends and family. Recently they have been asking her for extra jars and even paying her for them. In June 2006 Nina took a stall at a local farmers' market and sold almost all her jars of chutney, taking £500. Last week she had a stall at a craft fair and sold another £300 worth of stock. Inspired by her success she approached some local shops and now has orders for a further 500 jars which she plans to make over the coming month.

Starting to trade

Until Nina started selling her chutneys and pickles to the public she was not trading. Even when she was occasionally paid for a jar of her condiments, she simply had a cookery hobby. Now she is trading more regularly what was once a hobby has become a business. Like many small business people, Nina has been rather overtaken by events and she has probably become a self-employed business even though this was not necessarily her original intention. Irrespective of what she intends to do with the business at a later date, she must notify HM Revenue and Customs within three months of the date she started to be self-employed (probably when she went to the farmers' market in June 2006).

Pitfall: If she fails to notify the tax authorities she could be fined £100.

Nina completes HM Revenue and Customs form CWF1 'Becoming self-employed and registering for National Insurance Contributions and/or tax' which can be downloaded from **www.hmrc.gov.uk/startingup/register.htm** or completed by calling the Self-Employed Registration Helpline on 08459 154515.

Refer to Chapter 4 for further information.

Getting organized

Since we last met up with Nina she has made sure that she complies with all the necessary planning and hygiene rules laid down by her local authority and she has taken out public and product liability insurance. She has also started to keep records on a computer spreadsheet recording her income and expenses. She files all her receipts in a box file in case she or the tax authorities need to refer to them at a later date.

Nina decides not to register for VAT because she is unsure how long she will be running the business for. She decides to pay Class 2 National Insurance and not to opt for a small earnings exception to preserve her state pension entitlement.

Nina and her husband who is employed as an engineer earning £25,000 a year claim Child Tax Credit, so she informs HM Revenue and Customs about her new business. As the couple receive only the family element of the award their claim is not affected at this stage.

Refer to Chapters 3 and 4 for further information.

Buying new equipment

Nina is finding it increasingly difficult to transport her produce in her small hatchback car so she decides to exchange it for a larger estate model. In November 2006 she buys a second-hand vehicle costing £6,000. She trades-in her old car for £2,000 and she finances the balance with a bank loan repayable over three years. Nina also buys a new fridge for her business at a cost of £550. She makes a note to claim capital allowances on these items (see Claiming capital allowances)

Refer to Chapter 7 for further information.

Tax return time

Nina has now been in business for a year. She has been sent her first tax return to complete. Nina needs to decide on a suitable date to prepare her first accounts to. She is tempted to prepare them for a year to 31 May 2007 but in the end decides to keep her affairs simple by preparing accounts for the ten-month period 1 June 2006 to 31 March 2007.

Refer to Chapter 5 for further information.

Nina's accounting spreadsheet shows the following totals:

1 June 2006–31 March 2007	£
Sales	14,400
Jars and labels	−1,500
Ingredients	−2,800
Fridge	−550
Stall hire and entry fees	−650
Insurance	−300
Telephone	−420
Car costs	−5,400
Computer, office and administration	−525
Bank charges	−85
Advertising	−330
Car loan	−705
Nina	−5,000

Stock

Unfortunately Nina forgot to count her stock of chutneys and pickles on 31 March 2007 because she did not know that she would use that date as her accounting year end. She therefore counts the unsold chutney at 31 May and finds that she has 500 jars in stock. Nina works out that she made 700 jars of chutney and sold 600 of them in April and May so she must have had 400 jars in stock at her year end. She sells each jar for £4 and she estimates that each one costs £1 to make. She values her stock at cost as this is less than the sales price, so her stock of finished produce is £400. Nina also works out that she took delivery of a new consignment of empty jars shortly before her year end at a cost of £420. Her total stock is therefore £820.

Adjusting the accounting records for tax purposes

Nina examines her accounting records in more detail and finds that:

- Her insurance policy expires in August 2007. She therefore deducts £125 from her costs because five months' worth of the costs relate to the next tax year (£300 × 5 months/12 months).
- She receives a phone bill in April which relates to her previous accounting year so she includes a further £70 of telephone costs.
- Nina realizes that her car costs include both her vehicle running costs of £1,400 and the cost of buying the new car, i.e. £4,000. The car itself cannot be written off in the year in which she buys it because it is a capital purchase. Capital allowances can be claimed instead. Nina works out that she has used the vehicle 60% of the time for work purposes and 40% of the time for private journeys. She therefore reduces her car running costs by £560 (£1,400 × 40% = £560).
- Nina's car loan includes loan repayments of £555 and interest of £150. Nina realizes that she cannot claim a tax deduction for the loan repayments because this is also capital expenditure.
- Nina takes £500 each month from the business for her personal expenditure. These sums are her drawings and she cannot claim tax relief on them. She also takes one jar of chutney each week for personal use. She therefore adjusts her accounts by £172 (43 weeks at £4 per jar) for these items.

Refer to Chapter 5 for further information.

Use of home allowance

Nina works from home. She has not yet included anything in her accounting records for her home costs even though her gas and electricity bills have increased since she has been in business. Nina estimates that her costs of working from home are £5 per week (£215 for the 10 months). She decides not to include a deduction for part of the mortgage because she does not want to jeopardize the capital gains tax exemption on the family home.

Refer to Chapter 9 for further information.

Claiming capital allowances

Nina's accounting records include three items of capital expenditure:

- The new car costing £6,000;
- The sale of the old car for £2,000 (it was worth £2,400 when she started the business); and
- A fridge costing £550.

Nina also realizes that she now uses many items of kitchen equipment in the business (pans, funnels, food processor etc.) which she owned before she started trading. She values these at £500 and she works out her capital allowances as follows:

Description	Equipment (£)	Cars (60% business (£)	Private use (£)	Allowances (£)
Assets introduced	500	2,400		
Writing down allowance – 25% × 10 months/ 12 months	−104			104
Disposal of car		−2,000		
Balancing allowance		−400	160	240
Additions	550	6,000		
First year allowance: 50%	−275			275
Writing down allowance: 25% × 10 months/ 12 months		−1,250	500	750
Value carried forward to next accounting period	671	4,750		
Capital allowances				1,369

Refer to Chapter 7 and Appendix 1 for further information.

Income and expenditure

Nina now prepares her income and expenditure account on page SE2 of the self-employment pages of the tax return.

Income and expenditure 2006/07	Disallowable expenses (£)	Total expenses (£)	Calculations
Income		14,400	
Cost of sales		–3,480	Purchase of jars, labels and ingredients £1,500 + £2,800 – Closing stock £820
Gross profit		10,920	
Premises costs		–865	Stall hire £650 + use of home allowance £215
General administrative expenses		–1,190	Insurance £175 (£300 – paid in advance £125) + telephone £490 (£420 + bill received after the year end £70) + computer, office and administration costs £525 = £1,190
Motor expenses	560	–1,400	Motor expenses £1,400 – disallowable private use £500
Advertising and entertainment		–330	
Interest		–150	Loan interest not capital repayments
Finance charges		–85	Bank charges
Net profit		**6,900**	
Disallowable expenses		560	Private motor expenses
Goods taken for private use		172	
Capital allowances		–1,369	See capital allowance calculation
Taxable profit		**6,263**	Amount on which Nina pays income tax

Nina's sales are more than £15,000 per annum even though they are less than £15,000 for the ten-month accounting period. She cannot therefore enter just three numbers on page SE1 of the tax return and instead she must complete page SE2.

Refer to Chapter 5 for further information.

Balance sheet

In addition to an income and expenditure account, the tax return includes an optional balance sheet on page SE4. Nina completes this as follows:

At 31 March 2007	£	Comments
Assets		
Plant, machinery and motor vehicles	7,050	Car £6,000 + fridge £550 + introduced kitchen equipment £500
Stock	820	Closing stock
Prepayments	125	Insurance paid in advance
Bank balance	135	From Nina's accounting records
	8,130	
Liabilities		
Accruals	–70	Telephone bill received in April 2007
Loan	–3,445	Car loan £4,000 – £555 repaid = £3,445
Net business assets	**4,615**	
Capital account		
Net profit	6,900	See income and expenditure account
Capital introduced	2,715	Car £2,000 + equipment £500 + use of home £215 = £2,715
Drawings	–5,000	
Balance at end of accounting period	**4,615**	This figure must be the same as 'Net business assets'.

For further information about balance sheets, see *Teach Yourself Small Business Accounting*.

Working out the tax liability

Nina checks through her tax return and as she has no other sources of income and no other deductions to claim, she can now work out how much income tax she owes on her taxable profit.

Income tax liability 2006/07	£	£
Taxable profit		6,263
Personal allowance		−5,035
Income subject to income tax		**1,228**
Starting rate: 10%	1,228	122.80
Class 4 National Insurance: £1,228 × 8%		98.24
Nina's total income tax and Class 4 National Insurance		**221.04**

Refer to Chapters 2 and 5 for further information.

Submitting the tax return

Nina submits her tax return on 31 July 2007. As this is before 30 September 2007 HM Revenue and Customs will work out her tax liability and confirm Nina's calculation.

Pitfall: If Nina fails to submit her tax return by 31 January 2008 she will incur a fine of £100.

Refer to Chapter 3 and Appendix 2 for further information.

Paying the tax

Nina pays her income tax and Class 4 National Insurance on 11 January 2008. This is before the due date of 31 January 2008 so she avoids paying interest.

Nina is pleased to see that she does not need to pay any tax on account of her potential tax liability for 2007/08 because her total tax bill for 2006/07 is less than £500.

Refer to Chapter 3 and Appendix 2 for further information.

Moving on

We now catch up with Nina at the beginning of April 2008. She has just counted her stock so that she can prepare accurate accounts for the year to 31 March 2008 in due course. Her business is thriving thanks to good PR and she has just signed a contract to supply three spicy chutneys to a well-known food emporium for their Christmas 2008 range. As she will have to increase production significantly to meet the new order, she decides to rent a unit on an industrial estate at a cost of £6,000 a year. She spends £10,000 on kitchen units, appliances and equipment which she finances with a further bank loan.

Nina will be able to claim a tax deduction for the rent, business and water rates, power, insurance and security. She will be able to claim plant and machinery capital allowances on the cost of fitting out the unit provided that the individual items qualify as either plant or machinery.

Refer to Chapters 7 and 9 for further information.

Taking on staff

Nina needs to take on staff to fulfil her Christmas order so she recruits a cook, two part-time assistants and an office administrator to process orders and deliveries. Each member of staff is paid a basic salary of more than the National Minimum Wage with the promise of a bonus when the order is fulfilled. Nina decides to use an agency to administer her payroll and pay her employees each month.

Nina obtains a form P45 from three of the employees and sends these to the agency together with their pay and bank details. One assistant cook does not have a P45 so Nina asks her to complete a form P46 instead.

At the end of the month, the agency produces payslips for each employee and tells Nina how much to pay them. They also inform her how much PAYE and Class 1 employee's and employer's National Insurance to pay to HM Revenue and Customs by the 19th of the following month.

Nina will obtain a tax deduction for the employees' gross salaries and employer's National Insurance. She can also claim a tax deduction for the cost of recruiting the employees and the payroll agency fees.

Refer to Chapters 5 and 8 and Appendix 2 for further information.

VAT registration

Nina's sales have not yet reached the VAT registration threshold but she knows that they will do so within the next few months when she invoices her Christmas sales. She therefore decides to register for VAT voluntarily from 1 July 2008.

> Nina completes HM Revenue and Customs form VAT 1 online which she accesses from the VAT Online Registration Service by following the links from **www.hmrc.gov.uk/** 'VAT'. Nina reads the literature and checks with the National Advice Service on 0845 010 9000 that chutney is a zero-rate supply because it is food.

Nina learns that because all her sales are zero-rated that she will be entitled to VAT repayments, as a result there is no benefit to her to join either the cash or annual accounting schemes. She also belatedly realizes that she could have registered for VAT when she started her business and reclaimed the VAT on her purchases but she is not too dismayed when she realizes that she can reclaim the VAT on items she still owns back to the date she started in business because it was less than three years ago. She therefore makes a list of all her kitchen equipment and stock on hand at 1 July 2008. She locates the original invoices so she can include the items on her first VAT return.

Nina alters the way that she keeps her accounting records. She now needs to make additional entries to record the VAT on her purchases.

Refer to Chapter 10 for further information.

Completing the second tax return

Nina has not yet completed her tax return for the year to 5 April 2008. If she wants HM Revenue and Customs to calculate her tax bill, she must send in the form by 30 September. She therefore prepares her accounts to 31 March 2008 and enters the details on the form. The entries are similar to the previous year. Nina is pleased to see that her profit has nearly doubled but she is concerned about how much tax she will owe.

In due course HM Revenue and Customs inform her that she owes income tax and Class 4 National insurance for 2007/08 of £1,360. All the tax is due on 31 January 2009. She also learns that because this liability is more than £500, she has to pay the same sum again as two payments on account for the tax year 2008/09 (£680 on 31 January 2009 and £680 on 31 July 2009). As Nina needs to pay tax of £2,040 on 31 January 2009 (£1,360 + £680) she mentally notes that when she is paid for her Christmas orders she must put some of it aside to pay the tax before she takes extra drawings.

Refer to Chapters 3 and 5 and Appendix 2 for further information.

Completing the first VAT return

Nina asked HM Revenue and Customs to allocate her VAT returns for calendar quarters so that they coincide with her accounting year end. Her first VAT return is due for the three-month period 1 July 2008–30 September 2008 and must be submitted by 31 October 2008. During the first week of October, she completes the return online and is pleased with the refund she is owed.

Refer to Chapter 10 for further information.

Rewarding staff

By the end of October Nina's Kitchen has fulfilled its Christmas orders and as promised Nina pays her staff a bonus. She tells the payroll agency how much to add to their usual pay. They calculate how much PAYE and National Insurance must be deducted and tell Nina how much extra to pay each employee.

Pitfall: Nina has forgotten that she would have to pay employer's National Insurance on top of the bonuses. As a result it costs her more than she anticipated. She can however deduct the bonuses and employer's National Insurance as a business expense.

Nina takes her employees out for a seasonal meal to thank them for their hard work. The bill for the evening comes to £300. As this is less than £150 per head, Nina can deduct these costs as a business expense and there is no tax to pay on the perk.

Refer to Chapters 5 and 8 for further information.

We next meet Nina in late April 2009. Her business is still thriving. She has a repeat order for Christmas 2009 from the food emporium and now makes regular sales to two large department stores. She is also planning a range of anti-pasti.

Completing employer end of year returns

Nina has to file an employer end of year return this year consisting of a form P35 and a form P14 for each member of staff. The payroll agency completes the forms for her and she issues her employees with forms P60 showing the details of their pay, tax and National Insurance before the end of May. None of her employees has received any perks so she does not complete forms P11D and P9D.

Refer to Chapter 8 and Appendix 2 for further information.

PAYE inspection

In July 2009 HM Revenue and Customs come to inspect Nina's PAYE records. She obtains monthly printouts from the payroll agency which she makes available to the officer. He discusses her business operations and checks her bank payments. He tells her that she should have reported details of the office expenses she reimburses to her administrator on a form P11D because she does not have a dispensation in force. Nina therefore completes the form P11DX 'Dispensation of expenses payments and benefits in kind' to apply for a dispensation so that she does not have to report non-taxable benefits in kind in the future.

Refer to Chapter 8 for further information.

Completing the third tax return

Nina completes her third tax return to 5 April 2009 in August 2009. Apart from the fact that her profits have increased significantly, she has no further difficulties with the numbers. She wonders whether she can obtain a tax deduction for some of her childcare costs but learns that her own childcare costs are not a tax-deductible expense.

HM Revenue and Customs advise Nina that she owes a balancing tax payment for 2008/09 of £5,200 after deducting the two payments of £680 she paid on account. This tax is due to be paid on 31 January 2010. In addition Nina owes payments on account for 2009/10 of £3,280 per instalment, making her 31 January 2010 payment a total of £8,480.

Nina and her husband renew their tax credit claim. They discover that their claim will be significantly reduced for 2009/10 because of Nina's higher income.

Refer to Chapters 3, 4 and 5 and Appendix 2 for further information.

Paying a pension

Nina is concerned about her rising profits and increased tax bills. She has read that paying into a pension can save tax, so she consults a financial adviser who recommends that she starts paying £250 per month into a pension. Nina is pleased to learn that she only has to pay the pension company £195 each month and that they reclaim £55 per month from the tax authorities and pay it into her pension.

Refer to Chapter 11 for further information.

Paying a sick employee

In September 2009 Nina's cook falls ill and she has to pay her part-time assistants to cover his work. She notifies the payroll agency of the changes to her employees' pay and her cook's sickness. They calculate how much statutory sick pay (SSP) he must be paid and work out how much of the SSP Nina can recover against the monthly PAYE and National Insurance she pays to HM Revenue and Customs.

Refer to Chapter 8 and Appendices 1 and 2 for further information.

Loss

We meet Nina again in March 2010. Things have not been going well for her. Her new anti-pasti range has not been the success she hoped for and an expensive advertising campaign in a gourmet food magazine produced no new customers. She calculates that she has made a loss of £6,000 and is keen to submit her tax return to 5 April 2010 as quickly as possible to claim tax relief for it. First of all she needs to reduce the tax she is paying on account so that she does not have to pay income tax of £3,280 on 31 July 2010. She does this by completing form SA 303.

Nina sees that she has two possible ways to get tax relief for her loss:

- As the loss is in the fourth tax year of her business (2009/10), she can claim relief against her income of the three previous tax years but she must claim it against the earliest year first (2006/07).
- Alternatively, she can claim the loss against her profits for the previous tax year (2008/09).

In 2006/07 Nina's profits were only £6,263 and her tax bill £221.04. She will waste her personal allowance to claim the loss against this year and she will only receive a tax refund of £221.04 because that is all the tax she paid in that year. She will therefore choose to use the loss against her income of the previous tax year 2008/09 by making a 'Section 380 claim'. This will probably give her a tax refund of £1,800.

Refer to Chapters 3 and 6 for further information.

Completing the fourth tax return

Nina completes her fourth tax return to 5 April 2010 in May 2010. Her loss must be entered in the box 'Loss – relief to be calculated by reference to earlier years' on page SE3. Nina must also provide details of the claim she is making in the additional information box on the form (page SE4). HM Revenue and Customs will then refund the tax from 2008/09. Nina will also receive a tax refund for 2009/10. The £3,280 she paid on account of her tax liabilities for 2009/10 on 31 January 2010 will be returned to her as she owes no tax at all for that year.

Nina also has to enter details of her pension on the tax return this year. As she has made a loss there is no further tax relief to claim. Her annual contributions are less than £3,600, so are within the permitted limits in spite of the loss.

Once again Nina and her husband renew their tax credit claim. They are pleased to discover that due to Nina's losses, their original claim is restored and in addition they receive an extra payment for 2009/10.

Refer to Chapters 3, 4, 6 and 11 for further information.

Where next?

It is time to leave Nina. Her business has now been running for nearly five years and like many new ventures she has had her share of misfortune. During this time Nina has developed a basic knowledge of tax and business. With a reliable customer base she could continue running her self-employment for many years. She may alternatively consider expansion and incorporation, selling the business or closing it down. Whatever the future holds for Nina's Kitchen, Nina is now aware of the tax consequences that can occur at each stage in the development of her business.

appendix 1: rates and allowances

The following tables summarize the tax rates, allowances and thresholds for the 2006/07 tax year (6 April 2006 to 5 April 2007) referred to throughout the book. Where figures have already been announced for later tax years these are also provided.

Annual changes

Many of the allowances and thresholds change each year so if you are reading this book in 2008 and want to make tax calculations for 2007/08 (or a subsequent tax year) you will need to update the figures. There are three blank columns for the years 2007/08, 2008/09 and 2009/10 to enable you to do this. Most of the numbers do not change dramatically from year to year unless a particular tax is radically overhauled, there is a change of government or a need to raise more tax. Generally allowances and thresholds rise annually by the rate of inflation or the increase in earnings. Tax rates change less often and they frequently stay the same for many years.

Updating the tables

The annual increases in personal allowances and National Insurance are first announced in the Chancellor's autumn Budget statement. All other rates, allowances and thresholds are given in the spring Budget. National newspapers often print details of these or they can be accessed from HM Revenue and Customs website under 'Budget – rates and allowances'. The document summarizing the autumn rate and allowance changes is usually called PN2 (Pre-Budget Note 2); the spring document is called BN2 (Budget Note 2).

Once you have located the new rates, allowances and thresholds
for the relevant tax year, you should enter the numbers in the
grid supplied and use them in your calculations.

Income tax

Rates

Income is taxed at different rates according to whether it is:

- Dividend income;
- Interest; or
- Another source of income such as self-employed and
  partnership profits, employed earnings or rental income.

There are three rates of tax applicable to each source of income
and these are applied to a slice or band of your taxable income
(that is income after deducting personal allowances and other
reliefs such as losses). If you have multiple sources of income
including dividends and interest, the dividends are treated as if
they are the top slice, then interest as the next slice and finally
all the other sources. It is therefore possible for you to pay tax
at five different tax rates: 10%, 20%, 22%, 32.5% and 40%.

Income bands

	2006/07	2007/08	2008/09	2009/10
Income band	£	£	£	£
Band 1 (starting rate)	0–2,150			
Band 2 (basic rate)	2,151–33,300			
Band 3 (higher rate)	Over 33,300			

The rate bands change annually and can be updated from
www.hmrc.gov.uk/rates/it.htm.

You now need to look up the rate of income tax which
corresponds to Band 1, 2 and 3. The tax rates depend on the
type of income you receive.

Self-employed and partnership profits, employed earnings, rental income

	2006/07	2007/08	2008/09	2009/10
Income band	%	%	%	%
Band 1 (starting rate)	10			
Band 2 (basic rate)	22			
Band 3 (higher rate)	40			

Interest

	2006/07	2007/08	2008/09	2009/10
Income band	%	%	%	%
Band 1 (starting rate)	10			
Band 2 (basic rate)	20			
Band 3 (higher rate)	40			

Dividends

	2006/07	2007/08	2008/09	2009/10
Income band	%	%	%	%
Band 1 (lower dividend rate)	10			
Band 2 (lower dividend rate)	10			
Band 3 (upper dividend rate)	32.5			

Personal allowances

Every UK citizen including children and some people from overseas are eligible for a personal allowance. Higher allowances are paid to those who are aged 65 and over and aged 75 or more but the allowances are reduced if your income exceeds an income limit. The allowance cannot be reduced to less than the personal allowance given to those aged under 65.

Married couples and those in civil partnerships born before 6 April 1935 are eligible for the married couple's allowance. This allowance is reduced where your income exceeds the income limit but it cannot be reduced to less than a stated minimum. The allowance is usually given to the husband or partner with the higher income but can be claimed by a wife or the other civil partner, or shared equally.

	2006/07	2007/08	2008/09	2009/10
Description of the allowance	£	£	£	£
Personal allowance (aged under 65)	5,035			
Personal allowance (aged 65–74 depending on your income, see income limit)	7,280			
Personal allowance (aged 75 and over depending on your income, see income limit)	7,420			
Blind person's allowance	1,660			
Married couple's allowance (born before 6 April 1935, aged under 75 and depending on your income, see income limit)	6,065			
Married couple's allowance (born before 6 April 1935, aged 75 and over and depending on your income, see income limit)	6,135			
Married couple's allowance (born before 6 April 1935 minimum amount irrespective of your income)	2,350			
Income limit for age-dependent personal allowances and the married couple's allowance	20,100			

Personal allowances are deducted from your income before you pay tax. This means that they save you tax at the highest rate you pay. The basic personal allowance will therefore save a 22% taxpayer £1,107.70 (£5,035 × 22%) and a 40% taxpayer £2,014 (£5,035 × 40%). The married couple's allowance only saves you tax at the 10% rate of tax, so for those born before 6 April 1935 and aged under 75, it is worth a maximum tax saving of £606.50 (£6,065 × 10%).

Personal allowances change annually and can be updated from **www.hmrc.gov.uk/rates/it.htm**.

Enterprise Investment Scheme (EIS)

	2006/07	**2007/08**	**2008/09**	**2009/10**
Maximum investment	£400,000			
Rate of tax relief	20%			
Share-holding period	3 years			

These figures may not necessarily change each year. For further information see Chapters 4, 12, and 14 and **www.hmrc.gov.uk/ eis/eis-index.htm**.

Capital gains tax – individuals

Rates

Capital gains tax is charged at three rates. Each rate is applied to the gain based on a slice or band of taxable income including your capital gains. The gains (after deducting losses, reliefs and the annual exemption) are treated as if they are the top slice of your income. This means that if you pay 40% tax on your income you will pay 40% tax on any gains. If you pay basic rate tax on your income you will pay 20% capital gains tax (not 22%), unless the gains take your total income and gains into the 40% tax band.

	2006/07	2007/08	2008/09	2009/10
Band of income and gains	£	£	£	£
Band 1	0–2,150			
Band 2	2,151–33,300			
Band 3	Over 33,300			

The capital gains tax rate corresponding to each band is shown in the following table.

	2006/07	2007/08	2008/09	2009/10
Capital gains tax band	%	%	%	%
Band 1 (starting rate)	10			
Band 2 (lower rate)	20			
Band 3 (higher rate)	40			

This table can be updated from **www.hmrc.gov.uk/rates/cgt.htm**. Details of the indexation allowance are also shown here. You can claim indexation allowance on the cost of an asset bought before 5 April 1998 but only up to that date. From 6 April 1998 you can claim taper relief (see Chapter 2).

Annual exemption

The annual exemption is the capital gains tax equivalent of the income tax personal allowance. It is deducted from your gains before the tax is calculated.

	2006/07	2007/08	2008/09	2009/10
Annual exemption	£	£	£	£
Individuals	8,800			

This table can be updated by referring to **www.hmrc.gov.uk/ rates/cgt.htm**.

Taper relief on business assets disposed of after 5 April 2002

Taper relief reduces your gains from 6 April 1998. There are different rates for business assets and non-business assets. Different rates of business asset taper relief applied to disposals of business assets before 6 April 2002 and before 6 April 2000. Taper relief is unlikely to change each year but you should check the tables printed in Help sheet IR279.

Tax year	Number of whole years asset held for	% reduction	% chargeable
2006/07	0	0	100
	1	50	50
	2 or more	75	25
2007/08	0		
	1		
	2 or more		
2008/09	0		
	1		
	2 or more		
2009/10	0		
	1		
	2 or more		

Taper relief on disposals of non-business assets made after 5 April 1998

Tax year	Number of whole years asset held for from the date of acquistion or 5 April 1998 if later	% reduction	% chargeable
2006/07	0	0	100
	1	0	100
	2	0	100
	3	5	95
	4	10	90
	5	15	85
	6	20	80
	7	25	75
	8	30	70
	9	35	65
	10 or more	40	60
2007/08	0		
	1		
	2		
	3		
	4		
	5		
	6		
	7		
	8		
	9		
	10 or more		

Tax year	Number of whole years asset held for from the date of acquistion or 5 April 1998 if later	% reduction	% chargeable
2008/09	0		
	1		
	2		
	3		
	4		
	5		
	6		
	7		
	8		
	9		
	10 or more		
2009/10	0		
	1		
	2		
	3		
	4		
	5		
	6		
	7		
	8		
	9		
	10 or more		

Capital gains tax – companies

Companies pay capital gains tax as part of their corporation tax bill. They are not entitled to an annual exemption or taper relief. Gains are added to the company's profits and they are taxed at the corporation tax rates. A company's gains can be reduced by indexation allowance (see Chapter 2). The tables are published by HM Revenue and Customs and are available on **www.hmrc.gov.uk/rates/c_gains_subject_c_tax.htm**.

Corporation tax

Rates and thresholds

Company profits are taxed at one of two rates depending on whether the company qualifies as a small company because it has profits below the stated threshold. Marginal relief eases the transition between the small companies' rate of corporation tax and the main rate.

Financial Year	2006 – year ending 31 March 2007	2007 – year ending 31 March 2008	2008 – year ending 31 March 2009	2009 – year ending 31 March 2010
Small companies' rate	19%			
Small companies' threshold	£0–£300,000			
Marginal relief band	£300,001–£1,500,000			
Marginal relief fraction	11/400			
Main rate	30%			
Main rate threshold	£1,500,001 and above			

This table can be updated by referring to **www.hmrc.gov.uk/rates/corp.htm**.

Inheritance tax

No inheritance tax is charged if the value of your estate is below the level of the nil rate band. Above this limit inheritance tax on death is charged at 40%. The nil rate bands have already been announced for tax years up to and including 2009/10.

	2006/07	2007/08	2008/09	2009/10
Tax percentage	**£**	**£**	**£**	**£**
0% (nil rate band)	Up to £285,000	Up to £300,000	Up to £312,000	Up to £325,000
40% (charged on death)	Over £285,000	Over £300,000	Over £312,000	Over £325,000

National Insurance

As outlined in Chapter 2, National Insurance is divided into four classes.

Class 1

	2006/07	2007/08	2008/09	2009/10
	Per week £	**Per week £**	**Per week £**	**Per week £**
Lower earnings limit (LEL)	84			
Upper earnings limit (UEL)	645			
Employee's threshold (FT)	97			
Employer's limit	97			

	2006/07	2007/08	2008/09	2009/10
Employees	%	%	%	%
Under employee's threshold	0			
Between employee's threshold and upper earnings limits	11			
Above upper earnings limit	1			
S2P contracted out rebate	1.6			
Married women's reduced rate (Note 1)				
Under employee's threshold	0			
Between employee's threshold and upper earnings limits	4.85			
Above upper earnings limit	1			
Employers (Note 2)				
Under employer's limit	0			
Above employer's limit	12.8			
S2P contracted out rebate – salary schemes	3.5			
S2P contracted out rebate – money-purchase schemes	1			

Note 1: Available only to women married before 6 April 1977 making the required election and who have not subsequently divorced.

Note 2: Including Classes 1A and 1B National Insurance.

Class 2

	2006/07	2007/08	2008/09	2009/10
Weekly rates	£	£	£	£
Class 2 contributions	2.10			
Share fishermen	2.75			
Volunteer development workers	4.20			
Annual threshold				
Small earnings exception	4,465			

Class 3

	2006/07	2007/08	2008/09	2009/10
Weekly rates	£	£	£	£
Class 3 contributions	7.55			

Class 4

	2006/07	2007/08	2008/09	2009/10
	Per year £	Per year £	Per year £	Per year £
Lower profit limit	5,035			
Upper profit limit	33,540			

	2006/07	2007/08	2008/09	2009/10
Annual profits or gains	%	%	%	%
Less than lower limit	0			
Between lower and upper limit	8			
Above upper limit	1			

These tables can be updated by referring to **www.hmrc.gov.uk/rates/nic.htm**.

VAT

For further information about VAT see Chapter 10. These tables can be updated from 'Introduction to VAT' available on HMRC's website – follow the links from 'VAT'.

Rate

From	1 April 2006	1 April 2007	1 April 2008	1 April 2009
	%	%	%	%
Standard	17.5			
Reduced	5			
Zero	0			

Annual turnover thresholds

From	1 April 2006	1 April 2007	1 April 2008	1 April 2009
	£	£	£	£
Registration	61,000			
De-registration	59,000			
Annual accounting – joining	1,350,000			
Annual accounting – leaving	1,600,000			
Cash accounting – joining	660,000			
Cash accounting – leaving	825,000			
Flat-rate scheme – joining	150,000			
Flat-rate scheme – leaving	225,000			

Car fuel scale charges

From	1 May 2006	1 May 2007	1 May 2008	1 May 2009
Diesel cars				
12-month period	£	£	£	£
1400–2000cc – scale	1,040.00			
1400–2000cc – VAT per car	154.89			
2001cc or more – scale	1,325.00			
2001cc or more – VAT per car	197.34			
3 month poriod				
1400–2000cc – scale	260.00			
1400–2000cc – VAT per car	38.72			
2001cc or more – scale	331.00			
2001cc or more – VAT per car	49.30			
1-month period				
1400–2000cc – scale	86.00			
1400–2000cc – VAT per car	12.81			
2001cc or more – scale	110.00			
2001cc or more – VAT por oar	16.38			

From	1 May 2006	1 May 2007	1 May 2008	1 May 2009
All non-diesel cars				
12-month period	£	£	£	£
1400cc or less – scale	1,095.00			
1400cc or less – VAT per car	163.09			
1400–2000cc – scale	1,385.00			
1400–2000cc – VAT per car	206.28			
2001cc or more – scale	2,035.00			
2001cc or more – VAT per car	303.09			
3-month period				
1400cc or less – scale	273.00			
1400cc or less – VAT per car	40.66			
1400–2000cc – scale	346.00			
1400–2000cc – VAT per car	51.53			
2001cc or more – scale	508.00			
2001cc or more – VAT per car	75.66			
1-month period				
1400cc or less – scale	91.00			
1400cc or less – VAT per car	13.55			
1400–2000cc – scale	115.00			
1400–2000cc – VAT per car	17.13			
2001cc or more – scale	169.00			
2001cc or more – VAT per car	25.17			

Stamp duties

Stamp duty land tax on property

For further information see Chapter 9. The tables can be updated from **www.hmrc.gov.uk/so/current_sdlt_rates.htm**.

Rate bands	2006/07	2007/08	2008/09	2009/10
Purchase price including VAT	%	%	%	%
Residential				
Band 1 *(Note 1)*	£0–£125,000			
Band 2 *(Note 1)*	£125,001–£250,000			
Band 3	£250,000–£500,000			
Band 4	Over £500,000			
Commercial				
Band 1	£0–£150,000			
Band 2	£150,001–£250,000			
Band 3	£250,000–£500,000			
Band 4	Over £500,000			

Note 1: The limit is £150,000 instead of £125,000 for residential property in specified deprived areas.

Now look up the tax rates which apply to each band in the following table.

Rates	2006/07	2007/08	2008/09	2009/10
Purchase price including VAT	%	%	%	%
Residential				
Band 1	0			
Band 2	1			
Band 3	3			
Band 4	4			
Commercial				
Band 1	0			
Band 2	1			
Band 3	3			
Band 4	4			

Leases

Broadly, stamp duty land tax is charged on 1% of the discounted rental value over the lease term where it exceeds the upper limit in Band 1.

Other stamp duties

Rate	2006/07 %	2007/08 %	2008/09 %	2009/10 %
Stocks and shares	0.5			
Stamp duty reserve tax	0.5			

Capital allowances

For details of the conditions applicable to each allowance see Chapter 7 (Table 1) and Chapter 9. These allowances do not always change from year to year. The allowances most likely to change are first year allowances. For energy-efficient, environmentally beneficial and water-saving plant and green cars see **www.eca.gov.uk**.

Type of allowance	2006/07 %	2007/08 %	2008/09 %	2009/10 %
First year – small businesses	50	40		
First year – medium-sized businesses	40			
Writing down	25			
Energy-efficient	100			
Environmentally-beneficial	100			
Green cars	100	100	0	0
Water-saving	100			
Industrial buildings	4			
Agricultural buildings	4			
Flat conversion	100			
Enterprise Zone	100			

Employers

For further details see Chapter 8. The following tables can be updated from www.hmrc.gov.uk/employers/rates_and_limits. htm.

Statutory Sick Pay (SSP)

	2006/07 %	2007/08 %	2008/09 %	2009/10 %
Weekly rate	£70.05			
Weekly earnings threshold	£84			
Recovery percentage	13%			

Statutory Maternity Pay (SMP)

	2006/07 %	2007/08 %	2008/09 %	2009/10 %
Weekly rate – first 6 weeks	90% of pay			
Weekly rate – next 20 weeks	£108.85 or 90% of pay if lower			
Weekly earnings threshold	£84			
Recovery threshold	£45,000			
Recovery percentage – NIC under threshold	100%			
Compensation rate – NIC under threshold	4.5%			
Recovery percentage – NIC over threshold	92%			

Statutory Paternity Pay (SPP)

	2006/07 %	2007/08 %	2008/09 %	2009/10 %
Weekly rate	£108.85 or 90% of pay if lower			
Weekly earnings threshold	£84			
Recovery threshold	£45,000			
Recovery percentage – NIC under threshold	100%			
Compensation rate – NIC under threshold	4.5%			
Recovery percentage – NIC over threshold	92%			

Statutory Adoption Pay (SAP)

	2006/07 %	2007/08 %	2008/09 %	2009/10 %
Weekly rate	£108.85 or 90% of pay if lower			
Weekly earnings threshold	£84			
Recovery threshold	£45,000			
Recovery percentage – NIC under threshold	100%			
Compensation rate – NIC under threshold	4.5%			
Recovery percentage – NIC over threshold	92%			

National Minimum Wage

	From 1 October 2006	From 1 October 2007	From 1 October 2008	From 1 October 2009	From 1 October 2010
Hourly rate	£	£	£	£	£
Adults (*Note 1*)	5.35				
18-21 year olds (*Note 2*)	4.45				
16 and 17 year olds (*Note 3*)	3.00				

Note 1: Aged 22 years and older.

Note 2: Including adults attending approved training courses.

Note 3: 16 year olds who are no longer of compulsory school age.

Student loan repayments

	2006/07	2007/08	2008/09	2009/10
Earnings threshold	£15,000			
Percentange repaid	9%			

Repayment is at the percentage specified once a student's earnings reach the earnings threshold.

Company cars

For further information see Chapter 8. To update the table see **www.hmrc.gov.uk/cars/** and **www.hmrc.gov.uk/rates/travel.htm**.

CO$_2$ Emissions in grams per kilometre (gm/km)

2006/07	2007/08	2008/09	2009/10	Percentage of car's price taxed
–	–	120		10*
140	140	135		15*
145	145	140		16*
150	150	145		17*
155	155	150		18*
160	160	155		19*
165	165	160		20*
170	170	165		21*
175	175	170		22*
180	180	175		23*
185	185	180		24*
190	190	185		25*
195	195	190		26*
200	200	195		27*
205	205	200		28*
210	210	205		29*
215	215	210		30*
220	220	215		31*
225	225	220		32*
230	230	225		33**
235	235	230		34***
240	240	235		35****

*   add 3 per cent if car runs solely on diesel
* *   add 2 per cent if car runs solely on diesel
* * * add 1 per cent if car runs solely on diesel
* * * * maximum charge so no diesel supplement

There are discounts for cars running on alternative fuels.

Fuel charge

	2006/07	2007/08	2008/09	2009/10
Figure used to calculate scale charge	£14,400			

Vans

For further information see Chapter 8. To update the table see **www.hmrc.gov.uk/vans/**.

	2006/07	2007/08	2008/09	2009/10
Scale charge	500*	3,000		
Fuel charge	–	500		

* If the van is over four years old – £350.

Authorized mileage rate

Employers can reimburse business mileage driven in the employee's own vehicle up to the following rates without a tax charge arising. Where an employee reimburses their employer for the cost of private fuel at a rate at least equal to that stated there will be no benefit in kind charge. To update the table see **www.hmrc.gov.uk/rates/travel.htm**.

Single rate for all vehicles	2006/07 %	2007/08 %	2008/09 %	2009/10 %
Cars up to 10,000 miles	40p			
Cars excess over 10,000 miles	25p			
Passenger rate per mile	5p			
Motorbikes	24p			
Bikes	20p			
Fuel-only				
Petrol 0–1400cc	11p			
Petrol 1401–2000cc	13p			
Petrol over 2000cc	18p			
Diesel 0–2000cc	10p			
Diesel over 2000cc	14p			
LPG 0–1400cc	7p			
LPG 1401–2000cc	8p			
LPG over 2000	11p			

Pensions

For further details see Chapter 11.

	2006/07 £	2007/08 £	2008/09 £	2009/10 £	2010/11 £
Lifetime allowance	1,500,000	1,600,000	1,650,000	1,750,000	1,800,000
Annual allowance	215,000	225,000	235,000	245,000	255,000

Interest rates on unpaid tax

For further details see Chapter 3 and Appendix 2.

	From 6.9.06				
Income tax	7.5%				
Corporation tax	7.5%				

This table can be updated from the information at **www.hmrc. gov.uk/rates/interest-late.htm**.

Interest rates on overpaid tax

For further details see Chapter 3 and Appendix 2

	From 6.9.06				
Income tax	3.0%				
Corporation tax	4.0%				

This table can be updated from the information at **www.hmrc. gov.uk/rates/interest-repayments.htm**.

The following calendars set out the important dates and deadlines that individuals, employers and companies need to know about. Further details are given in Chapters 3 and 8.

Individuals

Tax returns

6 April	Beginning of the tax year. Tax returns issued.
30 September	Last date for submitting your tax return by post if you want HMRC to calculate your tax bill or if you have a tax underpayment of less than £2,000 which you want to be included in your tax code.
30 December	Last date for submitting your tax return over the Internet if you want HMRC to calculate your tax bill or if you have a tax underpayment of less than £2,000 which you want to be included in your tax code.
31 January	Last date for submitting tax returns. Forms delivered after this date attract a £100 penalty although it is not charged if the return is only one day late. If you owe tax of less than £100 the fine is limited to the outstanding tax.
5 April	End of the tax year.

| 31 July | Returns which should have been filed on 31 January but are still outstanding attract a further £100 penalty. |
| 31 October | From 2008 onwards the final date for filing paper returns. |

Income tax and capital gains tax payments

31 January	1st income tax payment on account due for the current tax year (usually 50% of the previous year's total tax bill).
31 January	Balancing income tax and capital gains tax payment due for the previous tax year (usually your total tax bill less two payments on account made on the previous 31 January and 31 July).
28 February	Payments due on 31 January which are still outstanding attract a 5% surcharge.
31 July	2nd income tax payment on account due for the current tax year (usually 50% of the previous year's total tax bill).
31 July	Payments due on 31 January which are still outstanding attract a 10% surcharge.

Interest is charged on all overdue payments (see Appendix 1).

Employers

Forms – due dates

5 April	End of the tax year.
19 May	Date for submitting employer end of year returns including forms P35, P38, P38A, P14 and CIS36.
22 May	Final date for submitting employer end of year returns including forms P35, P38, P38A, P14 and CIS36 if they are filed electronically.

31 May	Last date to give employees form P60 (summary of salary, tax, National Insurance and other income and deductions).
6 July	Date forms P9D, P11D and P11Db must be submitted to HMRC. Final date to give employees details of their benefits in kind.
19 July	Class 1A National Insurance due on relevant benefits in kind if paid by cheque. Late payments attract interest.
22 July	Class 1A National Insurance due on relevant benefits in kind if paying electronically. Late payments attract interest.

Payment dates – paying monthly by cheque

19 January	HMRC must receive December employer deductions.
19 February	HMRC must receive January employer deductions.
19 March	HMRC must receive February employer deductions.
19 April	HMRC must receive March employer deductions. Interest is due on any unpaid deductions for the previous tax year.
19 May	HMRC must receive April employer deductions.
19 June	HMRC must receive May employer deductions.
19 July	HMRC must receive June employer deductions.
19 August	HMRC must receive July employer deductions.
19 September	HMRC must receive August employer deductions.
19 October	HMRC must receive September employer deductions.
19 November	HMRC must receive October employer deductions.
19 December	HMRC must receive November employer deductions.

Payment dates – paying electronically

22 January	HMRC must receive cleared funds for December employer deductions.
22 February	HMRC must receive cleared funds for January employer deductions.
22 March	HMRC must receive cleared funds for February employer deductions.
22 April	HMRC must receive cleared funds for March employer deductions. Interest is due on any unpaid deductions for the previous tax year.
22 May	HMRC must receive cleared funds for April employer deductions.
22 June	HMRC must receive cleared funds for May employer deductions.
22 July	HMRC must receive cleared funds for June employer deductions.
22 August	HMRC must receive cleared funds for July employer deductions.
22 September	HMRC must receive cleared funds for August employer deductions.
22 October	HMRC must receive cleared funds for September employer deductions.
22 November	HMRC must receive cleared funds for October employer deductions.
22 December	HMRC must receive cleared funds for November employer deductions.

Payment dates – paying quarterly

19 January	Payment date for employer deductions.
19 April	Payment date for employer deductions. Interest is due on any unpaid deductions for the previous tax year.
19 July	Payment date for employer deductions.
19 October	Payment date for employer deductions.

Companies

Corporation tax payment dates

Nine months and one day after the end of the company's accounting period unless it is a large company and has to make quarterly payments on account.

Corporation tax return

Returns must normally be filed within twelve months of the end of the company's accounting period. Different dates apply if the accounting period is longer than twelve months.

appendix 3: glossary

This appendix provides quick definitions of the tax phrases and abbreviations found in the book.

Word or phrase	Description	Further reading
Accrual	Cost incurred in one accounting period relating to an earlier period.	Chapter 16
Administration	Formal way to manage: **1** an insolvent company's affairs and, **2** a deceased person's estate.	Chapters 13 and 15
Agricultural buildings allowance (ABA)	Tax allowance given on some farm buildings and infrastructure.	Chapter 9
Agricultural property relief	An inheritance tax relief.	Chapters 2 and 15
Annual allowance	Limit on the amount you can contribute to a pension each year and still obtain tax relief.	Chapter 11
Annual exemption	Amount of capital gains you can make each year before you owe any capital gains tax.	Chapter 2
Annuity	Pension.	Chapter 11

Word or phrase	Description	Further reading
Asset	A positive balance in a business such as property, equipment, cars, goodwill, stock, debtors and cash.	Chapters 2, 7, 12 and 15
Balance sheet	Accounting record showing your assets and liabilities at a particular date.	Chapter 16
Beneficiary	Someone 'benefiting' from an inheritance or trust.	Chapter 15
Bequest	Gift in a will.	Chapter 15
Business property relief	An inheritance tax relief.	Chapters 2 and 15
Capital account	Sum owed to a partner by a partnership.	Chapter 15
Capital allowances	Tax allowances given on your business equipment and cars.	Chapter 7
Capital expenditure	Assets of lasting benefit to the business (usually more than a year).	Chapter 7
Chattels	Personal property or assets.	Chapter 14
CIS	Construction Industry Scheme. Special tax arrangements for workers in the building trade.	Chapter 8
Company share option plan (CSOP)	Tax advantaged share scheme for employees.	Chapter 12
Connected person	Your (or your spouse or civil partner's) close relatives (and their spouses and civil partners). Your business partners (and their spouses, civil partners and relatives). Companies controlled by the same person.	Chapters 13 and 15

Word or phrase	Description	Further reading
Corporate Venturing Scheme (CVS)	Scheme to encourage investment by one company in another.	Chapter 14
Director's loan account	Sum owed by a company to a director (it is illegal to overdraw it).	Chapter 12
Dispensation	Formal agreement with HMRC which dispenses with the need for you to report non-taxable perks.	Chapter 8
Domicile	Country in which you have your family roots. Non-domiciled means that your natural home is not in the UK.	Chapter 2
DTI	Department of Trade and Industry	Chapters 8 and 13
Enquiry	Investigation into your tax affairs by HMRC.	Chapter 3
Enterprise Investment Scheme (EIS)	A scheme enabling people investing in small companies to obtain tax advantages.	Chapters 4, 12 and 14
Enterprise Management Incentives (EMI)	Tax advantaged share scheme for employees.	Chapter 12
ET	Earnings threshold for Class 1 National Insurance (see Appendix 1).	Chapter 8
EU	European Union	Chapter 10
Executor	Person responsible for administering your estate after you die. They may be a professional person or relative.	Chapter 15

Word or phrase	Description	Further reading
First year allowance (FYA)	A type of capital allowance.	Chapter 7
FSA	Financial Services Authority	Chapter 11
Gifts relief	A capital gains tax relief which defers tax on transfers of business assets.	Chapters 12 and 15
Goodwill	The amount a business is worth over and above the value of its assets depending on profits, customers, brands, expertise etc.	Chapter 12
Gross	Total amount before deducting something (often tax or VAT).	Chapters 8 and 10
HMRC	HM Revenue and Customs	Chapter 3
Incorporation	Forming a company.	Chapter 12
Indexation allowance	A capital gains tax relief for companies, and for individuals to 5 April 1998.	Chapters 2 and 15
Industrial buildings allowance (IBA)	Tax allowance given on some types of commercial property such as a factory.	Chapter 9
Input VAT	VAT on purchases or expenditure.	Chapter 10
Intestate	Dying without making a will.	Chapter 15
LEL	Lower earnings limit for Class 1 National Insurance (see Appendix 1).	Chapter 8
Lifetime allowance	Limit on the amount you can contribute to a pension over your lifetime and obtain tax relief on the investment.	Chapter 11
LLP	Limited Liability Partnership	Chapter 4

Word or phrase	Description	Further reading
Liquidation	Formal means of closing down a company, usually when it is insolvent.	Chapter 13
Marginal relief	A deduction from a small company's corporation tax liability to bridge the gap between the small company rate of corporation tax and the full rate.	Chapter 2
Net	Amount left after deducting something (often tax or VAT).	Chapters 8 and 10
Net relevant earnings	The measure of your income (excluding dividends) used to calculate how much you can pay into a pension.	Chapter 11
NICO	National Insurance Contributions Office	Chapter 12
Nil rate band	Part of your estate which is free from inheritance tax (see Appendix 1).	Chapter 2
Output VAT	VAT on your sales or income.	Chapter 10
Overlap profits/ relief	Profits taxed twice when you start in self-employment because you use an accounting year end date other than 31 March or 5 April. Relief is given when you change your year end or stop trading.	Chapters 5, 6 and 13
PAYE	Pay As You Earn – the system for deducting income tax and National Insurance from employees' and directors' wages.	Chapter 8

Word or phrase	Description	Further reading
Payment on account	Interim income tax payment made on 31 January and 31 July based on your tax bill for the previous year.	Chapter 3
Personal allowance	The amount of income you can earn or receive before you owe any income tax.	Chapter 2
Plant	Equipment, apparatus and furnishings.	Chapter 7
Pool	A group of assets on which capital allowances are claimed.	Chapter 7
Post-cessation expense	Expense incurred after closing down a business.	Chapter 13
Post-cessation receipt	Income received after closing down a business.	Chapter 13
Potentially exempt transfer	Inheritance tax term for a gift which may become liable to inheritance tax depending on when you die, the nil rate band (see Appendix 1) and other gifts made within the seven-year period.	Chapters 2 and 15
Prepayment	Advance payment.	Chapter 16
Probate	An official form giving the executors the right to deal with a deceased person's estate.	Chapter 15
PSA	PAYE Settlement Agreement	Chapter 8
Quoted company	Company listed on a stock exchange.	Chapter 15
Residue	The part of the estate left over after all the bequests have been paid.	Chapter 15

Word or phrase	Description	Further reading
Rollover relief	A capital gains tax relief to defer gains on the sale of business assets by reinvestment in new business assets (including on incorporation).	Chapters 2, 9, 12 and 14
SAP	Statutory Adoption Pay	Chapter 8
SAYE scheme	Tax advantaged share scheme for employees.	Chapter 12
SDLT	Stamp duty land tax	Chapter 9
Self-assessment	The system of tax operated in the UK under which the taxpayer is responsible for informing HMRC of their tax liabilities and paying their tax on the due date.	Chapter 3
Self-invested pension scheme (SIPP)	Type of self-directed pension scheme.	Chapter 11
Settlement	1 An agreement reached with HMRC about tax owing as the result of an enquiry. 2 A trust.	Chapters 3 and 4
Share incentive plan (SIP)	Tax advantaged share scheme for employees.	Chapter 12
Short-life assets	Equipment expected to last for less than five years.	Chapter 7
Small self-administered scheme (SSAS)	Type of self-directed pension scheme.	Chapter 11
SMP	Statutory Maternity Pay	Chapter 8
SPP	Statutory Paternity Pay	Chapter 8
SSP	Statutory Sick Pay	Chapter 8

Word or phrase	Description	Further reading
Standard-rated	VAT charged on certain items at 17.5%.	Chapter 10
State Second Pension (S2P)	Addition to the state pension based on your earnings.	Chapter 11
Statement of account	Document produced by HMRC showing your tax liability and the payments you have to make to them.	Chapter 16
Striking-off	Having a company removed from the register of companies.	Chapter 13
Taper relief	Relief given to reduce your capital gains. There is a higher rate for business assets and a lower rate for others.	Chapters 2, 6, 12 and 14.
Tax credit	1 A government payment to certain families, low earners and those with disabilities. 2 The tax associated with a dividend payment. 3 A means of tax relief for certain expenditure (research and development and land remediation).	Chapters 2 and 4
Tax return	Form on which you notify HMRC about your tax liabilities.	Chapter 3
Tax year	6 April to 5 April.	Chapter 3
Terminal loss	A loss made in the twelve months before ceasing your business.	Chapter 6
UEL	Upper earnings limit for Class 1 National Insurance (see Appendix 1).	Chapter 8
Unlisted company	A company whose shares are not quoted on a stock exchange.	Chapter 6

Word or phrase	Description	Further reading
Variation	A formal means of changing a will (or intestacy) within two years of death providing that certain conditions are met.	Chapter 15
VAT	Value Added Tax	Chapter 10
Writing down allowance (WDA)	A type of capital allowance.	Chapter 7
Zero-rated	VAT charged on certain items at 0%.	Chapter 10

appendix 4: further information

This appendix tells you how to access additional information about the subjects discussed in this book.

Organizations regulating accountants and tax advisers

Institute of Chartered Accountants for England and Wales (ICAEW). Members are denoted by the letters FCA or ACA – **www.icaewfirms.co.uk**

Institute of Chartered Accountants of Scotland (ICAS). Members are denoted by the letters CA – **www.icas.org.uk**

Institute of Chartered Accountants in Ireland (ICAI). Members are denoted by the letters CA – **www.icai.ie/index.cfm**

Association of Chartered Certified Accountants (ACCA). Members are denoted by the letters FCCA or ACCA – **www.acca-global.com**

Chartered Institute of Taxation (CIOT). Members are denoted by the letters CTA, FTII and ATII – **www.tax.org.uk**

The Association of Taxation Technicians (ATT). Members are denoted by the letters ATT – **www.att.org.uk**

The Association of Accounting Technicians (AAT). Members are denoted by the letters AAT – **www.aat.co.uk**

Organizations regulating solicitors

The Law Society of England and Wales – **www.lawsociety.
org.uk/home.law**

The Law Society of Scotland – **www.lawscot.org.uk**

The Law Society of Northern Ireland – **www.lawsoc-ni.org**

Organization regulating providers of financial services

The Financial Services Authority (FSA) – **www.fsa.gov.uk**

Government departments

HM Revenue and Customs – **www.hmrc.gov.uk**

Reference sources:

- Manuals – **www.hmrc.gov.uk/manuals/index.htm**
- Employer Bulletin – **www.hmrc.gov.uk/employers/
  bulletins.htm**
- Tax Bulletin – **www.hmrc.gov.uk/bulletins/index.htm**
- VAT Guides and Business Brief – follow the links from
  www.hmrc.gov.uk/library.htm

Inheritance tax – **www.hmrc.gov.uk/cto/iht.htm**

Stamp duty land tax – **www.hmrc.gov.uk/so/index.htm**

National Insurance – **www.hmrc.gov.uk/nic**

Valuation Office Agency (business rates) – **www.voa.gov.uk/
index.htm**

and **www.mybusinessrates.gov.uk/index.html**

Enhanced Capital Allowances – **www.eca.gov.uk**

The Department of Trade and Industry (DTI) – **www.dti.gov.uk**

The Insolvency Service – **www.insolvency.gov.uk**

Vehicle Certification Agency (Car CO_2 emissions) –
www.vcacarfueldata.org.uk/index.asp

HM Courts Service (probate) – **www.hmcourts-service.gov.uk/
cms/wills.htm**

Advisory services

Business Link – **www.businesslink.gov.uk**

Citizens Advice – **www.adviceguide.org.uk**

TaxAid – **www.taxaid.org.uk**

Community Legal Service – **www.clsdirect.org.uk/index.jsp**

Employers

The Advisory, Conciliation and Arbitration Services (ACAS) – **www.acas.co.uk**

Insolvency

Association of Business Recovery Professionals – **www.r3.org.uk**

Pensions

The Pensions Advisory Service – **www.opas.org.uk**

index

accountants **3, 5, 7–8, 41, 51**
  deciding whether to form a limited company **47**
  and employee status disputes **125**
  finding an accountant **7**
  and HMRC enquiries **40**
  and HMRC notification process **52**
  preparing accounts **65**
accounting year **30, 59–64**
  calculating profits **77**
  partners **63**
  sole traders **59–63**
adoption pay (SAP) **28, 124, 140, 279**
advisers *see* accountants
agricultural buildings **157, 159, 161**
agricultural property relief **237, 238–9, 241–2**
annual changes **3, 25, 259–60**
anti-avoidance measures **6**
assets
  disposal of **112–15**
  incorporating a business **199, 201–2, 209, 212**
  selling a business **226–7, 228–30**

bad debts **71, 178, 220**
balance sheets **250**
bank loans, interest on **54, 71**
the Budget **3, 27, 259**
  autumn pre-budget statement **27, 259**
business asset taper relief **155, 160, 205, 232, 265**
business bank accounts **31**
business property relief **237, 238–9, 241**

business rates **9, 54, 154**
buying business property **155–9, 162**
  claiming tax relief **156–9**
  financing the purchase **156**
  stamp duty land tax **156**

capital allowances
  calculating **77, 107–15, 277**
  cars **70, 103, 105, 106, 107–8, 115–18, 248**
  claims **67, 68, 103–5, 119–21**
    buying equipment before end of accounting period **121**
    disclaiming allowances **119–20**
    introduced assets **121**
    Nina's Kitchen case study **245, 248**
    short-life assets **120–1**
  closing a business **217**
  cost of equipment **104**
  disposal of assets **112–15**
  financing the purchase **105**
  first year allowances **105, 106, 107–9, 115, 277**
  incorporating a business **199, 202, 203**
  and insurance claims **195**
  leasing businesses **121**
  length of life **104**
  multiple acquisitions **110–12**
  selling a business **226, 227**
  writing down allowances **105, 106–7, 109–10, 115**
capital expenditure, VAT on substantial **178**
capital gains tax **9, 15–18**

assets liable for **15**
calculation **16–18, 263–8**
  annual exemption **16, 264**
  indexation allowance **16, 17**
closing down a limited company **219**
collection **16**
companies **15, 16, 268**
and death **240**
individuals **263–7**
key dates **286**
and loss claims **88, 91, 100**
minimizing when incorporating a
  business **199, 203–10**
and private investors **55**
selling a business **225, 226, 231–4**
selling business property **160–1**
selling a home you have worked
  from **153, 154, 155**
see also rollover relief; taper relief
capital losses **96, 97–100**
Capital Taxes Office **28**
cars
  capital allowances on **70, 103,
    105, 106, 107–8, 115–18, 248**
  employee perks **142, 143–4**
  motor expenses **66–7, 70, 73, 247,
    282–3**
  and VAT **175, 177, 273–4**
casual income **51**
checklist of taxes and duties **9–10**
Child Tax Credit **53, 245**
Child Trust Funds **10**
childcare
  costs **255**
  providing employees with **148**
CIS (Construction Industry Scheme)
  148–50
closing a business **213–22**
  limited companies **219–21, 222**
  unincorporated businesses
    214–18, 222
    allocating profits to tax years
      214–17
    capital allowances **217**
    cessation date **214, 215, 216**
    losses **217–19**
    overlap relief **217**
    post-cessation expenses **218**
    post-cessation receipts **218**
    stock **217**

commercial view on tax **3–6, 7**
Commissioners, appeals to **40, 41**
companies **5, 9**
  capital gains tax **15, 16, 268**
  corporation tax **9, 13, 13–14, 44,
    80, 268, 289**
  expenses **76**
  larger companies investing in your
    business **234**
  losses **96–7**
  National Insurance contributions
    25
  tax payments **37**
  tax returns **29, 33**
    late returns **34**
  see also limited companies
company directors **127, 128, 141**
  insurance for **197**
  loan accounts **208, 209**
  pensions **190**
construction industry **148–50**
  new scheme **149–50**
  sub-contractors **52, 148–9**
Corporate Venturing Scheme **234**
corporation tax **9, 13–14, 44, 80**
  key dates **289**
  marginal relief **14**
  rates and thresholds **268**
council tax **9**
credit sales, calculating income from
  65–6
criminal prosecutions for tax evasion
  6
CSOP (company share option plans)
  211

death
  benefits **193**
  passing on a business after
    239–42
  see also inheritance tax
direct taxes **9**
directors *see* company directors
discovery assessments **41**
dispensations on staff expenses
  145–6, 255
dividends **45, 46, 47**
  and corporation tax **13**
  income tax on **12**
  and pensions **190**

and share capital 210
domicile and inheritance tax 18, 19,
        20
drawings 74–5, 127, 247
dual expenses 72–3
duties checklist 9–10

EIS see Enterprise Investment
        Scheme (EIS)
EMIs (enterprise management
        incentives) 211
employees 123–50
    construction industry 148–50
    deductions from pay 133–37
    defining an employee 125–7
    expense claims 145–6
    insurance for 193, 197
    National Insurance 135–6
    paying 128–9
    payrolls forms 132–3
    perks 141–8, 254
        childcare 148
        tax-efficient 146–7
    redundancy payments 10, 221
    statutory payments to 28, 124,
        137–40, 256, 278–80
    student loan repayments 28, 124,
        136–7, 280
    taking on staff 131–2, 252
    tax codes 134–5, 142
    tax returns 255
    taxing 129–31
    see also PAYE schemes
employers
    key dates for 286–8
    National Insurance 9, 22, 23, 24,
        124, 140–1
    and pensions 193
    statutory payments to employees
        28, 124, 137–40, 256, 278,
        278–80
    tax obligations 124–5
    tax payments 37
    tax returns 30
        late 34–5
Enterprise Investment Scheme (EIS)
        55, 211, 263
    deferral relief 161, 210, 234
Enterprise Zones 158
entertainment costs 70, 177

equipment
    buying new 245
    closing a business 220
    depreciation on 71
    and VAT de-registration 183
    VAT on substantial capital
        expenditure 178
    see also capital allowances
European Union countries, VAT and
        trading with 179–80
excise duties 9
expenses 6, 54, 67–76
    capital allowances 67, 68, 103–5
    capital or revenue 73–4, 104
    claims by employees 145–6
    direct costs 67, 68, 69
    drawings 74–5, 247
    dual expenses 72–3
    good taken for personal use 75
    motor expenses 66–7, 70, 73, 247,
        282–3
    overheads 67, 68–71, 249
    post-cessation 218
    renting out unwanted property 161
    stock and work in progress 75–6
    and VAT 76
exported goods, VAT on 179

failing to budget for tax 5
failing to deal with your tax affairs
        5–6
family members
    employment status and pay
        127, 128
    giving away your business to
        237–9
    and share capital 210
Financial Services Authority 186
fines, for late tax returns 33–5
foster carers 79–80

GAAP (generally accepted
        accounting principles) 64–5
General Commissioners 41
gifts, exempt from inheritance
        tax 21, 237
gifts relief
    giving away your business 237, 238
    incorporating a business 206–8,
        212

goodwill
  incorporating a business **204, 206–8**
  selling a business **227**
Government economic policy **27**

HM Revenue and Customs (HMRC) **6, 28, 32, 35**
  Business Support Teams **150**
  and capital allowances **103**
  closing a business **214**
  Codes of Practice **28, 38**
  and the Construction Industry Scheme (CIS) **148–50**
  discovery assessments **41**
  and employee/self-employment status **50–1, 53, 125–7**
  and employees **131–2**
    perks **145–6**
  enquiries **5, 38–41, 195**
    appeals **40, 41**
  incorporating a business **200, 203, 204, 212**
  and limited companies **45, 211**
    striking off **219**
  notifications **49, 51, 52, 53**
  PAYE inspections **255**
  and PAYE systems **129, 131, 150**
  and pensions **187**
  registration **53**
  and self-assessment **28**
  selling a business **225, 227**
  starting to trade **49–50, 244–5**
  and statutory payments **137, 138–9**
  and tax payments **37, 38**
  and tax returns **29–30, 32–3, 253–4**
    late **33–5**
  and VAT **164, 170, 183, 253, 254**
    de-registration **220**
    paid to or reclaimed from **76**
    retail schemes **182**
    returns **173–4, 176**
  website **2, 3, 29, 35, 137, 259**
home responsibilities protection **194**
hotels **158**

imported goods, VAT on **179**
income
  calculating **65–7**
  and capital gains tax **264**

post-cessation receipts **218**
  recording **31, 249–50**
  understating **6**
income tax **9, 10–12**
  calculation **11–12, 80**
  and dividends **210**
  incorporating a business **200–1**
  key dates **286**
  limited companies **44**
  limited liability partnerships (LLPs) **48–9**
  loss claims **88–95**
  partners **10, 11, 25, 55**
  people living abroad **10–11**
  on perks **141–4**
  personal allowances **11, 261–3**
  rates **260–3**
    basic rate **11, 260, 261**
    higher rate **11, 260, 261**
    starting rate **11, 260, 261**
  and redundancy payments **221**
  and sole traders **43, 46, 55**
incorporating a business **198–212**
  closing down self-employment **199, 200–2**
  minimizing capital gains tax **199, 203–10**
  reasons for **211**
  starting a limited company **199, 203**
  when to incorporate **199**
indirect taxes **9**
individuals *see* self-employed individuals
industrial buildings **157, 158, 159, 161**
inheritance tax **9, 18–21, 237, 240–2, 269**
  agricultural assets **18, 20**
  business property relief **18, 19, 20**
  calculation **19–20**
  Capital Taxes Office **28**
  charges on **18–19**
  and domicile **18, 19, 20**
  exempt assets **18**
  gifts exempt from **21, 237**
  giving away your business **237, 238–9**
  nil rate band **19, 20, 21, 238, 269**
  pitfalls **21**

insurances **195–7**
directors' liability insurance **197**
and HMRC enquiries **40, 195**
key employees/directors **197**
life insurance **193, 197, 240**
medical insurance **196**
mortgage endowment policies
142, 153, 196
sickness insurance **196**
interest
on bank loans **54, 71**
on savings and investments **12**
on tax payments **37, 284**
investment income **10, 12, 13**
ISAs (individual savings accounts) **10**

late payments **37**
late returns **33–5**
leasehold business premises **155, 159**
leasing agreements **105**
leasing businesses, and capital
allowance claims **121**
life insurance **193, 197, 240**
limited companies **3, 43, 44–5, 46–7**
accounting year **63–4**
closing down **219–21, 222**
deciding whether to form **47**
directors' salaries and perks **44, 46**
dividends **45**
formal accounts **65**
giving away a business **239**
home-based **152**
incorporating a business **199, 212**
minimizing capital gains tax
199, 203–10
running a business with share
capital **210–11**
starting a limited company **199,
203**
length of time to keep records **32**
and loss relief **92**
monitoring your tax **80**
notification process **52**
and partnerships **48**
private investors **55**
selling a business **226–21**
and tax relief **47**
taxes paid by **44**
see also companies; company
directors

limited liability partnerships (LLPs)
48–9, 55
LLPs (limited liability partnerships)
48–9, 55
loans, interest on bank loans **54, 71**
local government taxes **9**
losses **87–101, 256–7**
capital losses **96, 97–100**
claiming income tax losses **88–92**
claims for business investments in
failed companies **101**
company losses **96–7**
in early years of a business **92–4**
transferring when incorporating a
business **199, 202**
when a business ceases **94–5,
217–18**

maternity pay **28, 47, 124, 138–9**
medical insurance **142, 196**
million pound scenario **4**
minimum wage **28, 124, 128, 280**
monitoring your tax **80–2**
mortgages
endowment policies **153, 196**
interest on **153**
pension mortgages **191–2**

National Insurance **22–5, 269–71**
calculation **24–5, 128, 135–6**
Class 1
employee's contributions **9, 22,
23, 24, 124, 252, 269–70**
employer's contributions **9, 22,
23, 24, 124, 140–1, 252, 254,
269, 270**
married women's reduced rate
270
Class 2 contributions **9, 22, 24, 43,
48, 49, 53, 271**
Class 3 contributions **9, 22, 23, 24,
271**
Class 4 contributions **9, 12, 23, 24,
28, 43, 48, 49, 55, 80, 271**
closing down a business **221**
collection **23**
and company directors **127**
deferred contributions **23**
and dividends **210**
and employee perks **142**

and general insurance premiums
197
incorporating a business 200
and limited companies 44, 45, 46
multiple jobs or self-employments
23–4
numbers 129
partnerships 22, 23, 48
and pensions 194
persons liable for 22
and redundancy payments 221
small earnings exemptions 23
and sole traders 43, 46, 47
and state pensions 194
and statutory sick pay (SSP) 137,
138
National Insurance Contributions
Office (NICO) 28, 200
National Minimum Wage 28, 124,
128, 280
National Savings certificates 10
Nina's Kitchen case study 244–58
buying new equipment 245
future developments 258
getting organized 245
losses 256–7
paying tax 251
pensions 256
renting premises 252
starting to trade 244–5
taking on staff 252
tax returns 246–51, 253–4, 255–6,
257
and VAT 253, 254
Northern Ireland law 3

overdrafts, interest on 54, 71
overhead expenses 67, 68–71, 249
'overlap' profits, calculating 61–3
overlap relief 94, 217
overseas residence
domicile and inheritance tax 18,
19, 20
tax liabilities 10–11, 15
overseas trade, and VAT 179–80, 184

P45/P46 forms 131–2, 252
partnerships 3, 9, 48–9
accounting year 63
and business property relief 241

capital gains tax 15, 16, 17
claiming capital allowances 119
drawings 74, 127
giving away a business 239
income tax 10, 25, 55
self-assessment 11
limited liability partnerships (LLPs)
48–9, 55
loans 55
loss claims 88–92
National Insurance contributions
22, 23, 48
notification process 52
selling the business 226
tax payments 35
taxes paid by 48
passing on a business 236–42
after death 239–42
giving away your business 237–9
paternity pay 28, 124, 139, 279
PAYE inspections 255
PAYE schemes 11, 37, 124, 125,
129–31, 150
closing down 220–1
and company directors 127
deductions 133–5
and gross pay 128
incorporating a business 201, 203
and limited companies 44, 46
and National Insurance 22
online filing 131
operating 130–1
and partnerships 48
and sole traders 43
PAYE Settlement Agreements 142
paying employees 128–9
paying your tax 35–7, 251
anticipating payments 55–7
balancing payments 35, 36, 255
companies 37
employers 37
interest on payments 37, 284
late payments 37, 38
payment dates 286, 287–8
payments on account 35, 36, 37
self-employed individuals and
partners 35–6
underpayments 37, 38–41
pension mortgages 191–2
pensions 6, 186–95, 283

death benefits **193**
and employers **193**
lump sums on retirement **10, 192**
paying into your own pension
186–93, 256
how much to pay **186**
self-administered pension
schemes **191**
paying a pension for someone
else **188**
pension simplification **186**
SSAS (Small Self-Administered
Schemes) **191**
state pension **47, 192, 194–5**
State Second Pensions (SP2) **195**
tax relief on **186–91, 193, 257**
and term assurance **197**
personal services, and
self-employment status **50–1**
pre-owned assets legislation **21**
premises **151–62**
buying business property **155–9,
162**
renting **155, 252**
renting out unwanted property **161**
selling business property **160–1,
162**
working from home **152–5, 162**
premium bonds **10**
profits **58–86**
calculating expenses **67–76**
calculating income **65–7**
calculating for tax **77–9**
choice of year end **59–64**
closing a business **214–17**
and foster carers **79–80**
planning for potential tax bills **56**
preparing accounts **64–5**
profit averaging **77–9**
and tax liability **80–6**
property
and capital gains tax **15**
income from **10, 11**

reasons to read this book **2–3, 7**
record-keeping **30–2, 31, 32**
redundancy payments **10, 221**
renting
business premises **155, 252**
unwanted property **161**

residence *see* overseas residence
retailers, and VAT **182**
retirement
age of and pension contributions
192
passing on a business **237–9**
risk-taking **5**
rollover relief **16, 17, 161**
incorporation **208–10, 212**
selling a business **227, 232–4**

savings income, tax on **10, 12**
SAYEs (Save As You Earn Schemes)
211
Scottish law **3**
second-hand goods, and VAT **182**
self-assessment **23, 28, 40, 53**
and casual income **51**
corporation tax **13, 28**
income tax **11, 28**
self-employed individuals
accounting year **30**
drawings **74, 127**
incorporating a business **199,
200–2**
key dates **285–6**
length of time to keep records **32**
National Insurance contributions
22, 23
notification process **52**
tax payments **35–6**
tax returns **29, 32–3**
late returns **33–4**
tax year **30**
see also sole traders; working from
home
self-employment status **50–1, 53,
125–7**
selling a business **223–35**
capital gains tax **225, 226, 231–4**
companies **226–31**
sole traders **224–5**
selling business property **160–1, 162**
services
personal services and
self-employment status **50–1**
providing overseas **180**
share capital, incorporating a
business **209, 210–11**
shareholders *see* dividends

shares, selling a business **226–7, 228–31**
sick pay (SSP) **28, 124, 137–8, 256, 278**
sickness insurance **196**
SIPPs (Self-Invested Personal Pensions) **191**
SIPs (share incentive plans) **211**
sole traders **3, 43, 46–7**
  accounting year **59–63**
    changing your year end **63–4**
    preparing accounts to another date **59, 60, 61–3**
    year end 5 April or 31 March **60–1**
  anticipating tax payments **55–7**
  capital gains tax **15, 16, 17**
  expenses **67–76**
  giving away a business **239**
  income tax **10, 11, 25**
  incorporating a business **199, 200–2**
  loss claims **88–95**
  National Insurance contributions **22, 23, 25**
  passing on a business after death **240**
  registering as self-employed **49–50**
  selling a business **224–5**
  taxes paid by **9, 43**
  see also self-employed individuals
Special Commissioners **41**
spending to save tax **4–5**
stamp duties **9, 28, 275–6**
  rates **276**
stamp duty land tax (SDLT) **156, 206, 227, 275–6**
Stamp Taxes Division **28**
starting a business **42–57, 244–5**
  anticipating tax payments **55–7**
  casual income **51**
  financing the business **54–5**
  limited companies **44–5, 46–7**
  partnerships **48–9**
  personal services **50–1**
  pre-trading expenditure **54**
  registering as self-employed **49–50**
  sole traders **43, 46–7**
state benefits **22, 54, 124**
  tax on **10, 11**

see also statutory payments
state pensions **47, 192, 194–5**
statutory payments **28, 137–40**
  adoption pay (SAP) **28, 124, 140, 279**
  maternity pay (SMP) **28, 124, 138–9, 278**
  paternity pay (SPP) **28, 124, 139, 279**
  sick pay (SSP) **28, 124, 137–8, 256, 278**
stock
  closing a business **217, 220**
  transferring when incorporating a business **201–2**
  valuing **246–7**
subsistence payments **70, 144–5**

taper relief **16, 17, 18**
  business assets **155, 160, 205, 232, 265**
  non-business assets **266–7**
  selling a business **230, 232, 234**
tax allowances **11, 261–3**
  annual changes **3, 25, 259–60**
  on business property purchases **157–9, 161**
  married couples' allowance **262, 263**
tax avoidance **6, 7**
tax credits **10, 28, 256, 257**
  and corporation tax **13**
  dividends paid with **12, 13, 45**
  notification of **53**
tax evasion **6, 7**
tax rates **3, 11, 259–63**
  annual changes **3, 25, 259–60**
tax relief
  on insurance premiums **195, 196**
  and limited companies **47, 55**
  loss claims **88–101, 256–7**
  for 'overlap' profits **61**
  on pension contributions **186–91, 193, 257**
  on property purchases **156–9**
  see also rollover relief; taper relief
tax returns **28–30, 53**
  balance sheets **250**
  companies **29, 33, 34**
  completing **32–3**

correcting errors **38**
employers **30, 34–5**
enquiries into **38–9**
and formal accounts **65**
full version **33**
HMRC enquiries **38–41**
income and expenditure accounts
    249–50
individuals **29, 32–3, 33–4**
key dates **285–6**
late returns **33–5**
Nina's Kitchen case study **246–51,
    253–4, 255–6, 257**
short return **32–3**
working out the tax liability **251**
tax system **26–41**
the Budget **3, 27, 259**
paying your tax **35–7, 251**
raising taxes **27**
records **30–2**
self-assessment **23, 28, 40, 53**
tax year **30**
see also accounting year; HM
    Revenue and Customs
    (HMRC); tax returns
tour operator's margin schemes
    (TOMS) **183**
travel and subsistence **70, 144–5**

unincorporated businesses **199**
closing down **214–18**

vans **144**
VAT (Value Added Tax) **9, 163–84,
    272–6**
annual turnover thresholds **272**
on business property purchases
    159
and cars **175, 177, 273–4**
complications **177–80**
date of supply **178–9**
de-registration **183, 220**
definition and case study **164–6**
and EU trade **179–80**
expenses **76**
imports and exports **179**

and limited companies **44**
partial exemption **178**
and partnerships **48, 49**
rates **170–3, 272**
reclaiming **76**
records and VAT returns **173–6,
    254**
  input VAT **176**
  invoices **174**
  output VAT **175**
  returns **174–5**
registration **66, 166–70, 183, 253**
  cancelling **183, 220**
  claiming back VAT before **170**
  compulsory **166–8**
  forms **170**
  incorporating a business **199,
    201, 202, 203**
  voluntary **169**
on selling a business **227**
and sole traders **43**
special schemes **180–3**
  annual accounting scheme
    181–2
  cash accounting scheme **181,
    183**
  flat-rate scheme **182**
  retailers **182**
  second-hand goods **182**
  tour operators **183**
and turnover **66**

wealth increases **4**
wills
  dying without a will **239**
  making a will **242**
working from home **152–5, 162**
  business rates **154**
  capital costs **154**
  mortgage interest **153**
  Nina's Kitchen case study **244–58**
  running costs **153–4**
  selling a home you have worked
    from **153, 154, 155**
  use of home allowance **154, 247**
Working Tax Credit **53**